T0110337

Praise for *The Good Teen*

"The most prolific developmental psychologist of our era has distilled his decades of insight into *The Good Teen*, a very accessible analysis of adolescence as it deserves to be understood."

—*Graham Spanier, Ph.D., president, Penn State University*

"With unchallengeable research and analysis, Dr. Richard Lerner's terrific and very important book, *The Good Teen*, totally refutes and rejects the fear and demonization of teenagers so prevalent in America today—and shows us how we must recognize the treasure that teens are and work to develop fully their great potential, for the teens themselves and for our society."

—*Former U. S. senator Fred Harris, chair of the Board of Trustees of the Milton S. Eisenhower Foundation*

"There is no one in America today who understands teenagers better than Richard Lerner. *The Good Teen* overflows with gemlike insights based on Lerner's own groundbreaking research, his 'positive youth' perspective, and his own experience as a caring and successful parent. Readers will find lots of useful advice about questions that arise every day in contemporary family life."

—*William Damon, Ph.D., professor of education and director of the Center on Adolescence, Stanford University*

"This outstanding book, written by one of the nation's leading authorities on adolescent development, is a critical read for all interested in youth. It merges scholarship with anecdote to produce a volume that is as informative as it is engaging. For any parent, youth worker, educator, or health professional as well, *The Good Teen* provides valuable insights that debunk the myth that this is an age of storm and stress."

—*Robert Wm. Blum, M.D., M.P.H., Ph.D., William H. Gates Sr. professor and chair, Department of Population, Family, and Reproductive Health, Johns Hopkins Bloomberg School of Public Health*

"At a time when poverty, inequality, and school segregation are increasing in a country with over 2 million incarcerated, the moral and political imperative of *The Good Teen* is to direct Richard Lerner's wisdom and research into a national youth investment policy for the truly disadvantaged that is resourced to scale."

—*Alan Curtis, Ph.D., president and CEO, Eisenhower Foundation*

"Richard Lerner is a rare developmental researcher who has taken on the challenge of setting the record straight on adolescence . . . and succeeded in doing a real public service."

—*Robert L. Selman, Ph.D., Roy E. Larsen professor of education and human development and professor of psychology, Harvard University*

"Richard Lerner has produced a user-friendly guide to parenting teens. He is optimistic throughout and presents many common-sensical suggestions that will enhance the lives of teens and improve the quality of life for everyone."

—*Joy Dryfoos, independent researcher*

"Richard Lerner has done a great job with *The Good Teen*. I loved it! I have raised three teens and I'm looking forward to raising one more in the coming decade. This is solid information for my wife and me to apply and learn from. And, if all else fails, the book is small enough to throw at them!"

—*Joe Pantoliano, actor, writer, director, and producer*

The Good Teen

The Good Teen

Rescuing Adolescence from the Myths of the Storm and Stress Years

RICHARD M. LERNER, Ph.D.

With Roberta Israeloff

A Stonesong Press Book
Three Rivers Press | New York

Published in the United States by Three Rivers Press,
an imprint of the Crown Publishing Group,
a division of Random House, Inc., New York.
www.crownpublishing.com

Three Rivers Press and the Tugboat design are registered trademarks
of Random House, Inc.

Originally published in hardcover in the United States by Crown Publishers,
an imprint of the Crown Publishing Group, a division of
Random House, Inc., New York, in 2007.

Library of Congress Cataloging-in-Publication Data
Lerner, Richard M.
  The Good Teen: rescuing adolescence from the myths of the storm and stress years /
Richard M. Lerner—1st ed.
  Includes bibliographical references and index.
  1. Adolescence.   2. Adolescent psychology.   I. Title.
HQ796.L3823 2007
155.50973—dc22   2007010070

ISBN 978-0-307-34758-9

A Stonesong Press Book

Design by Debbie Glasserman

First Paperback Edition

146028962

To Justin Samuel Lerner, Blair Elizabeth Lerner, and Jarrett Maxwell Lerner: from terrific teens to extraordinary young adults

Contents

The Good Teen

What We Can Learn from Tom and Huck

I think we can all empathize with poor Aunt Polly. How many times have we called to our adolescent children repeatedly, our voices growing louder and louder, and still received no answer? More than a quarter century before adolescence even became a field of scientific study, Mark Twain captured what for many parents was a universal view of teenagers: they were troublesome and troubled. And if Aunt Polly had a problem dealing with young Tom, well then, when it came to his friend Huck Finn, there was just no hope.

Yet one of the features that makes Mark Twain's novels endure is that their author surprised us each time we turned the page, following these two young adolescents on their adventures. Yes, both boys were more than a handful to deal with. Aunt Polly was always at her wits' end contending with all the mischief her nephew and his friend kicked up. However, by the time we finish *The Adventures of Tom Sawyer* and *The Adventures of Huckleberry Finn*, we discover that Tom's and Huck's problem behaviors were only a part—and a very small part—of who they were. Sure, the boys were mischievous, but they also showed great courage. At great risk to their own lives and even in the face of social disapproval, they stood up against crime and racial discrimination. They had character; they were loyal to friends and to family. They were also ingenious and able to solve problems, and they had enough "stick-to-it-iveness" to keep their promises and commitments, even against great odds. And they possessed the ability to love.

We can easily appreciate why Twain was such a captivating storyteller. He roped us in by making us believe that he was going to recount the adventures of two problem-filled adolescents. Instead, what he showed us was that although the boys had problems and flaws, they possessed extraordinary strengths. He encouraged us to overcome our own stereotypical expectations of teenagers and see these two boys as complete human beings. Overall, they were young people to admire and to value.

A METAPHOR FOR OUR TIMES

Twain's novels about Tom and Huck may be regarded as a metaphor for all American youth and perhaps all Americans. More than a century ago, his books conveyed the message that we should look beyond what may be an annoying characteristic or a shortcoming of our children and even of ourselves. Twain reminds us to keep our eyes wide open and allow the breadth of the person to be understood and appreciated. There is more to young people than just those irksome aspects of their behavior that may cause you worry. America and its youth had problems in the post–Civil War years during which Twain wrote these novels. Yet the individuals in this nation, and the nation itself, had considerable strengths, and these strengths, he believed, outweighed the problems.

Twain gave us this message of hope more than 125 years ago. Today, there are exciting results coming in from new research about America's youth. Much of this research comes from the 4-H Study of Positive Youth Development, a research project within my own laboratory, the Institute for Applied Research in Youth Development at Tufts University. Over the course of this book, I will tell you about the results of my research and, as well, the research of my colleagues across the nation who are learning similar things about the strengths present in all young people and about our hope for enhancing the positive development of all our children.

These innovative findings reinforce Twain's wisdom. Unfortunately, in the years that have passed between the publication of Twain's novels and the emergence of today's new data, many of us— parents and scientists included—have lost sight of the lessons we learned about young people from Tom and Huck.

All too often, parents have acted as if the only important aspects of their children's behaviors were those that caused problems. We think of adolescence as a time of storm and stress. Scientists, too, have regarded young people as lacking, as deficient, as unable to behave correctly and in a healthy manner. We characterize them as dangerous to others and as endangered themselves (because of their self-destructive behaviors).

Given this perspective on teenagers, researchers devoted their energies to finding ways to prevent young people from becoming all the bad things they could become. Therapists, too, used this deficit approach when treating young people. If their problems could not be prevented, then therapists searched for ways to reduce the impact of their shortcomings. Everyone focused on the problems. Experts of all types did not look to see if, in succeeding chapters of life, there were unnoticed strengths and admirable qualities that should be reinforced.

The Good Teen seeks to correct this imbalance. We do not need to see our young people as, essentially, repositories of problems.

Instead of dwelling on their weaknesses, we can concentrate on their strengths.

There's no denying that adolescence can be a tumultuous time and that teenagers sometimes act out, at times egregiously. It's not all smooth sailing. Just ask Aunt Polly—Tom gave her fits. All children do, at times. No adolescent is free of problems. So what's the best way to handle this reality?

It would have been incorrect for Aunt Polly to resort to strict punishment (once the preferred method for managing children's unruliness) or to think of it as her only option for treating Tom's behavior—although of course she certainly considered this alternative throughout the novel. It would be just as wrongheaded today to accept child-rearing options such as "tough love," "boot camp," and other flashy practices that advocate punishment to quell what we regard as children's inevitable rambunctious, disobedient, and troubling behavior. Such approaches are misguided and downright dangerous now that we have so much research to support the idea that all youth—no matter what their backgrounds or characteristics—have the potential to develop in more positive and healthy directions.

The Good Teen will explain how you can help your teenagers write an optimistic script for this phase of their maturation. Even if your children remind you of Tom and Huck, they will mostly likely grow up to lead successful, fulfilling lives, contributing positively to their own development and to that of their families, communities, and ultimately our nation and society. By taking to heart the messages emerging from this new research, which we will discuss, you can collaborate with your teenager at home, in school, and in your neighborhood to make certain that the story ends in a positive way. How? Keep your eyes open. Look for the bigger picture—the full story—about your child. Don't draw a conclusion about how the story will end by just reading the first chapter. Keeping this rule in mind may be very difficult at times, but it will pay off.

Consider Nancy. It was a Sunday evening, and Nancy found herself in the kitchen preparing a batch of pancakes for dinner. Ever since they were little, her kids—seventeen-year-old Eric and fifteen-year-old Donna—loved the idea of having breakfast at night. It had been a family tradition for more years than Nancy could remember. When the kids were younger, they used to help her, adding the ingredients, mixing the batter, and setting the table.

Now her husband, Rob, put out the plates because both kids were busy with more exciting activities. Eric had spent the day with his friends shooting a video for their English class. They'd been holed up for hours in Eric's bedroom—although Nancy couldn't imagine why anyone would want to spend time in his disaster of a room, decorated with dirty socks, laundry, and fast-food containers strewn on every available surface. Eric wasn't a straight-A student, but he loved taking challenging classes, such as AP English and history. In fact, he was talking about becoming a high school teacher after finishing college.

Donna had had a busy day also—soccer practice in the morning, and then her weekly stint at the soup kitchen where she volunteered. She'd just called to say that she'd be a few minutes late. "She left her backpack at soccer practice—again—and has to go back to the coach's house to get it," Nancy told Rob. "She's so forgetful! She knows she's supposed to be home on time for dinner. And I asked Eric to clean his room before his friends came over, and he said that he would. . . ." Her voice trailed off.

"I know, I know," Rob said. "They're frustrating, each in a different way. But you know what? They're really great kids. Think about it: at least Donna called. And no matter what Eric's room looks like, he's incredibly creative. He's basically directing and producing the video himself."

It was true, Nancy had to admit. Her kids may not have been perfect, but they were terrific. Years ago, Nancy remembered, people warned her about the maelstrom that would overtake family life when her kids became teenagers. "Just wait!" her friends had told her with dark foreboding. "You'll see. It's a roller coaster, a time characterized by endless fights, erratic behavior, endless limit testing, risky experimentation, disrespect, abrasive back talk, loss of academic focus, hair-raising moodiness, and wanton acts of outrageous behavior, not to mention life-threatening experimentation with drugs, alcohol, and sex. Little kids, little problems. Big kids, big problems."

But on the whole, adolescence hadn't been as bad as she'd been led to fear. Quite the opposite. In many ways, Nancy was enjoying her children more than she ever had. To watch them grow into people with their own opinions, to take their places in the community and at school, to become aware of and active in the larger world, to forge relationships with new people—it was gratifying in ways Nancy couldn't have imagined and never would have anticipated.

Does this family sound familiar? It could be yours. According to my research, it probably is, even though you may not realize it. Sometimes I think we all resemble Aunt Polly, standing on the porch screaming at Tom to come do his chores—and seeing our teenagers not as they are but as we expect them to be.

IT IS A MISTAKE TO EMBRACE THE STEREOTYPE

Think about it: when was the last time you heard a parent praise his or her teenager? When was the last time *you* did?

Most likely you're like Nancy. Whenever she met a friend in the library who asked how Donna was doing, Nancy would immediately say, "Forgetful and inconsiderate, as always." If she was asked to describe Eric, the first things she thought of were what a slob he could be and how he often lost track of time—as if these constituted his entire personality rather than just two aspects of it. Only during rare moments, such as during her conversation with Rob, was she able to stop dwelling on her children's faults and see their strengths.

Sometimes I am convinced that many parents do not even have a useful vocabulary to describe teens who aren't "troubled." Although we're comfortable acknowledging academic achievement (usually in the form of school grades), when it comes to other aspects of their lives, we mostly describe "good" kids as either those who have learned to manage or cope with their shortcomings or ones who don't have problems. That is, we resort to negatives: good kids *don't* do drugs, *don't* hang out with the wrong crowd, and *don't* engage in risky behavior. To many parents, the absence of bad things is the definition of a good kid. They think, "My child is doing well because she's not in trouble." Do we even have enough words to depict all the important, valuable, admirable, and positive things that a young person can do? Have we forgotten how to affirm their positive characteristics?

This collective amnesia is more serious than you may at first realize. Our lack of vocabulary isn't innocuous—it's a symptom of a much larger public and scientific problem that has serious implications, both for individual teenagers and for our society at large. By focusing our conversations with friends on risks and dangers, and by our fascination with reading the incessant media accounts that emphasize the negatives of the teen years, we've implicitly accepted a theory of adolescence that's based on deficits. When we view teenagers as deficient—as if something's wrong with or misssing from them—it affects them. Acknowledging our low expectations, hearing nothing but their shortcomings, they feel vulnerable. Ultimately, they may come to believe that it is inevitable that they will become involved in problematic or dangerous behavior. They may incorporate the sense of actually being "at risk" as living only a step away from getting in trouble or creating problems for others, whether it involves taking drugs, dropping out of school, becoming pregnant, or getting caught up in violent behavior.

Imagine if everywhere you turned people thought poorly of you— if every time you read an article or saw a TV news report about people your age, you realized that no one expected very much of you. Surrounded by these impressions, it wouldn't take long for you to feel burdened by the incessant accusations and suspicions. Some teens become convinced that their parents are just waiting to discover incriminating evidence or are always on the verge of asking invasive and accusatory questions: "Are you smoking cigarettes? Are you smoking dope? Are you having sex?"

What a dispiriting, disheartening outlook! Teens who grow up in this atmosphere can have their self-esteem deflated, their motivation and spirit dampened. After all, when people don't expect the best of us, we often respond in kind.

Sheila, for example, wanted her fourteen-year-old son, Andy, to help out with household chores. Since he loved their cat, Star, Sheila asked her son to be responsible for cleaning out the kitty litter box twice a week. At first, he was fairly responsible. But after a couple of weeks, Sheila found herself having to remind him. Within a month, she was nagging him all the time.

One day Andy was in the kitchen and overheard his mother on the phone talking to a friend, complaining about what a pain it was to constantly remind Andy to do his chores. "I'm sorry that I ever asked him to do this," he heard his mother say. "We always end up yelling at each other. But what I'm really worried about is that he doesn't know how to be responsible. He has to learn that life's not all play, that sometimes we have to do chores that we don't enjoy."

Andy waited until later that evening to say to his mom, "I heard you on the phone, and you have it all wrong. It's not that I don't want to help out around the house—it's just that I hate doing the kitty litter. I can't stand the smell."

Sheila was speechless. She'd known since he was a baby that Andy was very sensitive to smells. Of course it made sense that being in charge of changing the litter was not the best chore for him. After talking with him and asking about his preferences, they decided together that Andy would do the laundry. And because he had no natural aversion to this job, Sheila almost never had to remind him to do it.

But what also struck Sheila most painfully was how quickly she'd assumed that Andy had just been defiant and oppositional . . . because that's how teenagers are *supposed* to act. They're supposed to rebel, to resist doing chores, or doing anything their parents ask of them. They look for any opportunity to turn a discussion into an argument, and leave their parents no choice but to nag. Because Sheila accepted everything she'd heard about teenagers at face value, she never thought to wonder if there was another reason for Andy's behavior beyond "being a teenager."

WHY THE DEFICIT MODEL IS DEFICIENT

The negative implications of relying on a deficit model of teenage development involves more than disheartening individual adolescents and misleading their parents; it also leeches into decisions we make as a society. If we view teens as "broken," then it's our responsibility to "fix" them. This thinking explains the plethora of governmental and private programs designed to help teens who are in trouble, or to prevent problems from developing. Of course, some teens do have problems that require us to act. There are also situations in life that can and should be prevented. But today's governmental policies and social programs designed to address deficits are flawed in two ways.

First, problems are not the whole story. Focusing on a single "bad" behavior instead of placing it in the context of the whole person is like substituting a piece of a jigsaw puzzle for the completed picture. When we allow ourselves to become caught up in analyzing any single behavior, we never seem to find the time to consider the individual's totality. In this way, many of today's programs fall seriously short.

Second, these programs have not been very successful. Despite the hundreds of millions of taxpayer dollars—your money and mine—spent each year on problem prevention or problem remediation, the problems are by and large still with us. Although the numbers are decreasing slightly, kids are still taking drugs (although the drug of choice does seem to change periodically), still dropping out of school (especially in urban areas and among kids of color), still engaged in gang- and/or drug-related crime and violence, and still far too often getting pregnant and having babies. While there are some drug- and pregnancy-prevention programs that do help, the vast majority of programs have shown no convincing evidence of their effectiveness.

Because society has not spent enough time identifying factors that apply to teenagers who aren't at risk, or agreeing on the positive characteristics we would like to see all young people possess, we do not have good tools to fully evaluate the programs or social policies that are aimed at promoting positive change. We can't measure what we haven't named.

We need to think about spending tax dollars not just on fixing problems or on preventing them. We should think—as a society and as parents—about how to promote healthy, positive, admirable, and productive behaviors in our young people. And we need to find a new vocabulary to talk about our young people. Let's name the good things they can and should do. Let's measure these good things. Let's then find ways to make those good things more likely to be present in their lives.

We already have a few words to describe teenagers who are doing well, though as I mentioned earlier, we tend to reserve these for those youth who do well academically, in sports, or at their jobs. But when we talk about teens being good students, talented quarterbacks, or conscientious employees, we're still just talking about a very small portion of their behavior. What about the sense of themselves as competent and able people? What about their moral compass, their integrity, and their sense of spirituality? What about their social relationships, not just with you and their friends but, as well, with their teachers, coaches, mentors, and members of their community? Also, what about their compassion for those who have less than they do, their sense of caring, and their belief in a just world? And what about their commitment to keep themselves on the right track, to contribute to their own health and success and to the well-being of their family, community, and society?

We need words to describe all these characteristics of young people. We need to begin to talk about our teens by using these words, and we need to insist that policies and programs strive to identify, measure, and promote these important characteristics, as well as fix and prevent problems. Only then will we be able to think about teenagers as complete persons: living their lives every day, taking into account their strengths along with their weaknesses, weighing all they do wrong against all they get right. They're not problems to be fixed but resources to be developed. They're not immature or incomplete adults who need constant constraint and direction, but are active partners in their own positive transition to adulthood.

After all, as parents, this is how we thought of our children throughout every earlier stage of their lives. When they were infants, toddlers, and young children, we knew our role: to guide them through their developmental challenges to achieve mastery. We wanted nothing more than to see them walk, learn to use the toilet, build their vocabularies. We helped them achieve those goals, collaboratively. We thought of them as full of potential, capable of growing in positive ways with our loving guidance. They still are.

Maybe we don't need to change our teens as much as we need to change the way we think about them. Maybe it's time to set aside our preconceived notions of what adolescence is like and see our kids as they really are and as they can be. *The Good Teen* will help you do this.

TEENS BY THE NUMBERS

When we open our eyes to all that really characterizes our youth—and when we view them with a new, positive, and strength-based vocabulary—a different picture of adolescence emerges. This picture, according to my research, and buttressed by my own experience as a father of three grown children, indicates that much of what we accept as common wisdom about adolescents is a myth. Adolescence isn't the nightmare it's advertised to be. Most teens—and there are about forty million of them between the ages of ten and nineteen—have an undeserved bad rap.

Much of this gloom-and-doom portrait is derived from studies and statistics that bombard us, regularly showing up in newspapers, in weekly magazines, on television, and on the Internet. Yet these statistics are tethered to the deficit model, reporting on what's wrong with teenagers. The majority of these statistics hone in on four major areas where teens encounter the biggest risks:

- Drug and alcohol use and abuse, including cigarette smoking
- Unsafe sex, teenage pregnancy, and teenage parenting
- School underachievement, failure, and dropout
- Delinquency, crime, and violence

If you were to try to imagine what percentage of today's youth engaged in any one of the above behaviors, or in all four, I'm guessing that your estimate would be pretty high. Most people's would be—and for good reason: the media are constantly barraging us with dooms-day news about our teens.

So when we learn that about 10 percent of all teens engage in all four of the risk categories above, we probably experience that as very bad news. True, 10 percent translates into four million teens. That's a lot of teenagers taking serious risks, right? Wait—there's more bad news. Half of all teens, or 50 percent, engage in two of the four risk categories listed above. That sounds terrible.

I'm not going to say that's wonderful news; it isn't. There are too many kids who are playing Russian roulette with their lives. But before you despair, turn the statistic around: if four million teens are engaging in all four categories of risk, thirty-six million kids *aren't* risking their well-being in all these four areas.

Take drug use, for example. It's down among older teens but on the rise among younger teens. Yet this uptick is very recent and reverses a decade-long downward trend. Similarly, teens today are less likely to smoke than they were a decade ago, although the rates of decline are slowing and, for younger teens, stopping altogether.

When it comes to teen pregnancy, the rates are declining and have been since 1990. Today, about one million female teenagers, or 10 percent of all girls between fifteen and nineteen, become preg-nant . . . but 90 percent do not.

Let's talk about the dropout rate, which has also been falling. Today, only about 8 percent of American teens leave high school without a diploma. The bad news here is about inequity: though as many boys as girls drop out, children of color and those who are poor have higher rates of school failure. According to one study, black and Hispanic youth drop out at a rate of nearly 50 percent. A 2006 study from the Economic Policy Institute, however, shows that the rate is much lower, closer to 25 percent.

What about violence? The rates of juvenile crime and arrests for weapons charges, violence, and murder are all decreasing. Only 5 percent of youth are ever arrested and, of these, only 6–8 percent are arrested for violent crimes. Although high-profile school shoot-ings have increased public concern for student safety, school-associated violent deaths account for less than 1 percent of homicides among school-age children and youth. In a nationwide survey of high school students, 33 percent reported being in a physical fight one or more times in the twelve months preceding the survey, and 17 percent reported carrying a weapon (a gun, knife, or club) on one or more of the thirty days preceding the survey. As for bullying, which has also been in the news, an estimated 30 percent of sixth to tenth graders in the United States were involved in bullying as a bully, a target of bullying, or both.

Teenagers also face "internalizing" problems—that is, problems that affect no one but themselves. Take body image. One-half of teenage girls and one-quarter of teenage boys say that they're dissatisfied with their bodies. And the rates of obesity among children and teenagers have tripled in the last twenty years. However, the rates of serious eating disorders are lower than you probably imagine. Despite all the media attention focused on anorexia, only one-half of 1 percent of teenage girls develop it.

In terms of mental health, according to *America's Children: Key National Indicators of Well-Being 2005,* nearly 5 percent—or an estimated 2.7 million children—experience emotional or behavioral difficulties, as reported by their parents. These difficulties create problems at home, at school, and with peers. Additionally, boys as well as children from poor families were more likely than girls or children from well-off families to have definite or severe emotional and behavioral difficulties. These are sobering statistics. But if you ask how many children do *not* experience significant emotional or behavioral problems that interfere with their lives, the answer is 95 percent.

What are the statistics really telling us? For the past several years, important trends are headed in the right direction: fewer teens are dropping out, committing crimes, having sex, and abusing drugs. Yes, it's true that about one million teenage girls still get pregnant every year and 40 percent of these pregnancies end in abortion. But it's also true that nineteen million girls don't get pregnant. Yes, more eighth graders are smoking, and this is a problem because the earlier you start, the more likely you are to continue; however, fewer tenth and twelfth graders smoke. More teens may become sexually active at earlier ages than we'd like, but most aren't getting pregnant. And most teens aren't becoming alcoholics or drug addicts and are staying out of jail to finish high school.

Remember, in baseball, our national sport, a batter who retires with a batting average of .333 most likely receives a ticket to the Hall of Fame. But this sterling batting average means that on more than six out of ten trips to the plate, he made an out. That should help put the statistics in a better light.

Obviously, the snapshot of today's teens that emerges when you study the statistics is decidedly mixed: there's plenty of good news, but some bad news as well. Even in the bad news, however, I see rays of hope.

Take, for example, the statistics on teen voting. It's part of the national conversation that teens don't vote. Some pollsters attribute John Kerry's loss of the presidency in 2004 to the surprising and dismaying fact that despite Rock the Vote and other efforts targeted at getting youth to the polls, they didn't turn out. Statistics back up this claim: according to some studies, only about one-third of those eighteen to twenty-five years old vote.

But wait. When we look at another measure of civic engagement—the rate of volunteerism, for example—a very different picture emerges. About 33 to 50 percent of all youth ages fifteen to twenty-five engage in some type of voluntary community service. And these rates have been rapidly rising since the mid-1990s. In light of this, it's hard to conclude that teens are apathetic and withdrawn from civic life.

In short, the majority of teens aren't in serious trouble. They're works in progress, with strengths and weaknesses, each complex and complicated, each an individual, each possessing some characteristics and behaviors we love and cherish and some that drive us completely crazy. But on the whole, they're good kids who have good relationships with their parents, siblings, families, friends, teachers, and employers. They're upstanding citizens at home, at school, in the workplace, and in their larger communities. We ignore this reality at our own peril.

A POSITIVE VISION AND A NEW VOCABULARY

How do I know this? For the past thirty years, I've been studying adolescent development, much of that time using a new, strength-based theory of human development—Positive Youth Development. This perspective is rooted in a positive vision about youth, one stressing their strengths and potential for healthy growth. Instead of focusing only on preventing problems in children or fixing (treating) problematic behavior, Positive Youth Development strives to identify those conditions under which teens thrive—that is, grow to become model adults, who in turn bolster society's institutions. Boys or girls, able-bodied or disabled, impoverished or wealthy, religious or nonreligious, overachievers or underachievers, gay or straight, college-bound or not, whatever their culture, race, and environment—all have the potential to develop in healthy ways and contribute to society.

The roots of this theory, that our personal, moral, and civic lives are interconnected, arise from ideas as old as America itself. Benjamin Franklin, for example, believed that children who were honest and had integrity grew to be adults who could contribute meaningfully to their communities. We Americans have always believed that we have the capacity to overcome, to transcend our adversities and find ways to prosper and succeed. My research is, perhaps not surprisingly, finding that the wise ideas of the past correspond to the present reality, that there are data supporting this optimistic view of how young people develop—not just American youth, but all adolescents.

Thanks to a grant of several million dollars from the National 4-H Council—an organization that works with thousands of community-based 4-H clubs and programs across the country—I've been surveying thousands of teenagers nationwide. Much of what we have discovered will probably surprise you, as you will soon find out. For example, we've learned that teens who enjoy a healthy adolescence and a smooth transition to adulthood share similar characteristics and outlooks. We call this cluster the Five Cs, and they include competence, confidence, connection, character, and caring. When all of these are present, a sixth C emerges—contribution. Chances are good that most teens already possess at least some of these characteristics. But as you'll learn, there are many ways to enhance the strengths they have and to develop the ones they lack.

The Good Teen will also explain how we can help young people discover and tap the resources that already exist in their homes, schools, and communities so that they can create their own positive sense of self, enabling them to develop in healthy ways while contributing to society. Rather than turn our backs on our kids and call it "tough love" or send them off to "boot camp," we need to work with our teens to help them find what nourishes them. When we meet them with hope and optimism, they will respond in kind. By adopting the positive development outlook, we're dismantling the old, crippling myths of adolescence and thinking of this time of life as a period of great promise—a developmental era to be not merely endured or tolerated but truly enjoyed.

Positive Youth Development has been a hot topic in academic circles for about a decade. However, its ideas haven't yet filtered down to the general public. And although this approach grew out of rigorous developmental research and is currently considered to be at the cutting edge of scientific theory and research, it is also a very practical and accessible set of ideas that can be adapted for use in all families. The first step is to understand the core principles of the positive development perspective.

HOW TO USE THIS BOOK

I firmly believe that there's no teen who can't be launched on the course of positive development, and that it's never too late. *The Good Teen* can help you and your teen in many ways. In Chapter 2, for example, "Promoting Positive Development: From Theory to Practice," we'll explore the origins and theoretical underpinnings of positive development and how I came to embrace this framework. It will also expose one of the most persistent and damaging myths of adolescence: that there is only one stormy path through adolescence.

This particular myth has dogged our understanding of teenagers since they first became a subject of study, and its harmful shadow has handicapped us until very recently. Once we acknowledge the many possible routes through adolescence, it seems logical to help steer teens down the path that promotes their positive development. I'll explain how my colleagues and I first derived and identified the Five Cs and how these characteristics are the building blocks of successful development. I'll also discuss the notion of developmental assets, which are the social nutrients teens need to grow, and show how and why something I call the Big Three, my unique approach to parenting, helps to nurture the Five Cs.

The next six chapters constitute the practical, hands-on heart of the book. Each will explore and define one of the Five Cs (and the sixth C, contribution) individually, according to the positive development framework. You'll be given ways to recognize whether your child is already manifesting one of these characteristics without your realizing it. As we saw with Aunt Polly, it is often the case that if we're not versed in this new, optimistic approach, we can overlook or misinterpret behavior. In addition, each chapter will give you comprehensive and specific suggestions for nurturing and enhancing each characteristic using the Big Three approach.

Sadly, not all teens are able to access the Five Cs. As the tabloids remind us every day, many teens struggle simply to survive. Others face daunting challenges most of us can't even imagine. Yet my research—which involves another longitudinal study, of young gang members in a large urban area of the Midwest—indicates that if given the right support and resources, even the most troubled teen can be launched on the path toward positive development. In Chapter 9, "When Real Trouble Brews," I'll discuss some serious problem situations and tough issues, not just minor annoyances, of living with teenagers, and give advice on how to deal with teens who have difficulty thriving.

Finally, it's not sufficient to address parents within the confines of their homes about their own children. In Chapter 10, "Beyond Our Own Families: A Call to Action," you'll learn how and why positive development needs to move out of our living rooms and into our national debate. It's not enough for young people, their families, and their communities to enhance youth development. As a nation, we need to generate creative policies that focus on enhancing the positive characteristics of all young people. We need to begin a national dialogue about who young people are and what they can and should become, not merely what they must do. We need to join forces with our teenagers and with like-minded parents across the country so that we can align their strengths with the resources and supports in our own families and communities, and in the process build stronger neighborhoods, a stronger country, and a better world. To my way of thinking, we've spent too much time preventing risky behaviors and not enough time identifying the assets and building the skills of our youth and preparing them for the future. We need to focus less on drug prevention programs than on developing programs and policies that focus on young people's strengths.

As citizens, we need to do a better job of talking about the positive attributes of our young people. As we work together to accomplish this goal, we'll be looking at our teenagers through new eyes . . . and liking what we see.

After all, if Tom and Huck could turn out so well, so can all of our young people. So, too, can our nation.

Promoting Positive Development: From Theory to Practice

You can observe a lot just by watching.

—Yogi Berra

hen I began graduate school in the mid-1960s, intending to become a child psychologist, one of my professors assured me that everything I needed to learn was quite straightforward. She was very clear about this. "You can conceive of children in one of two ways," I was told. "You can believe that everything about a child is caused by his biology" (it seemed we were always talking about a "him" back in those days), "that is, by the genes his parents gave him. In short, his nature."

"Yes," I said, nodding. "Like a chip off the old block . . . the apple doesn't fall far from the tree . . . like father like—"

"Or," she interrupted, not amused by the way I linked her wisdom to the proverbs we'd all heard throughout our lives, "you can decide to not bother about anything going on inside the child—his genes, his thoughts, or anything else. Just think of the child as a black box."

A black box? "You cannot peer inside a black box," she explained. "You can never know for certain what is going on inside the box. And you don't have to, either. All you need to do is study the stimuli presented to the child and the responses that the child makes to the stimuli. By studying these stimulus-response connections, you'll learn everything you need to know about a child."

She went on to explain that by controlling the stimuli to which a child is exposed, you can control his responses, his behavior. In other words, by monitoring what parents, teachers, and other people do to the child, you can pretty much mold the child in any way. "Child development," she concluded, "is really all nurture, not nature, and it's all the information you'll have to learn."

Was that true? Could it really be so simple to become a child psychologist?

THE EPIC BATTLE: NATURE VERSUS NURTURE

I was aware that not everyone would agree with my professor. Many people studying psychology stressed what was going on inside the black box. Psychoanalysts such as Sigmund Freud, his daughter, Anna, and their colleague Erik Erikson claimed that a child's development was shaped by what they called the id, the ego, and the superego—things you couldn't even see, much less control in a laboratory. Others studied thought and/or language. Jean Piaget, a Swiss biologist, struck me as particularly interesting, albeit unusual. He was not even primarily concerned with children's responses, that is, their behaviors. He was concerned with the reasons they behaved in whatever ways they behaved.

When I asked my professor about Piaget, she dismissed him. "Why," she asked, "should we care about the child's reasons for his behavior when we can shape his behavior by controlling the stimuli he experiences?"

"Is that really all there is to know?" I blurted out.

My professor sighed. She realized she had another naive graduate student on her hands. "Well, it is certainly not as easy as I think you are suggesting, Mr. Lerner. There are so, so many stimuli and so, so many responses. Thousands of studies are done each year to discover the nature of stimulus-response connections. You'll need to learn all about these studies. And, of course, you'll need to learn how to do your own research. It's not easy to do good experiments. It's not easy to gain control over stimuli. It's no small task to be certain that teachers and parents always act in precisely the way you want them to.

"And then," she added a moment later, almost as an afterthought, "there's one other thing you'll need to learn. You'll also have to be able to explain why nature theories are wrong and why nurture ones are correct!"

"I see," I told her. "I think I understand." I walked out of my professor's office smiling. I was off to become a child psychologist.

What I didn't know then, as I skipped down the hall thinking what a snap graduate school would be, was that I was taking my place in an intellectual battle that had been raging for two thousand years as philosophers and scientists debated whether human behavior and development were caused by nature (genes) or nurture (the environment, learning, socialization).

Neither did I know then—though I certainly found out soon enough—that the study of adolescence was one of the chief battlegrounds for this debate. Indeed, the "nature army" had originally staked out this territory as their own, claiming, as Sigmund Freud originally put it and others echoed, "Biology is destiny."

Accordingly, teenagers were viewed as deficient adults—that is, as poorly behaved, quasi-grown-ups needing instruction and management. G. Stanley Hall, who pioneered the study of adolescents in 1904, thought of teenagers as creatures who needed civilizing, much the same way Aunt Polly thought of Huck Finn. Anna Freud viewed adolescence as a universally tumultuous time of huge upheavals and psychic disturbance. Erik Erikson also conceived of adolescence as a time of great danger: he wrote that teenagers were enmeshed in an identity crisis, and thought of them as "at risk" for becoming lost and uncommitted to society.

As to why they behaved like this, researchers had a ready answer: hormones made teenagers deficient. According to Anna Freud, the inevitable developmental disturbance of the teenage years was precipitated by puberty. Her colleague Erikson expanded on this theme, arguing that this hormone-induced disequilibrium brought on an inevitable crisis of self-definition, what he termed an identity crisis. Teens, it was agreed, had to act out and break away from their families in order to establish themselves. In fact, it was the *only* way to get through adolescence.

These, then, were some of the prevailing myths of adolescence:

· It was characterized by storm and stress.
· There was only one path through it.
· The difficulties were due to hormones, or "nature."

These ideas were originally promulgated by those who subscribed to the nature side of the nature-versus-nurture debate. Yet for nearly sixty years, just about everyone agreed. The idea that it was important to consider how we develop over the course of our lives wouldn't gain wide acceptance for about another decade. Adolescent development was a minor field of study. I certainly didn't want to get involved in it. I was busily devising experiments in which I could control stimuli presented to subjects and prove why the nature side of the nature-versus-nurture controversy was wrong.

WHAT'S WRONG WITH THIS PICTURE?

Then I encountered Sam Korn, the professor who would eventually sponsor my dissertation and serve as my mentor. My self-satisfaction came to an abrupt halt. He told me about the research being done by some of his colleagues—a team of psychologists, pediatricians, and psychiatrists—whose work didn't fit into a black box. The findings of two renowned child psychiatrists in the group, Alexander Thomas and Stella Chess, from New York University Medical School, were especially exciting.

Their clientele—highly educated, well-paid professional people from the New York City area—were at their wits' end. "Our children are unmanageable!" both the moms and dads complained, "Things aren't turning out as we expected. We've read and followed all the authoritative parenting books we could get our hands on. But it's no use. My child won't sleep through the night and I cannot tell when she will get up or how long it will take me to get her back to sleep."

That was bad enough. But some mothers weren't just complaining—they were also puzzled and distraught. "I'm not an inexperienced mother," many of these women began. "I've already raised a child. My oldest was terrific. I did everything the parenting books told me to do, and it worked like a charm. But with my second . . . forget it. Nothing seems to work. I'm doing exactly what I did with his older brother, and it's not working. And I'm not just talking about his sleep problems, though those are severe enough. I don't know when he's hungry. I don't know how much he'll eat. What he liked yesterday, he won't even put in his mouth today. He's driving me crazy! What am I doing wrong?"

The researchers noted other inconsistencies as well. For example, in the late 1950s and the early 1960s, when Thomas and Chess began their psychiatric practice, most "experts" assumed that if a child had behavior problems, it was his mother's fault. But they also couldn't fail to notice that some parents who were emotionally troubled sometimes had psychologically healthy kids, and some mothers who seemed to "do everything right" had very problematic children.

"Now, Mr. Lerner, tell me, what *is* wrong with these pictures?" Professor Korn asked me. "If you can determine how a child will behave by controlling the stimuli you present to that child, why aren't these children eating or sleeping as expected? And why, even in the same families, do the exact same parenting practices work so well for one kid and fail so miserably for his or her sibling? Why do troubled mothers raise healthy kids and vice versa? Why is there so much variation in how the children behave?"

Frankly, I was stumped. "What you're describing isn't supposed to happen," I said. "If you do the same thing, you get the same result. That's what the black-box theory is all about!"

"Richard," he said softly, "maybe it is supposed to work that way according to one theory. But suppose, as Thomas and Chess are learning, that the theory is not working so well. What if the world is more complicated than stimulus-response? What if we need to think more subtly about children and parents? Perhaps it's time we invented a new theory."

INTO AND BEYOND THE BLACK BOX

In fact, Thomas, Chess, and their colleagues (including my professor Sam Korn) were already on their way to developing an ambitious research project that would spawn a revolutionary new theory of child development, one that rejected the necessity of splitting the study of behavior into nature and nurture. Underlying this work was an evolving theory of interaction between people and their environment, between nature and nurture, which meant that we didn't have to emphasize one side of the equation over the other.

In Sam's class, for example, I also learned about the work of Donald Hebb, a psychologist who studied the brain and behavior. Hebb was impressed by the capacity of the brain to change its organization across life (indicating that the brain is not hardwired) and the ability of people to change their behaviors as well. He used the concept of plasticity to describe the capacity to systematically change our behavior across life. Plasticity is a fundamental asset in helping people lead successful lives. The ability to change our behavior in ways that advance our knowledge and skills, improve our ability to live successfully in the world, and help us find new paths to success is essential for healthy development. Although development also involves building on what went before in our lives, and therefore means that our lives are at least in part cumulative, plasticity means that we have the capacity to change direction if what we have been doing is no longer satisfactory to us or if circumstances change. In other words, because of plasticity, what happens later in life can be different from what went before.

Because of plasticity, we can be optimistic that we can change and improve the direction of our lives at any point no matter what our current circumstances. This holds true even for adolescents who may be engaged in a variety of problem behaviors. It is reassuring to know that plasticity lasts much longer than many scientists assumed: new studies indicate that it extends into the ninth and even tenth decades of life.

I also learned about research on "circular functions." Because of who we are as individuals (how we look, how we behave), we evoke different reactions in those with whom we interact—our mothers, for example, react differently to us than our teachers do. When we receive feedback from our environment, it changes us, which makes us change the way we act and interact, all of which allows us to develop into more complicated people. This interaction between person and environment is important; people relate to and are influenced by the society in which they exist, and the society in turn influences how people develop and behave. Because we influence those who influence us, the relationship becomes circular. That's how we become a source of our own development.

Understanding both plasticity and circular relations, Sam Korn and his colleagues cast child development in a new light. Instead of accepting the black box as is, Korn urged that we not only peer inside the box but also investigate all the family, social, and cultural influences surrounding the box. This view drew on biology, sociology, and history, as well as psychology, to understand a young person's development. He defined this development as the product of the entire system of relationships in which the child is engaged, which includes:

- How and what the child brings to any social situation—her genes, thoughts, or personality, for instance
- What the situation brings to the child—parents' expectations for the child, their child-rearing practices, and influences beyond the world of the family, such as economic pressures and professional responsibilities

In other words, to understand how and why children behave as they do, you need to understand *both* nature (genes) and the environment (nurture)—and the environment includes not only the family but also the entire social system beyond the family.

THE TUG OF TEMPERAMENT

But this approach doesn't explain why some children—and all teenagers, as it was assumed in those days—were considered so "difficult." Once again, Thomas and Chess helped us to understand this conundrum. As part of their groundbreaking New York Longitudinal Study, during which they observed the children of their clients over a period of years, Thomas and Chess decided to focus on temperament, which they defined as the behavioral style of a child. Temperament is a way of describing *how* children do whatever they do, though not *what* or *why* they do it. For instance, although all children eat and sleep, they don't all eat and sleep in the same way. The unique ways of sleeping or eating, their style of approaching these tasks, is what we call their temperament.

All parents are aware of their children's temperaments—it's what we talk about when we talk about their habits, their interpersonal style, the way they study, and the way they act in the world. For example, some children with regular or rhythmic temperaments get hungry at the same time each day and tend to eat the same amount at every meal. Some children will get hungry at all different hours of the day. These patterns tend to remain constant and carry over into adolescence. Some teens, for instance, eagerly join community organizations and welcome meeting new people; others are shy and tend to operate within a small circle of friends. Ultimately, Thomas and Chess isolated nine dimensions through which they could assess a person's temperament:

- Activity
- Distractibility
- Attention span and persistence

- Adaptability
- Approach or withdrawal
- Intensity of reaction
- Regularity (rhythmicity)
- Sensory threshold
- Mood

Thomas and Chess also noticed another important point about children's development: in some (but not all) children, these characteristics seemed to cluster into patterns:

- An "easy" child has regular routines, has a generally positive and undramatic mood, and adjusts well to new people and situations.
- A "slow to warm up" child hangs back and needs time to adjust to new people and environments.
- A "difficult" child has variable eating and sleeping routines, is often irritable, has more intense moods, and is slow to adjust to changes.

What they realized was that in most cases, children and teenagers who were labeled "difficult" shared many temperamental characteristics: they were intense in their reactions, were irregular in their habits, had a low threshold for sensory stimulation and so were considered overly "sensitive," and often weren't adaptable, so making transitions proved difficult. Children like this place heavy demands on a parent's patience and energy. In turn, the results of many studies indicate that in most American families, a child's difficult temperament is associated with poor parent-child relations. It is also likely that this child will encounter problems in the world beyond the family—with teachers and peers, for example.

It may be hard to imagine a case in which being a "difficult" child is an advantage. But it's not hard to find an example. Some researchers spent time among the Masai, a tribe living in Kenya and Tanzania, during a time of famine; for their study, they identified "easy" and "difficult" infants. When the researchers returned a year later, they found that many of the children were no longer alive—and that most of the dead were from the "easy" temperament group. Why? The difficult kids demanded more attention, food, and water. The easy kids adapted to scarcity, complained less . . . and died. In some situations, the old saying applies: the squeaky wheel gets the grease.

In this case, being "difficult" was a lifesaving advantage. Reading about these findings, I had to ask myself how any single characteristic could be considered bad. How could we label a temperament as intrinsically "difficult"? In truth, the children who stayed alive possessed unexpected strengths, especially when their natures were combined with the appropriate environment (the best nurture for them).

We don't have to travel to Africa to find examples like this. Most American families, for instance, would consider the incessant demands, shifting moods, and erratic schedules of a "difficult" child very trying. On those days when parents are especially exhausted, they can even claim that their oppositional, grumpy child is out to get them. But not every parent would react this way. According to some studies I found, many moms spoke with pride about their "difficult" kids. "He doesn't take any crap from anybody," they bragged.

These moms understood what Thomas and Chess discovered—there's no single way to interpret any one personality characteristic, or any constellation of characteristics. But Thomas and Chess didn't stop here. While refusing to characterize individual characteristics or even temperaments as good or bad, they pioneered the concept of "goodness of fit."

Suppose, for example, Julie has a low sensory threshold—sounds startle her, fabrics abrade her, bright lights irritate her. If she's raised in a rough-and-tumble family, with parents who love their music loud and their lights bright, she'll seem perennially out of step with them. They'll call her "overly sensitive" and "difficult." If, however, she's raised in a family that's quieter and more subdued, she'll fit in just fine. Or consider Sean, who has many characteristics of what we'd consider the "typical" teenager—his sleeping and eating patterns are very erratic. He'd be considered impossible in a family that ate its meals at regular intervals and synchronized its alarm clocks. However, he'd fit right into a more unconventional family. More than that, his irregularity would prove a real plus in a family in which the parents work irregular hours and who are able to be more spontaneous in their plans.

The concept of goodness of fit opened up a new world to me. Thomas and Chess' work challenged me to reject all splits when we think about child development. It makes no sense, they argued, to label and judge how a child behaves as "good" or "bad." We need to evaluate behavior in terms of the bigger picture; we need to look at and study the relationship between a child's characteristics and the family and broader social environment in which she lives. Instead of thinking in terms of black or white, which ultimately isn't helpful or useful, we need to adjust the dial and think in terms of shades of gray.

THE SEEDS OF POSITIVE YOUTH DEVELOPMENT

The same message was emerging from those developmental systems theorists, as Sam Korn and his colleagues came to be known, who were reconsidering basic notions of cause and effect as it applied to human development. If it's not helpful to separate characteristics into "good" and "bad," it's equally wrongheaded to separate nature from nurture. The two are inextricably linked.

Those who subscribe to the nature approach, they explained, conceptualize an arrow going in one direction, from genes to behavior. Similarly, those who subscribe to the nurture approach imagine that the arrow also travels in just one direction, only this one moves from the environment to the person. To conceive of a developmental system, however, as Sam Korn and his colleagues did, is to recognize that causal arrows don't travel in one direction but go every which way. That is, the arrow that links a person to her genetic makeup has a tip on both ends: genes influence behavior, but behavior also influences genes.

The same is true for environmental influences on our development—it's mutual. The environment doesn't simply act on us; we act on the environment. Again, the arrows that track cause and effect travel in both directions at once.

It made sense to use this lens on development to think about how children grow. They're not passive recipients of information, whether it's from genetics or the outside world. Instead, they contribute to and shape how they develop.

If development results from the way children relate to the entire environment surrounding them, then there was a chance that we could change a child's behavior for the better by changing the way he or she relates to the world. If we could isolate the right characteristics in families, schools, and communities—those that promote positive growth—then we could promote positive change in youth. This idea anticipates the concept of the Five Cs, which I will discuss later in the chapter.

MYTH-BUSTING

This was the "new theory" Sam Korn taught me, and I embraced it. I would develop the theory further, I reasoned, because this is what a Ph.D. candidate is supposed to do. But what would I study? When I asked Sam, he urged me to take an advanced seminar in child development.

Even in the late 1960s and early 1970s, adolescence was still considered a specialized and quite minor field of study within the field of child development. Most researchers still clung to the old ideas that persisted in Freud's shadow—that most of the important developmental milestones and events took place before the adolescent years. As a result, other than the inevitable biological and emotional changes occurring when puberty struck, there was little to discuss. Everyone, it seemed, agreed that there was only one path through adolescence and that it was a stormy one.

Yet I was not convinced by this unanimity. And I wasn't the only one. Many other researchers were discovering evidence that painted a very different, much more nuanced picture of adolescence than the one we usually heard.

Daniel Offer, for instance, a psychiatrist in Chicago, found evidence for multiple paths through adolescence for boys. Most boys experienced either "continuous growth," which involved smooth and gradual changes in behavior that caused no problem for them or their parents, or "surgent growth," which involved some significant growth spurts or changes in behavior. However, such change was *not* typically associated with crisis or problems. Only a minority of boys experienced what Offer termed "tumultuous growth," which he defined as characterized by "storm and stress."

Echoing these findings in a different vein, Jack Block, a psychology professor at the University of California at Berkeley, found adolescent development was characterized by plasticity, not rigidity, and that many of the paths through the period were in fact positive. He found five different ways through adolescence for males and six different ways for females. For both sexes, some were always positive, a few were always problematic, and most had negative and positive features.

In another study, researcher Albert Bandura, professor of psychology at Stanford University, observed that aggressive, antisocial boys had an adolescence associated with storm and stress. However, their problem behaviors were present throughout their childhood. Bandura concluded that one could not appropriately view the problems of these boys as resulting only from adolescence.

Based on my findings and those of others, one of the major myths of adolescence was shattered: that there's only one path through adolescence. If we accept that each teen's development is a culmination of how she interacts with a staggeringly wide variety of biological, psychological, social, and cultural factors—including her family, her peers, her physical environment, her own biological and psychological makeup, the institutions with which she interacts (such as schools, churches, workplaces, teams, and clubs), her society, her niche in history—then we simply can't argue for the existence of a "typical" teenager or believe that any single conception (or stereotype) of adolescence is generally true. Clearly, no two teens, not even identical twins, have the same experiences; none undergoes transitions in the same way, with the same speed, or with the same results. Development isn't simple but incredibly multifaceted.

The myth about teenage hormones was also being dismantled. Conventional wisdom had long held that hormones influenced a teenager's psychological, social, and cultural development. But now some of us were learning that hormones weren't always the prime mover but were in fact influenced by psychological, social, cultural, and historical issues. Several studies indicated that although girls who begin menstruating early may be those who become delinquent, this is likely to be the case when those girls socialize with older friends rather than with girls their own age. Girls who had friends their own age tended not to become delinquent even if they matured earlier than most of their peers.

Similarly, we used to believe that teenagers' ability to think diminished during adolescence, as if their hormones scrambled their brains. Instead, studies showed that in many cases a teen's cognitive abilities were enhanced during adolescence, especially in those settings in which teens feel comfortable. Studies such as these illustrated the ways in which hormones are influenced by the environment, busting one of the most entrenched myths of adolescence—that teens are driven by their hormones.

Soon another accepted myth of adolescent development crumbled as we discovered that most teenagers didn't feel an urgent need to break away from their parents. Sure, the peer group still exerts a lot of influence in terms of how teens talk, what they wear, and what music is on their iPods. But teens spend a surprising amount of time with their parents, value their parents' opinions, and adopt values about core issues, such as the importance of education and social justice, even spirituality, that resonate with their parents' beliefs. More than that, teens even tend to choose friends who share these beliefs.

Clearly, my colleagues and I were on to something. It was thrilling to discard the damaging myths plaguing adolescent studies, to reject the older black-and-white, good-or-bad snapshots we'd relied on when describing teenagers and to draw them anew with all the shades of gray at our disposal. It was exciting to discover how plastic teens were, to realize that there were many roads, not just one, through adolescence, and to realize that the potential for change existed at every level.

But how could I make my own contribution to this exciting new field? What exactly was *my* territory? Where and how could I stake my claim?

The answer came to me in a conversation, a kind of bookend to the conversation about the black box I'd had with my professor years earlier that launched me on my career. The conversation that gave me the answer began when my son Justin happened to walk into my study the day I was unpacking copies of my seventeenth academic book. As proud as a kid with a new bike, I showed it to him. He shrugged. Clearly, he was less than impressed. Then he asked me, "Why do you write those things, anyway? Do they ever help anybody?"

His simple questions cut me to the quick. In a single stroke he raised the issue I'd been busy avoiding as I set about establishing myself professionally. Sure, it was fascinating to understand how teens developed and to chart the many paths through adolescence. But I wanted to do more than understand. I wanted to understand how to promote positive and healthy change. And then I wanted to make that change happen.

BEING PREPARED VERSUS BEING PROBLEM-FREE

How to best promote positive change is a difficult question. As recently as thirty years ago, there were basically only two kinds of programs to help kids grow, and both were based on the soon-to-be challenged deficit model.

As we discussed in Chapter 1, one camp was made up of advocates of "remediation," professionals who tried to remedy, lessen, or soften problems once they arose. For example, those kids who had internalizing problems, such as anxiety, depression, eating disorders, and other psychological issues, were often sent to psychotherapists to find out what was "wrong" with them. Kids with externalizing problems—who acted out and were aggressive or defiant—might be packed off to "boot camps," "tough love" programs, or in some states "punk prisons," which tried to shock, humiliate, and intimidate them into submission.

A second group said, "Remediation programs are not good uses of either financial or human resources. Instead of trying to cure problems, let's try to prevent them from cropping up in the first place. After all, wouldn't it be better to prevent cancer from occurring by discouraging smoking than to try to cure it through surgery or chemotherapy once it appears?" This approach spawned a plethora of prevention programs, such as D.A.R.E. (Drug Abuse Resistance Education), which strive to give "kids the skills they need to *avoid* involvement in drugs, gangs, and violence" (italics mine).

But at about the same time, pioneering practitioners in the field of youth development programs noted the inadequacy of both these approaches. Rick Little (founder of the International Youth Foundation, or IYF) and Karen Pittman (executive director of the Forum for Youth Investment) argued that these programs didn't go far enough. Prevention programs teach kids what *not* to do without teaching them what they *should* do. Just because you've learned not to smoke or drink to excess doesn't mean that you have the skills to be a productive member of society. Adults, for their part, can try to prevent teens from engaging in unsafe sex, but that doesn't necessarily give teens the skills they need to enjoy a loving, intimate, honest, and enduring relationship with another person, or to teach them how to find the means with which to make a positive contribution—to their own lives and to society. Being problem-free doesn't mean that you are prepared.

In the early 1990s I was hired as a consultant by the W. K. Kellogg Foundation to work with Rick Little and Karen Pittman, and to help them use theory and research about adolescent development to improve the IYF programs. I soon realized, however, that I had a lot to learn from them. I agreed with them that we can't simply tell kids to "just say no." We have to tell kids how to say *yes*—to give them the skills they need to develop successfully, to make positive contributions to their family, their after-school or summer jobs, their neighborhood, and the world at large. I knew that we needed a new vocabulary that would describe the strengths teens possessed rather than one which focused on their problems.

CREATING THE FIVE Cs

By the mid-1990s, thanks to the contributions of many practitioners such as Rick Little and researchers such as Peter Benson, William Damon, and myself, such a vocabulary began to emerge. We identified a set of strengths that, if nurtured, would prepare teens for a successful transition to adulthood:

- *Competence:* the ability to act effectively in school, in social situations, and at work
- *Confidence:* an internal sense of overall self-worth and efficacy
- *Connection:* positive bonds with people and social institutions
- *Character:* respect for society and cultural rules, an inner moral compass
- *Caring:* a sense of sympathy and empathy for others and a commitment to social justice

Later, a sixth C was added—one that emerges when the other five are present:

- *Contribution:* the capacity of teenagers to participate effectively by caring for themselves, so as not to be a drain on others, and by giving of themselves at home, in the community, and in civic life

If you're reading this list and worrying that your teen doesn't possess these characteristics and he's already in trouble—stop! The list of Cs is intended not to increase your anxiety but indeed to reassure you. According to my research, your teen already possesses facets of many if not all of the Cs.

Think for a moment. Many teenagers feel competent in some area, whether it's on a volleyball court, in the classroom, or dealing with other people. Many feel a connection to at least one other person outside the family—a teacher, coach, girlfriend, or teammate. Some kids act with a great sense of character, that is, they know right from wrong and stand up for others who are being treated unjustly. And many teens have caring relationships with family and friends, demonstrating compassion for others in times of need.

Still, for teens as well as adults, it's difficult to achieve a score of 100 percent for any C. It's best to think of the Cs as qualities that can and should be strengthened. And that's the purpose of this book.

THE FIVE Cs IN REAL LIFE

The Cs represented a big conceptual advance for those of us working with teens and trying to enhance their positive development. But the list was largely theoretical, and many practical questions persisted. For example, did the Five Cs actually exist? Could they be promoted? If development results from the way children relate to the entire environment surrounding them, could we change their behavior for the better by changing the way they relate to their world? If we could isolate the right characteristics in families, schools, and communities, could we promote positive change for teenagers? This is what I wanted to find out.

I decided to conduct a longitudinal study, which means that I would observe the same group of people repeatedly over a period of time. In 2000, and continuing for four subsequent years, I collaborated with Carl Taylor, a colleague from Michigan State University, on a study called Overcoming the Odds (OTO). It focused on African American teenagers growing up in the same Detroit neighborhood. Each year, through 2004, we compared two groups of young people. In one group were male adolescents who were members of gangs; in the other were kids who belonged to sports programs, 4-H clubs, or church-affiliated programs, all of which promoted positive youth development. To say that the results surprised us is an understatement.

As anticipated, we discovered that the teens enrolled in community organizations had higher levels of positive development. But what totally surprised us, as much as a .200 career batter hitting three home runs off an ace pitcher, was our discovery that across a five-year period, a small but consistent proportion of gang members (about 15 percent) showed characteristics of positive development that were similar to those youth in the community organizations.

I can't emphasize the importance of our findings enough: despite the fact that they lived in challenged, poor communities, and despite the fact that the violence, drug use, and other myriad risks associated with gang membership would suggest to many people that there was no hope for these young people, some of them were in fact overcoming the odds against them and appeared to be moving on a positive life path. That is, even though these teens were considered by some people as beyond help, they managed to possess and maintain valued characteristics—such as positive identity, social competence, and positive values—associated with positive development.

What allows this to happen?

The answer is that they were able to take advantage of certain available resources in their environments that promoted their healthy growth. These resources, what I call developmental assets, nurture all the Cs.

IDENTIFYING THE RESOURCES AROUND YOU TO GROW THE Cs

I believe that if you examine the world in which children live, you'll find things that either help or hinder their positive growth. As parents, we need to remove elements that will harm our kids, and supply elements that will help them. When my children were infants, my wife and I (actually, mostly my wife) baby-proofed our home so our children wouldn't hurt themselves; we also hung mobiles and mirrors in their crib to promote their development.

As children grow, we continue to protect them from what's harmful and give them positive things that will help them grow. These positive things are the "developmental assets" I mentioned earlier, and they can be found wherever our kids eat, sleep, learn, and play.

- You may not think of *individuals* as resources, but they are. Every time your teen interacts with you, teachers, counselors, coaches, mentors, employers, or members of the clergy, he's drawing on a resource.
- Some of the most important interactions he has with the adults in his world take place when they embark on activities together. The experience that comes from *intergenerational activities* is another key resource.
- He also interacts with *institutions,* such as schools, religious institutions, community organizations, and sports teams, and these provide yet another resource for him.
- To take advantage of these above resources, he needs to have *access* to them—and this is another asset we'll talk about throughout this book.

Just as not all teens pursue the same path through adolescence, not all teens need the same resources. And not every resource is available to every teen. But some sources of positive development exist in every home, school, and community. By coming in contact with these resources on a daily basis, teens develop the Five Cs. In general, the more resources that exist in children's lives, the more likely they are to thrive.

But how do we ensure that teens take full advantage of what's around then? This is the job that falls to parents—introducing and connecting, or aligning, teens with the opportunities that surround them. And they do it by adopting my approach to parenting.

These are the Big Three (see page 39). To best understand my reasoning, ask yourself, "What is my goal as a parent?" The goal is to raise teens who are healthy and self-reliant and who become productive adults who can assume leadership roles in their lives and in their community and the world at large. To do this, teens need to be able

THE BIG THREE: HOW TO GROW THE FIVE Cs

When I began analyzing all the parenting how-to approaches, many of them based on excellent research, I realized that what I considered the most successful ones had three key elements in common. They all gave teens the opportunity to:

1. Have sustained, positive interactions with adults
2. Participate in structured activities that enable them to develop valued life skills
3. Become leaders of valued community activities

to practice their leadership skills. This goal involves the third item in the Big Three.

How can teens best learn to be leaders? They learn by watching important adults—parents, teachers, coaches, mentors, members of the clergy—as they live their lives. Without even always realizing it, teens observe adults engaged in those very life skills teens need to develop. These skills include the ability to manage their time, prioritize, delay gratification, and accept responsibility. This is the second item in the Big Three.

How can we help ensure that teens will be receptive to learning life skills from their parents and other adults? How can we help them be open to learning? We do this by creating and sustaining positive interactions with teens, by engaging in positive relationships. This is the first item in the Big Three.

Of all the Big Three components, the first—having sustained, positive interactions with adults—is the most important. By "sustained," I mean relationships that extend over long periods of time; by "positive," I mean relationships that are thoughtful, committed, caring, sincere, and meaningful—not "drive-by" relationships, or ones you can phone in. In effect, adults with whom teens have positive relationships are the delivery system for all the other developmental resources.

Although we will discuss each facet of the Big Three individually, it's essential to remember that they need to be present simultaneously—we can't separate one from the other. Think of a double play in baseball: for it to work, the first baseman, second baseman, and shortstop all have to be in position. Without any one of them, the play won't work.

TRANSLATING THEORY INTO ACTION

By articulating the Five Cs and the Big Three, my colleagues and I had developed a vocabulary that allowed us to think about the characteristics of healthy teens and about how to foster their positive development. But many of the previous questions still remained unanswered. Most important, did the Five Cs really exist? If so, could they be measured? Did the Five Cs really lead to the development of the sixth C, contribution? There were no studies to prove any of this.

In 2000, however, I had an opportunity to begin to answer some of these questions. Through Don Floyd, who is the president and CEO of the National 4-H Council and a good friend and colleague, I received a multimillion-dollar grant to conduct a comprehensive study about the Cs.

Working with the National 4-H Council made perfect sense, as 4-H is the nation's largest youth-serving organization. Each year it serves about seven million teens who are enrolled in one or more of its community-based in-school or after-school programs. The mission of these programs, as stated on its Web site, is, "To advance the 4-H youth development movement to build a world in which youth and adults learn, grow and work together as catalysts for positive change."

The 4-H Study got under way early in 2002. We began by studying a diverse group of 1,700 fifth graders from thirteen states across the country, and a sample of about 1,200 of their parents. We had a good mix of rural and urban kids, as well as kids from different racial, ethnic, and religious groups. By its fifth year of data collection our initial group of fifth graders were now ninth graders, and the study involved about 4,000 adolescents from twenty-five states and about 2,000 parents.

We chose to start with fifth graders because the existing research literature indicated that the incidence of risk behaviors among children this age is low. Since our goal was to chart the growth of the Five Cs and to assess whether risk and problem behaviors diminished as positive development grew, we thought it reasonable to start our research at a point in life before most problem behaviors took hold.

We gave surveys to each child and one parent or guardian per child. Most of the data were obtained from the children, who were approached mainly in school; the parent questionnaire was used mostly to gauge family income and educational levels. Although the study is ongoing, with new and exciting results being reported each year, it has already yielded significant new findings. We have learned that:

- The Five Cs do exist. We can reliably and validly measure them. They cluster together as a measure of positive development. And, as predicted, positive development is related to the presence of the sixth C, contribution.
- No matter how low a teen may score on an initial assessment of positive development, he or she can improve. This means that *all* young people can show gains in positive development and the healthy behaviors associated with it.
- Belonging to certain types of community programs, such as 4-H clubs, enhances the Five Cs.
- Families that spend time together—for example, who eat dinner together—are providing their teens with the most important resource to promote positive development.
- Whether one is looking within the family, the school, or the community, the key resource that is linked to positive development are the individuals within any setting: parents, teachers, coaches, and mentors.

PROMOTING POSITIVE DEVELOPMENT IN YOUR CHILDREN

Now that we know that the Five Cs exist and how we can help teens thrive, it's time to get the word out. The following chapters will talk about each C individually, giving you a sense of the breadth of its meaning and explaining how you can identify it in your child. You'll learn how to recognize and access the resources that exist in your child's environment, and how to promote and grow each of the Cs using the Big Three. You'll see how you might integrate opportunities to build the Cs into your child's life. Remember that even though we discuss the Cs one at a time, they are all inextricably interconnected. A competent teen, for example, will most likely have the confidence she needs to create connections with other people. Similarly, a teen with character will appreciate the importance of caring for others.

But before moving on, I want to talk about parenting styles and the one that is most conducive to developing these strengths.

PARENTING STYLES

As we all know, there's no single way to be a parent. But parents who are authoritative usually do best in implementing the Big Three. Authoritative parents believe in rules that govern behavior, both their kids' and their own; however, they explain the rules to their children and try to create partnerships with them. They feel that they are responsible for making their children understand why the rules of the family exist, and for helping their children develop the skills they need to govern themselves in appropriate ways.

Becoming an authoritative parent is an important and necessary first step toward using the Big Three to promote positive development. Authoritative parents implicitly have faith that their children can learn to think and behave in ways that will result in their healthy development.

But being authoritative, while necessary, is not sufficient. Parents need to understand the cause-and-effect relationship between increasing the number of resources in a child's life and promoting the Five Cs. They need to understand the rationale behind the Big Three so that they can use this approach effectively. They need to commit themselves to keep at it— that is, to work throughout the teenage years to make certain that their child's transition to adulthood will be as smooth and full of potential as possible.

This type of parenting is *not* the same as being authoritarian. Authoritarian parents govern their children through strict rules; they also use punishment, often physical punishment, to enforce their edicts. These parents do not take their child's perspective into account in running the household or in setting its rules. Because obedience is their chief goal, they are not concerned with nurturing a teen's leadership capabilities.

In the same way, "helicopter" parents—those who hover too close, always eager to micromanage their teens' lives—won't give teens the room they need to develop in positive ways. But the other extreme isn't healthy, either: "hands-off" parents, who believe that teens are old enough to manage on their own without any guidance, and are too absent from their teens' lives to provide them with the skill-building opportunities they need.

In short, parents who become authorities about positive development and who bring assets into the lives of their children by enacting the Big Three substantially increase the likelihood that their teens will prosper and thrive all through adolescence. This assertion is not based on my personal opinion; it is founded on more than thirty years of research. Every recommendation I make in this book derives not from conjecture but rather from the interpretation of state-of-the-art research that has been conducted in my laboratory over three decades and, as well, in the laboratories of colleagues across the nation and throughout the world.

LOOKING AHEAD

I'm guessing that some of you have read this far and are saying to yourselves, "This sounds like a great theory, and I'm sure it works with some parents and teens. But it will never work in my house. My kids are like black boxes: I don't know what makes them tick. And if I don't, you don't, either."

That's true—I don't know your teens, and I don't know all the intimate details of your household. Certain suggestions I make may well resonate much more than others. Not everything clicks with every reader. Reading any parenting book is always a matter of picking and choosing what you can use. And I can't say for certain that the advice I offer in this book will work all the time, in every family, in exactly the way we want it to, 100 percent of the time. Nothing about parenting is an all-or-nothing proposition.

On the other hand, I trust our research. I have faith in the power of the Five Cs to help teens make a smooth, healthy adjustment to adulthood. I fully believe that every child has the potential to develop in a positive way. Over the course of this book, I hope I can convince you to trust in your teens' strengths as well.

The task ahead may seem daunting. At moments we all lose hope. But hope is an essential part of positive development. A child with a hopeful future is likely to be motivated to stay on a path toward positive development. A parent who maintains a hopeful attitude about her child's future can only help her along this path.

Before we can make even the smallest change, then, we need to cultivate hopefulness, but we also have to believe that we have the capacity to effect a change. This conviction in our own ability to make things happen, to be an agent of change, is a belief in our competence. It's the first C, the foundation upon which all the other Cs rest, and the one I'll explore in the next chapter.

Competence

I am only one,
But still I am one.
I cannot do everything,
But still I can do something;
And because I cannot do everything
I will not refuse to do the something that I can do.

—Edward Everett Hale

The summer my daughter, Blair, was nineteen, she traveled to Europe with a friend who, after a few weeks, left Blair to visit family in Italy. This meant that Blair would fly home alone from Paris—a prospect that fazed neither her nor us. Both before her trip and during it, she'd carefully attended to every travel arrangement by herself, down to the tiniest detail. Everything up to this point had gone off very well, and Blair had no reason to expect otherwise now that she'd be traveling alone. We had every faith in her, and she shared that faith in herself.

But when she arrived at the airport that Friday morning and tried to board the plane, she discovered that there was one important detail among the many hundreds she'd considered that she'd somehow overlooked: her passport, which had been valid when she left the United States, had expired while she was traveling. As a result, the plane flew back to the States without her.

She called us, frantic, hysterically crying—what should she do? We were frantic ourselves, scared out of our wits for her safety and welfare. All we had to connect us across that vast ocean was a fragile cell phone, which we all clung to like a lifeline. I even offered to fly to Paris on Saturday in order to return with her on Monday, an offer she eventually declined. "I can manage, I'll be OK," she said. This was the first time we heard her say anything like that during the call.

Now that she'd regained some composure, we worked together to compose a plan of action. The first order of business was to call the U.S. embassy, where she learned that nothing could be done until Monday morning. That meant she'd have to find a place to stay. She had little money and knew less French. With our help, she was able to find a hotel. It was far from ideal. The room was dingy and the clerk surly—he acted as if it were a huge inconvenience to merely transfer our calls to her room.

Once she was settled, we spent hours helping her figure out ways to pass the time until Monday morning. Although we kept trying to tell her that there were worse places to spend a weekend than Paris, she wasn't having any of it.

But in fact, she managed very well. By Saturday she'd moved to a new, more comfortable hotel. On Sunday she not only got precise directions from the hotel to the embassy but also practiced getting there so that she'd know exactly what connections she'd need to make on Monday morning, how much time it would take, and how much the fare would be.

With each phone call, she sounded more and more herself. By the time she emerged from the plane at Boston's Logan Airport, she was looking somewhat triumphant. She had accomplished what she'd needed to do in order to get herself home, and returned home a more competent young woman than she'd been when she left. In fact, she was more competent than she would have been had she remembered to renew her passport in the first place!

What do we really mean when we describe our kids as competent? We usually intend it to mean "able" or "up to a task." Think about it. Suppose you were to meet the parents of a child that your own child has lost touch with over the years, although they were once close. You'd naturally ask how their child is doing. You'd intend it as an open-ended question—wanting to know how the child is faring in the world, if she's meeting the challenges of her life, if she's successful and productive.

All too often, though, when we try to define competence as it refers to our children, we end up talking about school. We share information about grades, AP classes, extracurricular activities, and college visits.

If only it were that easy—if only doing well in school guaranteed success in life. Sure, there are some correlations. Performing well in school is linked to success in life and to how much your child will earn over his or her lifetime.

But being competent actually encompasses many more behaviors than being inducted into the honor society or taking five AP classes. Blair, for instance, happened to be a wonderful student. But the ways in which she proved her competence during the snafu at the Paris airport had little to do with academic competence. In fact, being competent in school is only one piece of a much larger picture.

BEYOND GOOD GRADES: DEFINING COMPETENCE

Competence is the ability to perform adequately in the world. Most simply, it refers to what you can *do* (as contrasted with how you *feel*). It means being able to accomplish what is needed so as to have effective interactions with other people and social institutions. Someone who is competent knows how to make things work out for him. Like a chain reaction, the more competence you have, the more competently you act, which hones your skills and leads you to be more competent.

Teens may demonstrate competence in five arenas: academically, cognitively, socially, emotionally, and vocationally. Each of these areas encompasses many more qualities than you may probably realize.

Academic Competence

Most narrowly, academic competence refers to the ability to get good grades on tests, papers, and report cards. But within the positive development perspective, academic competence involves much more. A young person with academic competence says to herself, "I'm a part of this system. I understand its rules: I contribute to it, and in turn I feel accepted by it." Academically competent teens are good school citizens—they join teams, audition for plays, and participate in events and student government. They also know how to negotiate the entire school environment and adapt it to their needs.

Annie, for example, a high school sophomore, was eager to participate in the highly competitive International Baccalaureate program her high school was initiating. Her teachers and parents were leery of letting her join the program. She'd been an average and unenthusiastic student, and this very rigorous program seemed tailored for those with more motivation. Annie, however, was undeterred. To support her admission, she sought out her teachers and guidance counselor to persuade them that because the courses had an international orientation, they would prove more interesting to her, and that she always worked better when challenged.

After numerous meetings and interviews, Annie was accepted into the program. Her first grades were sobering. But two years later, she proudly completed the very difficult curriculum. Statistically, Annie finished squarely in the middle of her peers in terms of her overall average and test scores; her performance was far from the best but equally far from the worst. But in terms of her total academic competence, Annie deserved an A. She had recognized that this specialized program would inspire her, and she worked with deliberation and passion to achieve her goal. Because she was able to recognize and take advantage of a scholastic opportunity that advanced her abilities, her high school experience was greatly enriched.

Cognitive Competence

This refers to intellectual abilities that transcend those needed to succeed academically; it includes an ability to articulate and argue cogently for one's opinions or to acquire information about topics that are of interest whether or not these topics arise or are assigned in school. If your teen listens to the news, watches the History Channel, maintains a blog, does crossword puzzles or Sudoku, is an avid reader, or is on the debate team, then he's cognitively competent.

Creativity—writing poetry, improvising at the piano, creating collages—is another manifestation of cognitive competence. The ability to imagine or see new ideas, relations, or products is very highly related to visual and verbal cognitive abilities.

Jonathan, for instance, the son of a family friend, believed from a very young age that duct tape was the answer to all of life's little annoyances: he used it to fix his shoelaces when the plastic tips came off, to attach coins inside his sneakers so he would have exact change for ice cream at the park, and even to keep his jeans up when he didn't feel like wearing a belt.

But Jonathan's most creative use of this product occurred at sleep-away camp the summer he was thirteen. He found himself living in a bunk with six other boys, all of whom just happened to be as tall as he was. Luckily, the bunk had its own bathroom; unfortunately, the toilet was positioned directly in front of a set of shelves on which the boys hit their heads every time they flushed. Jonathan cut a five-foot length of duct tape and attached one end to the ceiling and the other end to the flusher handle. Now his bunkmates could flush by standing up straight and pulling down on the tape. Problem creatively solved!

Cognitive competence can also be reflected in curiosity or inquisitiveness about different areas of knowledge and in the ability to figure out how to acquire this knowledge. Teens who are devoted to hobbies—whether they collect baseball cards, stamps, or figurines—are expanding their knowledge base when they consult the Internet, go to the library, or attend trade shows. They also learn patience and perseverance.

Social Competence

Social competence entails knowing what's expected in differing social situations and being able to act accordingly. If your child has satisfying and sustained relationships, she's socially competent. The number of friends she has doesn't matter as much as the quality of these relationships. But the definition of this competence also includes knowing how to act toward people of different ages, stations, and walks of life—teachers and employers; peers, friends, and siblings; waiters, salesclerks, and telemarketers; and eventually, perhaps, employees. A competent person knows how to conduct herself during a job interview, how to turn down a solicitation for a charity, how to participate in a committee meeting, and whom to turn to for help.

Teens sharpen their social competence skills in the course of their everyday lives. Sports—even individual sports, such as tennis—give teens an arena in which to learn about mastery, teamwork, commitment to others, and the importance of coping with both failure and success in socially acceptable ways. When families attend a place of worship together or participate in community events—such as road races, street fairs, Memorial Day parades, and Fourth of July picnics—teens learn social skills along the way.

Finally, social competence is about knowing how to handle strangers, those who you perceive as threatening, those in need, and those who cause you problems. At eighteen, for example, Rachel went off to the college she'd long dreamed of attending. She was a little less enthusiastic about her roommate, Beth, who had a propensity for leaving wet towels on the floor and for "borrowing" her sweaters without asking. As if that wasn't bad enough, within the first month of school Beth's new boyfriend, Ed, basically moved in—with a lot of his stuff. The dorm room, which had been tiny enough to begin with, became uninhabitable. "He sleeps over all the time," Rachel complained to her mother. "They give me dirty looks at night, as if they expect me to pick up and sleep elsewhere. I do, but by imposing on my friends. I hate feeling homeless. But worst of all, on the nights I stay they have sex after they think I've fallen asleep."

Her mother was outraged. I would have been, too. Unfortunately, this situation is all too common. Being "sexiled," or exiled from your dorm room because of your roommate's romantic life, is something many teens have to cope with. Rachel's mother wanted to complain to the dean of freshmen. Rachel begged her not to. "At least go to your resident advisor; maybe you can move to a new dorm," her mother said. But Rachel didn't want to move. Neither did she want to alienate her roommate or Ed, whom she actually liked.

In the end, Rachel's mother agreed to let Rachel handle her "sexile" her own way. What Rachel proposed was that she, Beth, and Ed meet with the resident advisor. "Look," she said to the couple at that meeting, "I just don't want to be in the room when you're having sex. I don't mind sleeping out a few nights a week if we can agree on these in advance," she continued. "And if you're in the room together when I'm out, leave me some kind of sign, like a towel on the doorknob."

"It's working out," Rachel told her mother a few days later. Not only did she again feel welcome in her own room, but she was proud of herself for finding a solution to a seemingly intractable problem by herself—and doing it in a way that accommodated everyone.

Emotional Competence

If your teen is doing well in school and has satisfying relationships, then she's already demonstrating her emotional competence, which entails the ability to identify, manage, and regulate one's emotions so that they help rather than hinder one's progress in the world. It's about knowing how to take turns, to delay gratification, to share and get along with others, and to cope with different contingences, such as success and failure.

Jeremy, for example, age fourteen, was a gifted drummer who looked forward to joining the high school jazz band, a collection of the school's most elite musicians. When he showed up for the audition, however, he was told he was ineligible to try out since he wasn't a member of the marching band. Jeremy was deeply disappointed. He'd attended music assemblies at the high school when his older brother was a member of the jazz band, and had been dreaming for years of joining the group himself. "It's one thing if I failed the audition," he complained bitterly to his parents, "but not being given the chance to try out? That's just flat-out unfair. I can't accept it." A day later, he told his parents that he'd decided to stop taking drum lessons.

For nearly a week, Jeremy didn't pick up a drumstick. But the night before his lesson, his parents heard him practicing. The next morning, he said that he'd changed his mind: he'd continue taking lessons. "Why should I spite myself over a stupid rule?" he asked. That he was able to assimilate his disappointment in ways that didn't further deprive him of the things he loved was a sign of his sophisticated emotional competence.

To be emotionally competent is to understand also that we need to take into account other people's emotions and reactions. Jed, thirteen, grew up loving musical theater thanks to his parents, who took him to plays from the time he was barely out of diapers. In middle school, he met a group of friends who shared his passion—who thought nothing of bursting into song when discussing a production they were involved in. At the same time, Jed knew not to behave that way when he was around his friend Armand, who was much quieter and more restrained. Thanks to his emotional competence, Jed was able to modulate his interactions with people and was sensitive to the fact that his exuberance would overwhelm his quiet, more analytical friend.

Vocational Competence

Teens who are able to work—whether it's holding a part-time job after school, having a summer job or internship, or participating in a work-study program—are demonstrating their vocational competence. They learn to get along with people who have power, such as bosses and supervisors, with one's co-workers, and with those who may be subordinates. It's also about learning to seize the initiative, assume responsibility, follow directions, and complete tasks. Competence in the workplace demands patience, perseverance, and the ability to attend to work that may not prove intrinsically interesting.

Seventeen-year-old Bonita took a job as a unit supervisor at a sleepaway camp for urban kids. Although she'd spent two years as a counselor, she now found herself in a supervisory position, responsible for several cabins of campers, counselors, and junior counselors. One night, one of the counselors, a friend of hers, snuck out of her cabin to meet her boyfriend; they were discovered by one of the camp directors on the far side of the lake, which was off limits. Bonita found herself in the uncomfortable position of having to discipline her friend by taking away her off-campus privileges for the next two weeks. Bonita was told that she'd been lax in her supervision. Meanwhile, the counselors in her unit gave her the cold shoulder for what they perceived as a too-harsh punishment for one of their own. Bonita spent a couple of very uncomfortable and lonely weeks. One day at lunch she began talking to another unit supervisor, a girl she hardly knew. Soon they were comparing notes about what a difficult position they were in, supervising counselors so close in age to themselves, feeling disliked both by those above them and by those they were supposed to be supervising. The two young women decided to meet after lights-out every other evening to compare notes and to support each other. Bonita felt better for the first time in days after this conversation. Thanks to her vocational competence, she was able to seek out the help she needed to do a good job for the rest of the summer.

Take a moment now to assess your teen in terms of his or her competence in the five areas we've discussed. Use the chart on page 54 to determine in which areas your teen is already competent, and in which areas he can improve. Revisit it as your child grows, so you can see how competence increases with age.

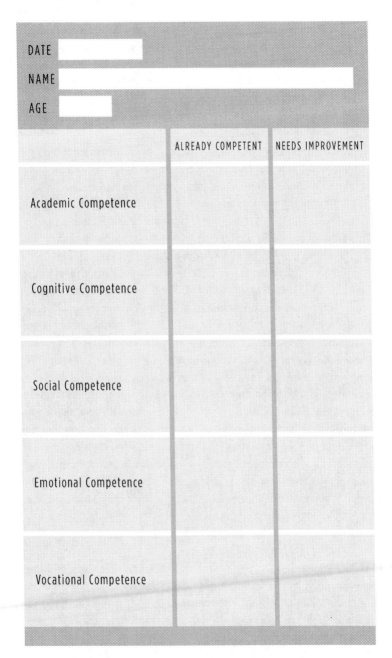

	ALREADY COMPETENT	NEEDS IMPROVEMENT
DATE		
NAME		
AGE		
Academic Competence		
Cognitive Competence		
Social Competence		
Emotional Competence		
Vocational Competence		

As I hope you can see, many teens are admirably and, at times, surprisingly competent when we train ourselves to notice their strengths. But very few teens—very few adults, in fact—are equally competent in all areas. A strength in one area, however, can buttress or compensate for a relative weakness in another. For example, if your teen is very socially competent but less so when it comes to academics, you can try to help her use her social networking ability to her advantage in school. Thanks to plasticity, competence can be nurtured where it doesn't exist and enhanced where it does.

To understand how to nurture and enhance competence in all these areas, it's first important to understand the roots of competence.

INTRINSIC MOTIVATION: THE WELLSPRING OF COMPETENCE

If you put a plant on a windowsill, its leaves will turn and grow in the direction of the sun. Similarly, teens will naturally turn toward those activities they enjoy; they have a natural thirst to succeed in areas that are of interest to them and that they value, not because they'll get a reward. Dara, who's always been athletically inclined, spends hours perfecting her layup; Tony, who was just asked to join a neighborhood band, practices playing the trumpet throughout the day, tapping out the fingering on his desk, table, or even his thigh. Liza is happiest when she's updating her blog. These teens are able to see for themselves that the more time they invest, the better they become.

A desire to learn things or accomplish tasks for their own value is called intrinsic motivation. Extrinsic motivation is when we work toward an external reward, such as money or a good grade. The problem is that once the reward is earned, the motivation often dries up.

Intrinsic motivation, on the other hand, is very compelling—and parents can use it to enhance their teens' overall competence. Suppose your thirteen-year-old daughter loves collecting seashells. It sounds like a pretty innocuous hobby, one that wouldn't have much impact on her competence. But approaching it from the positive development perspective, you'll recognize many new and exciting possibilities. For example, if your child wants to maintain and increase her collection, she'll need to decide:

- With whom she wishes to share her hobby and with what level of enthusiasm she should talk about it to others (emotional competence)
- How she can travel to the seashore, which involves finding someone to take her and making a plan that accommodates all those involved (social competence)
- How to transport the shells back home, clean, organize, and safely display them (cognitive competence)
- How to learn more about her collection by maintaining it and by doing research, which will ultimately improve her vocabulary and reading ability (academic competence)
- Whether to take summer classes in biology so that she can pursue her interest in becoming a marine biologist (vocational competence)

Any activity your child truly enjoys can be a gateway through which to enhance her overall competence. Just as your child doesn't need to be Ms. Popularity as long as she has at least one good friend, she also doesn't need a portfolio stuffed with interests as long as she has one or two she genuinely cares about.

Gaining mastery in these areas doesn't happen overnight. But you can help it develop over time by being sensitive to all the factors we've discussed so far, such as understanding your child's temperament, thinking of yourself as an authority in positive development—and using the Big Three. Here's how.

Like What She Likes

The first step is to carefully observe those activities your child naturally gravitates toward. Notice what she does in her free time. Try to remain objective about this—to really notice what your teen likes, not what you wish he or she would like. The number of boys who

BIG THREE #1:	MAINTAIN A SUSTAINED, POSITIVE RELATIONSHIP

· Find something your child likes to do (drawing, listening to music, collecting sea shells) and support her interest in it.
· Find ways to support the interest without taking it over or compromising your standards.
· Learn to praise and criticize productively.

were pressed into a Little League uniform because their dads clung to their own baseball dreams is a sad commentary about parent-child relations. If you feel the urge to live vicariously through your teen, find a softball team and join it yourself.

Once you've identified the area or areas, support her interest in it. This can be more delicate than it at first appears. You'll need to rely on your own emotional intelligence and knowledge of "goodness of fit" in order to gauge how much interest on your part your child welcomes before she begins to experience it as an intrusion. As we know from our discussion of temperament, some kids are more approachable and appreciate parental involvement, while others are more jealous of their independence and prefer to work alone.

For example, my younger son, Jarrett, casually announced at dinner one night that he'd decided to study fiction writing during his freshman year at college. I wanted to jump up and hug him because I know what a terrific writer he is and have so much faith in his ability. But if I did this, he'd pull back, as he had in the past. Because he's what I'd call "laid back" and I'm what he'd call "manic," our temperamental styles don't always mesh. So all I said was, "Hey, that's cool," and kept on eating. It wasn't until after he left the kitchen that I jumped up and said, "Isn't that fabulous news!"—to my wife, not to my son.

My older son, Justin, on the other hand, is completely different. If he shows me a movie script he's written and I say, "Yeah, I like this a lot," he says, "No, Dad, tell me what you really think." Because his personality is a lot more like mine, he wants me to be effusive. If I'm not, he takes my lukewarm reaction as negative. You have to know what level of response your child is looking for. Adjusting these levels is a parent's responsibility, not the teen's.

Some teens bristle if parents take any interest at all in their efforts. In these cases, it's best to wait until you're invited to respond. You can increase the likelihood of this happening by hanging out with your child while she is pursuing her interest and supporting the process rather than the product. That is, instead of saying, "You scored so many baskets today—you're getting really good at it," say, "You spent over an hour practicing today!" In this way, you're commenting on her commitment, energy, perseverance, and her tenacity.

Support, Don't Commandeer

It's essential that you support the activity without appropriating it. Nothing throws cold water on intrinsic motivation as much as a parent's overinvolvement. Teens who sense when their parents are too invested in their accomplishments often react by abandoning the activity altogether. It's much better to say something like "You have a terrific sense of rhythm" than "You're coming along so great on the guitar, I'm going to find you the best teacher in the area."

Sixteen-year-old Will, for example, volunteered to organize the car wash that the foreign-language club was sponsoring. He assumed that his mother, a fund-raiser for a local charity, could help him with the logistics. She was so delighted, however, that instead of facilitating the project she took it over. Shut out, Will felt his initial enthusiasm drain away. Remember, if you are asked to help, your goal is to nurture your teen's intrinsic motivation and love of learning. The less control you exert, the more opportunity your child has to build skills.

"Drag Racing? I Don't Think So!"

What happens when your child's passion leads her in directions you find loathsome or even dangerous? Your teen may be a devotee of hip-hop music that you find offensive, or violent types of anime (Japanese comic books). What then?

Let's take an easy situation first. Suppose your daughter spends all her babysitting money on makeup and subscriptions to fashion magazines instead of browsing at the local bookstore. If your interests don't coincide, remind yourself that it's important for teens to stake out their own territory. You may even find something of interest. It's possible that by leafing through *Allure* or *Lucky* with your daughter, you will learn about a vitamin supplement that could strengthen your nails, or a more flattering hairstyle. It's also possible that your daughter's interest in the field will persist throughout adolescence and she will decide to become a fashion designer or a magazine editor. These are her decisions to make.

Or take the case of Ward, age twelve, who became so completely absorbed in the world of wrestling that the rest of his life—family, school, friends—ground to a halt. His mother, Jeannie, hated everything about wrestling; she couldn't stand the voices of the announcers, the leather getups, the chicanery, the boasting, the slang—"Royal Rumbles," "Monday Night Raw." It actually pained her to think that she'd raised a son who could be so devoted to it. But one day Ward, who had never read an entire book, even those assigned in school, came home with a five-hundred-page book by Mankind (Mick Foley). He'd bought the book with his own money and proceeded to read it cover to cover. "I'd come upon him, hunched over this book, this awful book," Jeannie remembers, "but then I'd think, 'At least he's reading.'" Ward then began collecting and organizing memorabilia. His friends recognized him as an expert, and he reveled in their recognition. Years later, after Ward had moved on to cultivate more age-appropriate interests—recently he's become fascinated with photography—the book remains on his bookshelf. Wrestling, it turns out, was the bridge leading Ward to engage with the world.

Which brings us to another reason you shouldn't panic if your teenager pursues an interest that's not on your radar screen. Teenage passions, however fiery, rarely endure. Think about it—most of the things you cared most about as a teenager have probably long since burned out. A child's interests naturally evolve over time. From a positive development perspective, this willingness to embrace new challenges is a sign of a curious and engaged mind.

But let's talk about a more serious situation. Suppose your teenager becomes fascinated with video games that feature death and destruction. Because playing such games involves taking actions (albeit simulated) to kill people or to destroy homes and communities, you have to let your child know that you can't support this interest. One of the most important roles of parents is to establish clear standards and boundaries, not to win popularity contests. If this genre of game is repugnant to you, tell him so. Draw the line and forbid it. Explain why; help him understand that it is not just exposure to violence that you object to (for instance, watching the evening news, reading the newspaper, or viewing some television shows expose a child to violence) but his active participation, through the games, in violent acts that you will not tolerate. Let him know that until he's old enough to make his own informed decisions, you have to take responsibility in cases like this.

Sometimes kids actually *want* us to say no—they may have qualms but are worried about saving face with their friends. If you set a limit for them, you're giving them the cover they need to say to their friends, "I'm still cool; it's my parents' fault that I can't pursue this."

As you close one door, however, open another by turning a potential confrontation into a teachable moment. Ask your son, for instance, what he loves about video games—is it the story line? Graphics? Music? In this way, you're extracting and isolating a positive feature of his interest that you can support and encourage him to pursue. Maybe he can take a course in animation, or music lessons. The twenty-four-year-old son of a family friend was hired by the quality control division of a leading gaming company to sample new ideas. "It's my absolute dream job," he told me. "I can't believe I'm getting paid to do what I love." He doesn't credit his parents, but I do: when they refused to let him play Grand Theft Auto, he turned to role-playing video games, which emphasize strategy, problem solving, and community building.

Productive Praise

Another important element of maintaining a positive relationship with your child is learning how to praise wisely—to communicate your excitement without becoming overbearing. Find some aspect of the work that reflects one of your child's strengths and then emphasize it. For instance, if your child asks your opinion of her shell collection, find one or (ideally) several positive things to say. Point to the obvious hard work and effort that were required. Mention the creativity shown in the work, or the fact that it is unique, interesting, or important. Stress your pride that she is doing something that has these assets.

You can also note how her work has influenced you—that you're excited by her efforts. Say that through her you've learned that her activity is engaging, worthwhile, or important—for example, "Thanks for showing this to me. I love talking about it with you." Or tell her that you'd love to learn more about her hobby when she has the time.

Considerate Criticism

Suppose your child directly asks you to critique a drawing of hers that isn't very good. You can still find ways to reinforce your positive regard for her work by finding something that she did well. Perhaps the shading is accurate, or she made good use of color. In the absence of any redeeming qualities, you can praise the fact that she took on a creative project and saw it through.

Sometimes teens ask for a general appraisal of their work. If your fifteen-year-old son brings his portfolio to you and asks, "Do you really think these drawings are any good?" you might reply, "Well, yes, I think they're quite good. But I also know there are a lot of different types of styles of drawing and that different artists have different opinions. Artists say that whether something is good or not depends on what the artist is trying to accomplish. What sorts of things are you trying to do? Do you have any ideas about what you'd like to do to change the drawings?"

This encourages your son to think about ways he'd like to change—not necessarily improve—what he's done. It will also shift the focus away from what he produced to a discussion of his goals, his motivations, and his understanding of art in general. In other words, he may think less about judgment than about his commitment to his art, which will often end up stoking rather than extinguishing his desire to return to the drawing board and become even better.

Finally, be alert to changes, whether dramatic or subtle, in your teen's intrinsic interests. Some teens move from a passion for playing piano to devoting themselves to understanding how machines work. Many girls who are athletic may begin as ballerinas but eventually become more interested in competitive sports. The teenage years are a time of great change, and moving through many interests can be a sign of a great capacity for curiosity and growth.

Build on Strengths

When we think about helping our kids learn life skills, we often imagine that it's a one-way street: that we impart information our children lack. In other words, we're actively communicating and they're passively listening.

BIG THREE #2:   BUILD LIFE SKILLS

- If your child asks for help or is amenable to hearing your suggestions, take a strength-based approach—that is, help her enhance the skills she has and develop new skills.
- Suggest your teen learn to "chunk" tasks—that is, break down big jobs into smaller, manageable components.
- Help your child see that the competence she brings to the tasks she loves can be generalized to other important facets of life.

But according to the positive development approach, children learn best by interacting with others. Suppose, for instance, that your daughter, who plays the violin in the school orchestra, is having a hard time keeping track of her sheet music. When she gets a new piece, she throws it haphazardly into the same folder in which she keeps older pieces she's already mastered; as a result, she can never find the piece she needs when it's time to practice.

Your child says: I hate practicing! I can never find my music!

Quick response: If you'd organize your music, you'd be able to find everything you need. Let me show you how you can do that. It's easy.

But knowing teenagers, she'd probably say, "Back off. This is my system and it works for me"—even though it doesn't.

Positive development response: You have an amazing collection of music by now. And I love hearing you play. I'd love to be able to remember when you learned each of these pieces and when you performed it. You could do this just by dating each piece and putting it in a loose-leaf binder. Is this OK? Would you like me to help you do this?

The last response shows her that you recognize her skill, which is one of her strengths, and that you value all the time and energy she's invested in learning to play. You're also helping her realize that creating and maintaining good organizational skills will help her work more efficiently.

Learn to "Chunk"

But suppose that with or without help, the task proves too difficult for her. Nothing undercuts our feelings of competence so much as confronting a job that looms too large. The way to circumvent frustration is to create small, simple, manageable tasks out of big, complex ones. For example, you can help your daughter chunk her violin music by suggesting, "Let's see, what would be the easiest way to begin? How about if you separate out all the easiest pieces first?" Another way to chunk the task would be to suggest that she begin by identifying the most recent pieces she's played and then work backward. Either strategy will result in the same goal—she'll learn that she can attack a big project by finding a smaller aspect of it to accomplish first. It's also helpful to praise her as she completes each step of the process.

Portable Skills

Another competence-enhancing life skill to learn is the ability to generalize. When teens realize they can become competent in other areas besides the ones in which they're intrinsically interested, they have the opportunity to dramatically enhance their overall competence. In truth, no activity is an isolated endeavor. Everything we do can act as a bridge to something else. Even the most unlikely leisure activity, one that seems to have no socially redeeming value, can spur skill building and enhance competence. Take Richie, a seventeen-year-old who spent every free second involved in role-playing games on his computer. His parents were very concerned about him—although he was a bright boy, he was a classic underachiever in school, and they blamed his fanatical interest in gaming. One day, however, Richie casually asked his mother who Thor was. Instead of answering him outright, Susan said, "Let's look it up." Together, they discovered that Thor was the principal god in Norse mythology.

Richie then explained that a character in his game was named Thor. "Maybe there are other names from Norse mythology that appear in the game that you're not aware of," she suggested.

"How would I know who's a god and who isn't?" Richie asked.

"That's a good question," Susan said.

"I guess I could look up Norse mythology on the Web," he finally said.

To her surprise, that's exactly what Richie did. A week later, he mentioned during dinner that he'd found several great mythology Web sites. Soon he was chatting with real interest about how cool it was that the Greek and Norse gods were so similar. And a few months later, when he had to choose an elective to take during his senior year, he selected a class on mythology, and began talking about spending a summer at an archaeological dig in South America. His computer game, as it turned out, was a portal to a new passion.

Sometimes chunking and generalizing work together to create competence. Mark, a high school junior, took a part-time job at a local appliance store. He thought he'd just be performing menial tasks, but his boss wanted him to learn about the merchandise he'd be selling. When Mark complained to his dad that he didn't know where or how to begin, his dad said, "Remember what happened when you wanted to get your learner's permit?" Mark *did* remember. He'd been so eager to learn to drive that he insisted on going to the motor vehicle department the day he turned sixteen. "We'll take you," his parents had told him, "as soon as you find out everything you need to know: what you need to bring with you, where we have to go, when the office is open." Although Mark hadn't shown any interest in research or in using his computer for anything other than instant-messaging his friends and playing games, he quickly amassed all the relevant facts.

Recalling that incident, Mark realized that he could become more vocationally competent in ways his boss had requested by searching for information online.

Teens also have to competently manage their own health care, especially if they have medical conditions. My friend's son Jon, for example, had to have his spleen removed when he was fifteen—and then had to overhaul his life to cope with the challenges of having no spleen. Knowing that he'd be on his own at college within three years, his mother insisted that he memorize his complete medical history, including the date of his surgery, dates of hospitalizations, names of medications, and exact dosages, and that he refill his prescriptions himself.

When he arrived at college, Jon and his parents met with the school's medical director to inform her of Jon's condition and to establish a new protocol. When Jon did became ill during his first semester at college, he knew just what to do: he checked himself into the emergency room. Although he was scared, and although his mom was ready to make the four-hour drive to sit by his bedside, she refrained and let Jon handle it himself. When he was released, he created a new support system, telling his roommate and friends what they should do if he fell ill again.

Focus on Skills for Daily Life

In addition to the more general life skills discussed above, it's important to help your teen learn how to handle everyday situations that test his competence. The following list is adapted from the Targeting Life Skills model used by 4-H, and draws on their concepts of Heart, Hands, Head, and Health to organize these skills. Although the list isn't complete, it suggests some of the basic skills your teen needs to acquire or strengthen. As you read through it, be sure to evaluate your child's competence in relationship to his age. That is, while it's beyond the scope of a twelve-year-old to send out resumes when applying for a job, every teen should know how to handle social situations with some degree of competence.

HEART—CARING, RELATING
  My child knows how to:
        Answer the phone and doorbell
        Comfort a friend or relative who is ill
        Send out thank-you notes
        Introduce him/herself and others in social situations

HANDS—GIVING, WORKING
  My child knows how to:
        Serve as a contributing member of a committee
        Apply for a job
        Dress for and behave during interviews
        Turn down a job in ways that maintain relationships
        Open a bank account and deposit paychecks

HEAD—MANAGING, THINKING
  My child knows how to:
        Keep track of long-range assignments

Make haircut appointments

Handle difficult and emergency situations, such as having a fender-bender, making certain contact information is provided when babysitting, and knowing how to flip the circuit breaker if power is lost in a room

Navigate his/her physical environment using maps and other aids

HEALTH—LIVING, BEING

My child knows how to:

Eat healthfully

Maintain good hygiene

Keep track of his possessions

Be responsible for taking prescription medication

BIG THREE #3:	GIVE TEENS THE OPPORTUNITY TO BECOME LEADERS

· Actively involve your teen in making decisions important to the completion of the task.

· Turn mistakes into teachable moments.

Taking the Reins

The third component of the Big Three—leadership and actively involving teens in the decision-making process—is frequently overlooked and neglected. Sometimes we're so harried that we simply make all the decisions ourselves in a frantic effort to save time and streamline the process. Sometimes we discount and perhaps even devalue the contributions we imagine teens will make. But when we do this, we're shortchanging our children and undermining their burgeoning sense of competence. If we want them to grow into competent adults, we have to give them the chance to exercise this particular muscle when they're younger. And the truth is, once you begin looking at life through the lens of positive development, there are countless opportunities to instill leadership in your teens.

As mentioned earlier, it's always best to begin with an area in which your child is intrinsically interested and then generalize to other tasks. For example, Jane, thirteen, loved food—both cooking it and eating it. When she was younger, she'd accompany her mom to the supermarket and help prepare dinner. But when she got older, she was ready for more responsibilities. "How about you plan dinner for this Friday night?" Jane's mother asked her one day. Jane was thrilled. First, she buried herself in her cookbooks. Next, she made a shopping list. Soon she was scouring the kitchen cabinets to see which ingredients were on hand and which she'd have to buy. Then she realized that she'd have to actually get to the stores—she wanted to stop off at a local bakery as well as the supermarket—which meant that she'd have to coordinate her schedule with her mother's. This seemingly simple task required enormous organizational (cognitive) skills.

But possibilities for leadership extend way beyond the kitchen. Suppose Jane's mother asked her to coordinate a family trip to a restaurant in the nearby city. Then Jane would have to figure out which restaurant would suit everyone's taste, decide when to make a reservation, alert everyone as to how to dress, and perhaps find an activity earlier in the day that would engage her younger brother, who wasn't interested in food. All of these tasks would draw on Jane's emerging social competence.

This is how Blair was able to plan her trip to Europe with such skill. Although it was the first time she went overseas alone, she'd been helping us plan family trips for years. Poring over maps and timetables with us, she learned to prepare for contingencies, anticipate delays and obstacles, and develop backup plans. After all this domestic experience, traveling to Europe didn't feel so foreign at all.

It's also important to start thinking about helping your child take initiative outside the family unit. Remember, teens spend their days in two other environments: school and the community. They are eager to work with adults besides their parents and long to be listened to, respected, and treated as real working partners. When they're actively participating and not simply receiving the benefits of various programs, they're accessing another important developmental resource: intergenerational activity. By partnering with adults to create new programs, teens come to appreciate all the hard work that goes into creating positive change in the world.

Jane, for example, could be encouraged to propose that her high school offer a course in gastronomy. This would involve approaching a school official, and perhaps culminate in making a presentation to the PTA or to the school board of education. She could also approach the local Y and neighborhood kitchen supply or food store owners to see if classes could be run at these locations. She might be asked to conduct a survey among her peers to see how many would be interested in taking a cooking class. Ultimately, she might discover that she enjoys asking people about their interests; soon, her fascination with food might morph into an interest in politics, survey research, or marketing. The possibilities are endless.

It's often the case that teens are frustrated when they venture out of the family orbit. But even failed plans can boost competence. Take Jeremy, the drummer who wasn't allowed to audition for the jazz band in his school. Feeling as if he was being shortchanged, he composed letters to the chairperson of the music department, the assistant principal of the high school in charge of instruction, and eventually the assistant superintendent. Each of these officials told Jeremy that they couldn't make an exception for him. Even though all of his appeals were ultimately denied, Jeremy achieved a bird's-eye view of what it means to go through channels, to negotiate the bureaucracy, and to use the system to try to get what he wanted—skills that shore up his vocational competence years before he takes his first job.

Learning from Mistakes

The fact remains that even the most competent teen will have lapses of judgment that range from trivial to serious. That they make mistakes doesn't make them "bad" kids; in fact, some of the best and most enduring lessons teens learn about competence arise from their worst mistakes—if parents handle these mistakes with a positive development perspective.

When my son Jarrett turned sixteen, for example, my wife and I bought him a new Mazda SUV. Two nights later, Jarrett went for a drive to visit his friend. It was raining hard, and turning a corner, Jarrett lost control and rammed into a utility pole, knocking it down.

If this isn't bad enough, wait till you hear what happened next. Although the car was idling in a puddle with live electrical wires strewn about, Jarrett got out of the car. But that's not all. Remembering that he'd left the engine on, he went back into the car to turn the engine off. And then he got out of the car again.

At some point, Jarrett phoned me, and as I drove to the scene of the accident all I could think about was how incredibly stupid he'd been to risk electrocuting himself not once but three times. By the time I arrived, the police were already there. I parked my car a distance away. An officer intercepted me, took one look at my face, and said, "I know you want to murder your son, but first give him a big hug. He's scared to death."

Although I had fully intended to punish Jarrett, I soon realized that the accident and its aftermath were punishment enough. Without his car for over two months while it was being fixed, Jarrett had to rely on friends and family for transportation—an imperfect solution since everyone was always on the go. Not only was he chastened by the experience, but he also learned valuable lessons about anticipating road conditions, becoming more aware of the importance of peripheral vision while driving, and—perhaps most important— how to handle himself in case of an emergency. I felt doubly reassured—that he'd never again step into a pool of standing water with live wires sparking around him, and that he was a much more competent driver.

Lauren, seventeen, the daughter of close friends, also became more competent the hard way. One summer, her parents and younger brother went on a five-day vacation, leaving Lauren home so that she could work and attend soccer practice. She was to stay with a close friend and was allowed home only to shower and change. One evening, Lauren phoned her mom asking if she could have five girlfriends at the house for pizza and a movie. "I knew all the girls," said Judy, Lauren's mother, "so I said sure.

"A few days later, when we arrived home," Judy continued, "the house was spotless—there was food in the fridge and a plate full of chocolate chip cookies on the table. Things were so perfect that we knew something was up. My husband went into the basement and noticed a badly plastered hole in the wall. Another wall showed the imprint of someone's backside. It couldn't have been more obvious that something really horrible had happened.

"We stormed into Lauren's room and dragged her downstairs to face the music. To her credit, she told us the truth right away: although she'd invited five kids, about a hundred and five showed up. In fact, the entire football team put in an appearance—'Boy, do they need anger-management classes,' Lauren added at this point. The story didn't end there," Judy said. "It went on to include multiple beer kegs, a couple of fistfights in the driveway, cops being called . . . I couldn't listen anymore."

Lauren's parents ended up grounding her for two weeks. She was forbidden from using her car at all, even to drive to school, which was a huge blow to her since she'd just bought it with her own money and had long dreamed of driving herself to the first day of her senior year.

Even so, Judy was left wondering if this punishment was too soft. Some of her friends thought it was. But Judy couldn't help thinking that she'd handled the situation appropriately. After all, Lauren was generally a good kid—an honor student, a dedicated soccer player, sociable, a good friend, well liked, helpful around the house, and a good worker. And though she'd acted irresponsibly, she'd been able to rescue the situation by relying on what Judy realized were her daughter's many competences:

· When things began really spiraling out of control, Lauren reached out to kids at the party she knew she could rely on as well as some neighbors to help her clear the house—an example of social competence.

- Knowing nothing about plastering holes in walls, Lauren learned what she needed in order to repair the damage—an example of cognitive competence.
- Although cleaning the house was a huge priority, Lauren arranged the cleanup around her work schedule so that she'd keep her job—an example of vocational competence.
- Finally, Lauren accepted her punishment maturely and managed her emotions in the face of her parents' considerable anger—an example of emotional competence.

Thanks to the positive development perspective, Judy realized her daughter's instance of incredibly bad judgment didn't entirely blot out her many competencies. On Lauren's part, she more than learned her lesson. In the years since this party, she's never had people over to the house without letting her parents know. She became very aware of the importance of personal property, and of the legal consequences that arise when minors are concerned. Perhaps most important for her transition to adulthood, she knows that sometimes you have to anticipate the worst. Hosting a hundred uninvited guests taught her that she's not always in control and that events can take on a life of their own. She no longer dismisses what appears improbable, as many teenagers do. This knowledge will serve her well in years to come.

LOOKING AHEAD

As we've seen, a competent teen is able to take the initiative to pursue, refine, or even change her interests, knowing that she'll find her own way. Helping your teen nurture the competencies she has and develop the ones she doesn't, in all the ways we've discussed above, will enable her to make the transition to adulthood with less disruption and emotional trauma, whether she attends college, enters the military, or joins the workforce. That's not to say that any one task or set of tasks won't overwhelm her, but rather that she will have the tools she needs to earn a salary, contribute to society, and have a full life.

What happens to teens who don't become competent? I have a simple answer: they turn into George Costanza—the hapless, ineffectual bumbler from *Seinfeld*. Though chronologically a grown man, emotionally he was mired in an endless adolescence, distracted by trivia, avoiding the big questions, unable to take the reins of his life. Similarly, children whose competence isn't nurtured can't act independently. They remain attached to their parents, who worry about them constantly. Often they turn out to be followers—easily manipulated, they can end up joining cults or following charismatic leaders who have their own agendas.

In contrast, the research I'm conducting right now—research on teens who don't have these deficits and who aren't "problems"—indicates, in broad strokes, that the more all the Five Cs are promoted, the less teens are at risk for trouble. And the C that anchors all the others is competence. When kids feel free to devote themselves to do what they love, they learn about commitment and stick-to-itiveness. More importantly, they gain a sense that they can master their world—just as Blair saw that she could survive in Paris for a weekend on a shoestring budget and knowing no French. She returned home not only with a valid passport but also with a new sense of herself as a competent person.

Still, you can be the most skilled and competent teenager in the country and not show it. That's because the next C, confidence, activates competence the way gasoline powers a motor, as we'll explore in the next chapter.

Confidence

One cannot afford to be a realist.

—Albert Bandura

Fourteen-year-old Aaron had been playing bass guitar for five years. He'd just recently formed a band with a couple of his friends, and they began appearing at parties and at their middle school's variety show to rave reviews. In June, his band was invited to play at the last dance of the year, a monthly Friday night gathering in the gym. Aaron was so excited that he wrote a special song for the occasion. The night of the band's final rehearsal before the gig, Aaron was unusually quiet. When he finished dinner, he went up to his room and closed the door.

His parents, Eve and Jim, who had arranged their evening to drive him to and from rehearsal, knocked on his door. All they heard inside was the blare of the TV. "Don't we have to leave now?" Jim shouted, trying to make himself heard.

"I'm not going," Aaron shouted back.

"What do you mean, you're not going?" Jim said. "You have a rehearsal! Your friends are depending on you. You can't disappoint them."

"I'm not rehearsing and I'm not playing tomorrow. I suck at guitar. I can't play anything good. I don't know what I was thinking. Just leave me alone."

Jim walked into his son's room anyway. Aaron was sitting on his bed with his guitar, fingering the frets. Jim muted the TV.

"What's that you're playing?" Jim asked.

"Nothing," Aaron replied. "Just chords." He continued softly strumming.

For a while father and son did not speak. Then Jim said, "Well, it may be nothing to you, but I'll tell you, it sounds pretty good to me. You make it sound so easy."

"It's just a simple chord progression," Aaron said.

"Well, you're terrific at it. I couldn't do it," Jim said, getting up to leave.

Jim joined Eve in the kitchen, where they heard Aaron continue to play. After a few minutes the sequence of the chords changed as Aaron segued into the song he'd written, tentatively at first and then more assertively. A few minutes later, Aaron appeared in the kitchen, holding his guitar case.

"So can you take me to rehearsal?" he asked.

Aaron's nervousness wasn't about competence—he knew he could play guitar—but about confidence. He'd simply lost faith in himself. Yet he was able to recover pretty quickly. And although he probably didn't credit his father for his rapid turnaround, the truth is that Jim took the perfect approach to his son's situation. He stressed the facets of his son's musicianship that *were* impressive and pointed out that what Aaron was doing at that very moment—playing chords—was a part of the skills he needed to have to succeed. As you'll soon see, Jim's interaction with Aaron reflects many ways you can boost this very important C.

BEYOND OPTIMISM: DEFINING CONFIDENCE

Confidence is defined as the perception that one can achieve desired goals through one's actions. A confident teen believes that she has the ability to succeed and act in ways she wants to. She believes that she has the abilities or skills to perform well academically, socially, and in those other areas of life that are important to her. Teens learn confidence when their parents instill and enhance their sense of self-determination, independent thinking, and self-esteem.

Competence, as we learned in the previous chapter, is about what you can do. Confidence is about how you feel—or rather what you believe you can do. It is a more interior quality. We're confident if we perceive ourselves to be competent. These two Cs often go hand in hand: the more competent you are, the more likely it is that you'll feel confident. In turn, confidence can reinforce competence. Believing you can succeed allows you to work at developing a skill. There's a great deal of wisdom in the old adage "Practice makes perfect."

But sometimes the cycle breaks down, as it did for Aaron—when he lost confidence, knowledge of his competence alone couldn't come to his rescue. In these cases, our perceptions become reality; what we think is real may feel more "real" to us than the actual, verifiable reality. One of my friends has a son who is exceptionally good-looking. Yet when she compliments him, he shakes his head in disagreement and says, "You only think that because you're my mom. No one else does." And he really believes it. Similarly, a teen with twenty friends, who's never home and whose cell phone never stops ringing, can feel unpopular. An all-star tennis player can perceive herself to be a klutz. It's hard to argue with self-perceptions, which constitute our internal reality. But there are many ways you can help modify your child's perceptions.

CONFIDENCE AS SELF-PERCEPTION

Susan Harter, a developmental psychologist and professor at the University of Denver, has studied teenagers' self-perceptions. Specifically, she wanted to know how teens think about confidence—that is, what qualities they think they need in order to consider themselves effective in a specific area of life.

Harter's work yielded a list of characteristics that combine to create a sense of "self-perceived competence." That is, when kids feel competent in these areas—when they believe that they have the abilities to do well—they consequently experience themselves as having confidence.

In addition, she discovered that confidence is expressed differently at different ages. Although some of the characteristics of confidence remain the same throughout the adolescent years, others evolve as teens mature and acquire new roles, responsibilities, and interests. For example, sixteen-year-olds are concerned about job competence, but ten-year-olds aren't.

Researchers, including Harter, often divide adolescence into three periods: early, middle, and late. Although there are no "magic numbers," I've found it useful to think of early teens as between the ages of ten and thirteen, middle adolescents as ages fourteen to sixteen, and older adolescents as ages seventeen to twenty.

Early Adolescence (Ages Ten to Thirteen)

The six components of early adolescents' self-perceived competence, according to Harter, include the following:

- Scholastic ability—the perception that one is good at schoolwork
- Athletic ability—the perception that one is good at sports
- Physical appearance—the perception that one is physically attractive
- Peer acceptance—the perception that one is liked
- Global self-worth—an overall sense of satisfaction with oneself, a general good feeling about oneself
- Behavior/conduct adequacy—the perception that one knows how to behave and to follow the rules of home, family, and community

These characteristics persist throughout adolescence with a few changes: as you'll note next, behavior/conduct evolves into a more sophisticated understanding of morality, and scholastic achievement also broadens into intellectual pursuits and creativity. In addition, several new characteristics are added at each stage, noted in bold.

Middle Adolescence (Ages Fourteen to Sixteen)

During this period, nine characteristics of self-perceived competence develop:

- Scholastic ability
- Athletic ability
- Physical appearance
- Peer acceptance
- Global self-worth
- Conduct/morality—the perception that one understands the moral underpinnings of behavior and acts in accordance with society's rules
- **Close friendships**—the perception that one has certain relationships that are more intimate than others
- **Romantic relationships**—the perception that one has an emotionally meaningful relationship with a person toward whom one feels affection or even love and, eventually, sexual attraction
- **Job competence**—the perception that one has the skills to perform well in a work or job setting

Late Adolescence (Ages Seventeen to Twenty)

In the last part of adolescence, self-perceived comptence becomes even more complex. Reflecting an almost adult-like conception of the self, there are now thirteen components to it:

- Scholastic ability
- Athletic ability
- Physical appearance

- Peer acceptance
- Global self-worth
- Morality—the perception that one can make moral decisions independent of society's dictates
- Close friendships
- Romantic relationships
- Job competence
- Sense of humor—the perception that one can be witty and funny, and can partake in humorous exchanges with people, appreciating the lighter side of life
- Relationships with parents—the perception that it is important to have good relationships with parents and that such relations are valued
- Intellectual ability—the perception that one possesses general intellectual prowess and the ability to succeed in real-life settings apart from school
- Creativity—the perception that one can generate new and important products or ideas, as distinct from intellectual ability

HOW VALUES AND CONFIDENCE INTERSECT

Not only does our perception of confidence change with time, it's also highly individual. For some, confidence is grounded in appearance: they care about how they look more than anything else. Others may care most about how many people they know rather than the number of books they read, or vice versa.

Jacquelynne Eccles, professor of psychology at the University of Michigan, tells us that teens differ in what they expect to be good at, and they also differ in terms of the qualities they value—that is, they vary in regard to the qualities they believe are essential to their positive self-regard. The impact that specific activities have on confidence varies according to how much your child expects to succeed in a given area of life and how valuable to her such success is. When she values sports, for instance, then and only then will her expectation of success matter for her self-esteem.

For example, both Nan and Annette may perceive themselves to be terrible field hockey players. The difference between them, though, is that Nan would give up her honor society pin to be a better player. As a result, she takes every mistake on the field very much to heart. Annette, on the other hand, couldn't care less about field hockey. She joined the team because she likes spending time with her friends and because being on a team is what kids in her school do. When she misses an easy goal, she's able to shrug it off: her confidence isn't bruised. Or consider Max and Fred, two friends who are both good students and get similarly high grades. Both may therefore expect to do well in school. However, only Max values good school performance; Fred is more interested in becoming a professional guitarist. In this case, Max's self-regard will be influenced by his school achievement, but Fred's won't.

UNDERSTANDING CONFIDENCE

What does this detailed notion of confidence mean for parents seeking to promote positive development?

First, it underscores that confidence is not a single, global concept. Although a few lucky teens may experience themselves as generally confident, for most kids confidence is not something they either have or don't have. The vast majority of teens experience confidence differently in different situations—they feel confident in science class but not on the basketball court, or with girls but not with bosses. Second, parents need to recognize that confidence is linked to age. An eleven-year-old probably won't care about how badly he rakes a neighbor's leaves because he's too young to focus on vocational competence; a sixteen-year-old is likely to care. Finally, thanks to the multifaceted nature of confidence, even the least confident teen can be helped. If your daughter is full of self-doubt in one area, you can direct your attention to an area in which she's confident to help improve her overall positive self-regard. There are many ways to creatively address the problem of low confidence, and I'll detail them for you later in this chapter.

In short, self-confidence, like a muscle, can be built up. With regular practice, and by relying on the Big Three outlined below, you can increase what they already have and develop what they don't.

BIG THREE #1: **MAINTAIN A POSITIVE RELATIONSHIP**

- Enhance global self-worth by telling your child every day that you love and value her, and create tangible expressions of it.
- Share your own experience with self-confidence issues to strengthen your relationship with your child.

Enhancing Global Self-Worth

Whether teens are thirteen or nineteen, whether they live in the city or in the country, whatever their socioeconomic status, gender, religion, or ethnic heritage, the bedrock of confidence is having positive self-regard. By creating and sustaining a positive and close relationship with your child, you're naturally fueling his sense of global self-worth. The late Urie Bronfenbrenner, a preeminent scholar of human development, remarked that all adolescents need at least one adult in their lives who cares unconditionally—what he termed "irrationally"—for them. Clearly, all children deserve one such person; all kids would do well if they had such a reliable loving presence in their lives 24/7.

Daily Dose of Love

You can boost your child's confidence by telling him every day that he is loved and valued. Praise not only what he accomplishes but who he is. If and when applicable, talk about his generosity, thoughtfulness, honesty, good judgment, character, punctuality—any of the ways in which he functions well in the world. Help your child aspire to feel as if he is unique because of the particular set of good things he does, and that he therefore has something special to contribute to his world.

This sort of feedback will go a very long way toward boosting your child's confidence. However, such efforts are not enough. Although the nuclear family is important—probably central—it is not everything. Children need to know that they are supported by a "convoy of social support," as University of Michigan psychology professors Robert L. Kahn and Toni Antonucci call it. They need to know that more people than just their parents are invested in their health and well-being.

A child's nuclear family constitutes his first circle of support. In the second circle is the extended family—grandparents, cousins, aunts, and uncles. Neighbors compose the third level, and close family friends the fourth. In the next circle are people from the school and community with whom your teen has relationships—mentors, coaches, teachers, school administrators, religious teachers and leaders, employers, and leaders and sponsors of community organizations. Nowadays, there's yet another circle of virtual support surrounding teens; they can "reach out and touch" others thanks to their cell phones, e-mail, and instant messaging. This notion of a convoy of support reinforces the essential positive development belief that none of us goes through life on our own, that we're all embedded in social systems and are defined by our relationships, as we'll explore in Chapter 5, about connection.

Having a convoy is particularly useful in times of family crisis. No child is immune from tragedies. Parents get sick and die; sometimes a parent becomes chronically disabled, is called into military service, or leaves the house because of separation or divorce. Acknowledging this harsh reality, some of us have designated someone like a loving uncle or godparent to step in as a second-in-command in times of tragedy. But even this isn't enough. Your children need to know that the entire convoy is there, ready to support them. This way, they are more likely to feel more resilient, as if they can make it in a challenging world.

Creating Tangible Expressions of Your Love

Boosting confidence through the closeness of your relationship isn't a quick fix: it's nourished over your lifetime together and can be expressed in many creative and concrete ways. You can, for example, create a DVD on which you compile all the videos you've taken of your child through the years, and give it to her on her birthday. You can also create a photo album, or a scrapbook of all the programs, plays and athletic events she's participated in. You can devote a shelf in the family room to her trophies and awards. These artifacts are confidence boosters. They serve as constant reminders that you have confidence in and admiration for her, and that these feelings of love and devotion remain steady, even as her feelings of confidence may waver.

Sharing: "You're Not the Only One"

Another way to nurture a close relationship, especially as teenagers grow, is by letting them know about your own life. Teens may not fully appreciate that we were once young—that we stayed in unsatisfying relationships because we were too insecure to break them off, sweated out failing grades, and mistreated our siblings. But sharing some of these stories—in ways that feel appropriate—can really cement your relationship, especially when your teen is encountering problems.

Moira, for example, who was eighteen, had been dating a boy her parents didn't approve of for over a year. Al appeared disrespectful—he showed up late for their dates, often honked the horn for her to come out rather than coming to the door, and frequently made fun of her, even in front of other people. She'd dismissed her parents' concerns with a disdainful expression; they had no idea what her relationship was really about and knew nothing of how good Al was to her when they were alone. This relationship formed a wedge between Moira and her parents—she came and went in the house, barely acknowledging her parents.

One day, however, Moira learned that Al had been seeing another girl on the side. She was devastated. She tried talking to her friends, but they were dismissive: dump him, they told her, and move on. "I can't turn my feelings off like a faucet," she said to herself. Feeling utterly alone, she began to cry even though (or perhaps because) she knew her mother was in the next room. When her mother came in to ask what was wrong, Moira fell into her mother's arms and told her everything.

To her surprise, her mother was very understanding. "I was in a relationship like that once myself," her mother admitted.

"What happened?" Moira asked. She'd never sounded so interested in what her mother had to say. The older woman shared with her daughter that she had once been in a similar relationship and that she'd waited too long to break it off. She concluded by saying, "So you see, I think I know how you feel. It may be best to cut your ties to Al. I didn't do that, and it left me with bad feelings about men that took years to go away."

"I'm worried that I'll feel the same," Moira admitted.

Soon after this talk, Moira broke up with Al. It was a difficult breakup. Until this point, having a boyfriend was the primary source of her confidence. But she discovered, slowly, that this wasn't as important to her as it had been. She found herself appreciating her parents, particularly her mother, who hadn't tried to influence her but had just listened and shared her own experiences. When Moira went to college a few months later, she was amazed to discover that she was one of the few people who called her parents because she wanted to, not because she felt obligated to.

BIG THREE #2:   BUILD LIFE SKILLS

- Create a Confidence Profile and use it to encourage your teen to build and expand on the skills he has.
- Compensate for low confidence in one area by targeting an area of strength and helping your teen generalize this feeling to other areas.
- Extract success from failure by enabling teens to become their own models.
- Offer support in ways that buttress rather than undermine confidence.

Creating a Confidence Profile

Just as you assessed your teen's competence in Chapter 3, you can assess and track your teen's confidence based on the categories of self-perceived competence.

After completing this profile, you're in a good position to draw many helpful conclusions. Suppose your twelve-year-old daughter tries babysitting but discovers that she's not really interested in it. Because she's too young for job competence to be relevant to her, you don't necessarily have to worry that she doesn't have the skill set required for work. If your seventeen-year-old daughter, however, takes an after-school job at the local bookstore only to be fired after a month because she was habitually late, you may become more concerned. At this age, job competence is part of her self-perceived competence profile.

How can you help her? Try asking her what she enjoys doing—not necessarily as a job. Simply ask her how she likes spending her time. Ask her what she daydreams about doing. Your goal is to build on strengths to bolster self-confidence. Everyone respects expertise. By excelling in something, your teen can enjoy a big boost.

For example, if your son does well academically in school, suggest that he investigate more challenging scholastic opportunities. Many colleges, for instance, including local community colleges, offer exciting summer programs, internships, or study-abroad opportunities for high school students. If your high school student is seeking a paying job, suggest that she look into tutoring younger students—a job that not only is lucrative and rewarding but also will build her academic, social, and vocational confidence. Other paid jobs, for instance, working in a fast-food restaurant or in retail sales, may not have this combined benefit. If your daughter excels at soccer, suggest that she try out for even more competitive teams, perhaps a travel or all-star team. Maybe she could begin coaching or refereeing younger children at soccer in a community league or a more specialized volunteer organization, such as an athletic league for children with physical or emotional disabilities. If your older teen plans on returning to a previous summer job, such as being a music counselor at a local day

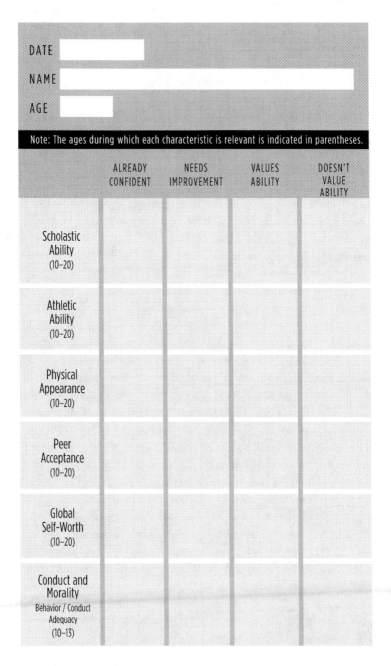

	ALREADY CONFIDENT	NEEDS IMPROVEMENT	VALUES ABILITY	DOESN'T VALUE ABILITY
DATE				
NAME				
AGE				

Note: The ages during which each characteristic is relevant is indicated in parentheses.

	ALREADY CONFIDENT	NEEDS IMPROVEMENT	VALUES ABILITY	DOESN'T VALUE ABILITY
Scholastic Ability (10–20)				
Athletic Ability (10–20)				
Physical Appearance (10–20)				
Peer Acceptance (10–20)				
Global Self-Worth (10–20)				
Conduct and Morality Behavior / Conduct Adequacy (10–13)				

	ALREADY CONFIDENT	NEEDS IMPROVEMENT	VALUES ABILITY	DOESN'T VALUE ABILITY
Moral Reasoning (14–16)				
Close Friendships (14–20)				
Romantic Relationships (14–20)				
Job Competence (17–20)				
Sense of Humor (17–20)				
Relationships with Parents (17–20)				
Intellectual Ability (17–20)				
Creativity (17–20)				

camp, suggest that he apply for a position as camp music coordinator. In other words, help your teen see that there's always another step and another way—both will bring more confidence.

Compensating for Low Confidence

Obviously, no one, child or adult, is equally competent in all areas. Nor, as we learned above, do we value all areas equally. Once you identify those developmentally appropriate areas in which your child's confidence is high, and which he also values, you can use these areas to help nurture his overall sense of confidence. In other words, when your teen is having problems with his self-regard in one area, talk with him about the different areas of competence he has. This discussion will help your child understand that there are many ways to feel good about oneself.

Sometimes it's important to help teens refocus their energies even within a single area of interest. Manny, for example, now seventeen, had always been great at baseball. Short but agile and quick, he made the all-star and travel teams from the first year he joined the Little League in his city neighborhood. But when his family moved and he tried out for his high school baseball team, he found himself up against three second basemen, all of whom had a better eye at the plate than he did. "I didn't make the team," Manny explained. "They had higher batting averages than I did, and there was no way around that."

Manny's mom, noticing Manny's disappointment, refocused his attention. Knowing that he was one of the fastest runners among boys his age, she encouraged him to try out for track instead. Manny turned out to be an excellent sprinter. "My confidence went way up when I joined the track team," Manny said. "Baseball always came naturally to me; I didn't have to work at it. But when I joined the track team, I had to learn a lot of new things. That made me believe in myself more—I saw that I could work and do well if I put my mind to it. And I felt so good running—it just made me feel good all around. I could relax a bit. I said to myself, 'Listen, you're good at this at least; you don't have to worry about every little thing.' I figure if I can be competitive at track, I can do just about anything." Next Manny began to make some friends in the new school. "I think kids respect you when they see you can do something well," he added. "I don't think I would have made friends as quickly if I hadn't made the track team."

For Manny, gaining confidence in a specific area—sprinting—enhanced his overall confidence. It's also true that drawing on your overall sense of confidence can fund a new venture. Dean, for example, found himself fascinated by break dancing when he was a sophomore in high school. He taught himself the moves by printing out instructions from the Internet. At first he practiced only in his basement, but gradually he became bolder and practiced in his driveway, and ultimately he tried some moves one day at school. "I fully expected to look like an idiot," Dean said. "I knew the other kids would probably laugh in my face. But I also knew that break dancing was just something I liked—it wasn't who I was. Overall, I'm pretty OK. I mean, the kids know I'm pretty athletic. So if I embarrass myself a little doing something new, I can take it." Ultimately, Dean became so good at it that he and a few friends began a break-dancing club, and their act at the variety show brought down the house. "It was a good experience for me," Dean explained. In a sense, he borrowed "credit" for his break dancing from his general savings account of confidence.

EXTRACTING SUCCESS FROM FAILURE

What about when your teen (who usually gets good grades) comes home from school, slams the door shut, and throws his books on the kitchen table out of sheer frustration because he failed a surprise math quiz? At times like this, it seems as if his lack of confidence is reality-based.

He says: I hate math. I suck at it.

Quick response: No, you don't. I wish you had a higher opinion of yourself.

Positive development response: You have the quiz with you? Let me take a look at it. I see you got a 60. That means that you got more than half the questions right—six out of ten, in fact. Why don't you show me one of those questions you got right? Explain to me how you reasoned it through to come up with the correct answer.

This is the tack that Jim, Aaron's father, took in the anecdote that opened this chapter. Aaron lost faith in his ability to play guitar, so his father commented on what Aaron was doing right—namely, playing chords and chord progressions. Focusing on this enabled Aaron to realize he could take the next step toward conquering his insecurity and play the song in its entirety. Once he did, he was ready to go to rehearsal.

Perhaps without realizing it, Aaron's father structured the situation so that Aaron was able to model his own success. The possibility that young people can serve as their own model grows out of an ingenious 1989 study conducted by Dale H. Schunk, a former student of Stanford psychologist Albert Bandura and now a professor of psychology at the University of North Carolina, and Antoinette R. Hanson, a professor of psychology at the University of Houston.

The researchers, after learning which students in a class were doing poorly in math, videotaped these students solving math problems. Just as a stopped clock is correct twice a day, even the poorest math student gets an occasional problem right. These instances were videotaped and compiled into one tape. The researchers then spoke with each of these students individually, explaining that they were interested in understanding how kids performed on math lessons and that they wanted to speak with the child because they knew he was a good math student. Of course, the child protested that the researchers had selected the wrong child to interview. The researchers then invited the child to view the tape with them—and there the child saw himself being successful at math.

After viewing their own successful behavior, the children in this study perceived themselves in a whole new light—as being able to do well in math. Seeing themselves being successful, they came to believe they could improve. They also became more interested in math, more motivated to work hard to succeed. And they did—their math grades went up.

This study has profound implications for learning. As the authors of the study write, "The perception of progress is an important cue in gauging self-efficacy." Or, as Bandura puts it, "Self-belief does not necessarily ensure success, but self-disbelief assuredly spawns failure."

It has another important implication: you can learn to value a task over time. Math wasn't initially important to the kids in the study described above, but they came to value it as their confidence in their mathematical abilities rose. As we learned earlier, we tend to want to work at those tasks we value.

You don't have to videotape your child doing her homework to help her benefit from the results of this study. Instead, help your child learn to monitor and evaluate her skills, so she will have the chance to revise the strategies she employs to find solutions until she hits upon one that works. In this way, you're allowing your teen to observe herself and to serve as her own model. Beyond this, you're encouraging your teen to serve as an agent of her own positive development—which is a key concept in the developmental systems model discussed throughout this book.

But what if your teen doesn't care about becoming better in a specific area? I, for example, am a terrible cook, but I don't care. That means I have absolutely no motivation to ever pick up a frying pan, much less learn how to make a soufflé. But I do care about playing the piano, and I'd like to get better at that.

What parents have to do is find ways to help their teens value those areas in which they need to do well. For example, suppose your daughter receives a score of 65 on an English term paper and has to redo it.

She says: I don't care about English.

Quick response: It doesn't matter what you care about; your teacher expects you to do the work, and so do I!

Positive development response: You may not care about English, but let me ask you this: do you care about going to that party next weekend? Because you can't go unless you get your English paper done. You'll need to spend your time working on the paper.

When you respond like this, you're using the Premack Principle, named by Dr. David Premack, a University of Pennsylvania psychologist. Actually, my grandmother was familiar with this principle years before it was named. She knew that if I didn't want to wash the dishes, she'd tell me that the only way I could go out to play ball was if I washed the dishes first. So my getting what I wanted—playing ball—was contingent, or dependent, on my doing something I didn't want to do.

This is consistent with the positive development perspective in that by using this principle you're not punishing your child; instead, you're making opportunities available to her, but only after she completes a previous task. She'll get what she wants once she works at something less desirable. As parents, we need to figure out which pairs of behaviors go best together; we need to craft behavioral sequences so that less-desired activities will become more attractive because they are the gateway to something more attractive.

Offering Support that Bolsters Confidence

It's natural to want to support teens in all their endeavors. But not all support is equally helpful. In fact, parents' unsolicited help with homework can have negative effects, as was learned from a fascinating 2005 study by Ruchi Bhanot and Jasna Jovanovic, a former student of mine.

The researchers asked fifth through eighth graders to describe how they perceived their abilities in English and math; at the same time, their parents were asked how they viewed their child's ability in these areas, and to record their own opinions on how boys and girls differ in regard to achievement in math and English. Then the students were given checklists to fill out after any interaction they had with their parents while they were doing homework in these two subjects. The researchers found that when parents monitored homework and provided help that their children didn't request, competence sometimes increased and sometimes decreased. However, kids' *confidence* levels always went down when such unsolicited help was offered. Children experience such help as intrusive, and it diminishes how able they feel.

This study has other important implications for gender differences, as we'll explore later in the chapter. But its findings on how to offer support is clear: parents need either to be invited to help or to be collaborators with their children so that the advice they have to offer is received as welcome rather than as an intrusion.

Suppose your tenth grader comes home complaining about a science project he has to put together for his biology class in a week's time. A biology major yourself, you're bursting with advice, suggestions, and ideas. But if you care about his confidence, bite your tongue and keep your plans to yourself—until he asks for your help. If you take over the reins of the project, your child will feel as if he is simply following your lead. In this case, even if he succeeds, the research of Bhanot and Jovanovic indicates that such success won't lead him to conclude that he can be successful on his own.

BIG THREE #3:	GIVE TEENS THE OPPORTUNITY TO BECOME LEADERS

- Ask your teen for help with challenges to your own sense of confidence.
- Help your teen "de-center"—shift her focus away from herself so she can better appreciate the perspective of others.
- Encourage your teen to take the initiative and seek out facts that will help bolster her confidence.

Asking for Help

All of the parents discussed in the last section helped their teens become more competent by suggesting skill-building activities. It's also important for parents to model these life skills. You can talk and suggest until you run out of breath, to little or no effect, while sometimes the smallest gesture ends up influencing a child enormously.

If you're facing a challenge that requires you to gain confidence in a new area, let your child help you.

A good friend of mine, for instance, recently accepted a job as an associate director of a foundation, a field only tangentially related to the one in which she'd worked for the past twenty-five years. She was eager to get started but also felt cowed by how much she needed to master in a short time. One evening at dinner, she mentioned that she'd been asked to prepare a special report for the board of the foundation and didn't know how or where to begin. As she described how inadequate she felt to the task, she saw her fifteen-year-old daughter's ears prick up. "I bet you can find lots of information online," the girl volunteered. "I could help you search for it if you'd like."

My friend gratefully accepted her daughter's help, and together they found a template for the type of report she needed to write. From that day on, my friend made a concerted effort to talk candidly about her new job—her successes and her frustrations—in front of her daughter. She wanted her daughter to see how much time and perseverance the new job required, and that although her confidence waxed and waned on a day-to-day basis, she generally grew more confident over time. Sometimes we want to hide our personal struggles from our teens, but they benefit greatly when we let them accompany us on our own journeys through adversity, success, and failure.

It's also a good idea to ask teens for guidance with specific questions. Tasks that often drive parents to frustration—learning to work iPods, digital cameras, and DVD players—seem to come naturally to teens raised on a steady diet of technology. Not only are many eager to help, but they also take pride in the fact that they are in a position to help, which in turn boosts their confidence.

Helping your Teen to De-center

When your twelve-year-old wakes up with a pimple on her forehead, she naturally assumes that everyone will see it when they look at her. When your fifteen-year-old daughter sits in math class praying that the boy in the seat in front of her will turn around and smile at her, she's convinced that no one else has ever longed for love as much as she. When a month before the senior prom your eighteen-year-old is dumped by the girl he's been going out with, he knows that no one has ever been treated so cruelly. Teens construct what my Tufts University colleague David Elkind calls a "personal fable" about themselves, in which they are the one-of-a-kind star, so unique that the world has never known another like them. Sometimes they're the best, and sometimes they're the worst; what's salient is that they consider themselves singular. At the same time, they also construct an "imaginary audience," believing that they are at center stage at all times, so everyone cares about their pimples and love affairs as passionately as they do.

Having an imaginary audience and constructing a personal fable are both aspects of what Elkind has termed "adolescent egocentrism." That is, teens become so preoccupied with their own thinking that they fail to distinguish between their thoughts and the thoughts of others. They feel as if they are transparent, so everyone else can see what they're thinking and feeling, and whatever they are thinking is shared by all around them. Dwelling on themselves—constantly focusing on their deepest desires and their most glaring deficiencies—may make them overly self-conscious and reluctant to act. Such feelings may then have a negative effect on their confidence.

The best way to counter adolescent egocentrism and the lack of confidence it may breed is to help your teen de-center, to move away from the intense focus on herself. Encourage her to pursue interests outside herself, to get involved with a wide range of activities and people. Activities that engage people of different ages, such as attending meetings at school to plan trips or becoming involved with a neighborhood food drive, are particularly helpful in expanding teens' horizons. Whatever collaborative activity your child chooses, she will soon discover that what she's going through isn't unique. She'll also learn that she's not the center of the universe. As egocentric worries diminish, confidence has room to grow.

Maxine, for instance, had just transferred from a school for kids with learning disabilities to a public high school for ninth grade, where she became part of the collaborative program. She was very nervous about fitting in. Specifically, she worried that the kids in her regular classes would know that the other teacher in the room—a special ed teacher—was there to help her and the other special ed kids. In truth, the students who weren't in the collaborative program had no idea why there was a second teacher in the room; they simply accepted the fact. But Maxine was convinced that the special ed teacher was attached to her by a cord visible to everyone.

Things didn't improve much until auditions were announced for the school play. Maxine had gotten one of the leads in her old school but felt too nervous to try out now. She wasn't sure she'd be able to remember all the lines, and she didn't want to fall behind in her schoolwork—she knew how much extra time rehearsals consumed.

"Being involved in the play would be good for you," her parents told her. Then they asked, "Is there a way you could participate without feeling so stressed?"

"I guess I could join the tech crew," Maxine said. This turned out to be a perfect solution: Maxine became part of the sound team and felt very much part of the collective enterprise without feeling as if she were putting too much pressure on herself. She felt accepted by her peers and valued for her contribution, and as a result her overall confidence received a huge boost.

Encouraging Your Teen to Become a Fact-Finder

Although confidence is about how we feel, having facts at your fingertips can help counter low confidence. Take the area of physical appearance, about which nearly every teen feels vulnerable.

Suppose, for instance, your son is upset because he's not "buff" enough. He's goes to the weight room at his high school gym religiously and had the wrestling coach work out a bodybuilding program for him, but still hasn't bulked up. One day, he mentions that he wants to buy supplements one of his weight-lifting buddies has been talking about. You worry that the supplements are really steroids.

Quick response: No way! Those pills are so unhealthy!

Positive development response: Why don't you do some research online about those pills? It's always a good idea to get all the information you can about any medication, since everything has side effects.

See where his research takes him. He may discover all the negative side effects of suspicious supplements on his own. He may find out about vitamins and minerals that really would help him bulk up. He may, however, find himself in a dead end, saying, "OK, so the pills aren't healthy, but I don't know what else to do to increase my muscle mass."

Quick response: I think you're fine the way you are.

Positive development response: I understand your concern. Let's figure out whom we can call on or where we can go for advice about what will work for you. Do you have any ideas about what we should do first?

This sort of response, while not disputing his own feelings, throws the ball back in his court. He may want to buy new clothes, for instance—perhaps T-shirts a size smaller will highlight his just-emerging biceps. He could pick up a men's magazine for other tips on how to dress to best showcase his physique. Or maybe he'll want to change his look in other ways: buy a new pair of sunglasses, for instance, or cut his hair short.

Or suppose your daughter is unhappy with her weight. If you *have* a daughter, she probably is. According to the studies of researcher Robyn Silverman, another one of my former students, whose groundbreaking research at Tufts University focused on young girls' weight issues and confidence, girls as young as seven can have a distorted self-image and want to weigh less. Sadly, as girls age, their desire to lose weight increases and intensifies. By the time they reach late adolescence, 50 to 75 percent of girls are actively dieting. Some studies have detected a positive association between girls who overestimate their size and feelings of depression. Other studies seem to indicate that girls who are dissatisfied with their overall appearance experience difficulties in terms of low self-esteem, depression, and anxiety. Unfortunately, the way in which a girl views her body when she's young can affect her later in life as well.

Apparently, no girls are entirely safe from this low-confidence epidemic. Although body image problems were once considered the bane of European American suburban girls exclusively, newer research is showing that girls of various ethnic groups and women of color are also grappling with the problem. In addition, eating disorders, which in the past were seen as afflicting affluent girls, are now affecting girls who are raised in lower-income families as well.

How can you help inoculate your daughter against a weight-induced confidence drain? Ask her to do some fact-finding. Perhaps you and she could consult one of the many fashion magazines to see which type of necklines, fabrics, sleeve lengths, and jeans would have the most flattering effect, paying special attention to the "do and don't" advice. Perhaps she can learn about new cosmetics and new ways of applying makeup to enhance her features. My research has shown that the face and head are prime cues for others' judgments of our attractiveness. By tweaking her appearance so that she likes the way she looks, she's taking a leadership role in shoring up her own confidence.

At the same time, you may not want your daughter to worry that you think she *needs* to change her appearance to boost her confidence. To prevent her from thinking this, you can:

- Make an appointment for a new hairstyle yourself and ask her to join you.
- Take one of her girlfriends to make it a "girls' day out," complete with manicure and pedicure.
- Create your own spa day with your daughter at home. Have fun together by taking turns doing each other's hair, trying out different soaps and moisturizers you may have on hand, or creating "kitchen cosmetics"—spa-like recipes for natural beauty products you can make from items in your refrigerator (the ingredients are found in many magazines geared to teenage girls as well as on the Internet).

- Change your family's dietary habits to focus on healthy eating.
- Encourage other family lifestyle changes. Institutionalize exercise regimens—taking a walk after dinner, for instance, promotes better sleeping patterns.

Spending time on lessons of grooming, nutrition, and dietary habits, facial and hair care, and style of dress isn't trivial. It gives adolescents the sense that they have control over the physical impression they make on others. By showing a teen that she herself has the power and ability to alter something as concrete as physical appearance, she gains confidence that she has control over her destiny, that she is a capable, effective "producer" of her own development.

Encouraging your teenager to do some fact-finding works in other areas as well, such as encouraging vocational confidence. Lydia, for example, took a summer job as a cashier in the local branch of a national department store. She liked having her own spending money but complained all the time—she couldn't just talk to customers but had to follow "stupid scripts" imposed by the store; she had to deal with ridiculous customers; and she had to push store promotions, such as inducing people to sign up for credit cards that they really didn't need. She began talking about quitting.

"I wonder if there's a way you can expand your job responsibilities," her father commented during one of their discussions about her unhappiness at work. "Is there a way for you to take initiative?"

"I doubt it," Lydia replied. But during one slow day, Lydia began rifling through some drawers and found an employee manual that listed all the levels of employment. She began reading it, and ended up taking it home with her. To get a promotion, she learned, she needed to impress her supervisors with her initiative. It wasn't long before an opportunity arose. As Lydia told it, "The store hired a bunch of new trainees just before the Fourth of July weekend, and there were too many on the floor; no one was sure where to go. I was on the cosmetics register with two trainees, but business was slow so I suggested that one move to housewares, which was much busier. When the girl's supervisor came to check up on the trainee, I told the supervisor what I'd done. I thought she'd be angry, but instead she asked if I had any other ideas. I did—like getting rid of those scripts—and she took me seriously."

When Lydia came home that evening, she told her parents that she'd had a taste of what being a manager was like, and she liked it.

GIRLS AND CONFIDENCE

As you know by now, I'm interested in teenagers in all their diversity. My research cuts across all genders, socioeconomic groups, religions, and ethnic identifications. So far, I've scrupulously avoided focusing on one particular set of needs as compared to considering adolescents in general.

But the issue of confidence has special resonance when it comes to girls. Writers such as Carol Gilligan and psychologist Mary Pipher, author of *Reviving Ophelia,* have argued that girls in early to middle adolescence may have their confidence challenged for several reasons. As a consequence, their faith in themselves may plummet.

Stressful Transitions Take a Toll on Confidence

My own research, as well as studies by other longitudinal researchers, is consistent with the suggestions of Gilligan and Pipher. For many girls, making the transition from elementary to middle school is associated with drops in self-esteem and grades. In the 4-H Study, for instance, we find that although girls score higher than boys on every measure of positive development, including contribution, when they are in the fifth through seventh grades, they nevertheless show a consistent decrease in confidence—and in other indicators of positive development.

In part, the decrease in confidence experienced by girls is related to the type of school they attend. Research by the late sociologist Roberta G. Simmons and by Dale A. Blyth, director of the Center for 4-H Youth Development at the University of Minnesota, indicates that waning confidence and a drop in self-esteem and grades are associated with the transition to middle school; girls who attend

K-8 schools do not experience such declines. Some researchers have proposed an "accumulation of risk" idea to account for this difference. In other words, at the time that girls are making their transition to middle school they are also typically undergoing the transition to puberty—that is, they're at the age of menarche, or first period. It may be, then, that girls who attend middle school are making too many transitions at once. The reality of transferring to a new school, meeting new people, and coping with the physical and physiological changes of early adolescence may place too much stress on them, overtaxing their coping resources. Because boys don't reach puberty until two years later than girls, they don't have to cope with so much change at once.

There is some good news here, however. The decrease that girls experience in their confidence and grades seems to be more of a dip or a detour rather than a permanent change. Simmons and Blyth found that by the time girls enter ninth grade, their self-esteem and grades rebound. Research that I conducted with my wife, Jacqueline Lerner, a professor in the Counseling and Applied Developmental Psychology program at Boston College, confirms this finding. Based on this understanding, parents can use the Big Three to help ease the crisis of confidence in their adolescent daughters.

To maintain a close positive relationship with your teenage daughter, parents, and especially moms—or older sisters or aunts, if moms are not available—can talk about their own transition stresses and about how they bounced back. When girls hear these stories, their sense of being unique (starring in their own personal fable) decreases, thus diminishing their overall adolescent egocentrism. Honest talks like this also convey an important promise: "There's light at the end of the tunnel. I made it through. So did all my friends and so did your sister. You will, too."

At the same time, parents can explain to girls that it's not uncommon for them to have a hard time adjusting at this stage of life because they are trying to deal with so many changes all at once. Show your teen you fully understand what she is experiencing and emphasize that there is nothing "wrong" with her if her confidence is shaken. Give your teenage daughter the information she needs to understand what is happening to her body and social relationships. Explaining a situation and labeling feelings are very useful tactics in dispelling mystery and reducing anxiety. The very fact that you are discussing these issues with your daughter indicates to her that you view her differently: she's no longer a child but has reached a new, more mature status. In short, although passing from childhood to young womanhood can be scary, you can attenuate this reaction by showing that you not only are there for her but also regard her as capable of understanding and coping with more adult challenges.

Your teenage daughter has many opportunities to take the lead during this phase of her life. She'll most likely be interested in going shopping by herself or with a few friends—and she certainly can begin to do this, within guidelines you propose. She should also be afforded some privacy in the doctor's office so she can talk to her pediatrician without you in the room.

After these forays on her own, engage her in conversations about her experiences by asking questions that begin with "how" or "why" rather than yes-or-no questions: for example, "How did your shopping go? Were you able to find what you needed? Is there anything you need me to help you with? What did Dr. Smith have to say?" Within guidelines you set, you can also let your daughter decide how she'll partition her time between schoolwork, chores, extracurricular activities, and simple "downtime." Ask her to suggest a plan and, as well, a system to monitor and evaluate how she is doing. In collaboration with you, allow her to follow the plan she has set. This opportunity will enable her to gain experiences in coping with the changing demands on her body and her time. By taking a leadership role in planning how to contend with all these changes, she'll gain confidence sufficient to enrich her path through this transitional time.

Gender Stereotypes Influence Confidence

Despite the pronounced impact of the social and physical transitions teenage girls undergo, the impact of gender on confidence cannot be underestimated. For example, studies have shown that by the time girls reach middle school, they are less confident when it comes to math than boys are, even when they perform as well as or better than boys. Why is this so?

According to several studies, parents' stereotyped beliefs about gender and ability have a profound effect on both children's performance and their confidence levels. Parents who believe that boys do better in math and science tend to overestimate how well their sons will perform in these subjects and underestimate their daughters' performance in these areas. But perhaps even more significant is the finding that these stereotyped beliefs influence children's perceptions of their own abilities—and this happens whether or not children have actual ability in these areas. One study of sixth-grade girls showed that even those girls who received higher grades in math than their male counterparts were more likely to underestimate their mathematical ability—which coincided with their mothers' diminished view of their abilities. And perhaps most interesting of all, the study found that "this reliance on stereotypes about math was truer of mothers than fathers."

In the Bhanot and Jovanovic study mentioned earlier, results indicate that girls pick up on their mothers' gender-stereotyped beliefs—the stereotype that girls are worse in math—especially when moms give unasked-for help with homework. That is, when moms spend extra time helping their daughters with math—help girls didn't ask for—these girls in effect seem to say to themselves, "My mom believes that boys do better at math than girls."

To counter this tendency, moms need to carefully monitor the way they interact with their daughters about homework. Rather than intruding where they're not wanted and unwittingly reinforcing harmful stereotypes, moms of daughters who are struggling can encourage their daughters to seek help in math and science from others—tutors, for example, if this is affordable. If this option isn't available, there may be a homework center your daughter can use, either in her school or in the community. If Dad is available, he should offer to help—because he knows his daughter can do well in this subject area.

At the same time, make sure that your daughter is aware of all the women who have made important scientific discoveries and contributions—Madame Curie, for example; Sally Ride and other women astronauts; and Rosalind Franklin, the unsung molecular biologist without whose pioneering work Watson and Crick might never have stumbled upon the structure of DNA.

BECOMING CONFIDENT BUT NOT CONCEITED

As you boost your child's confidence in the ways discussed above, you'll want to make sure that healthy confidence doesn't morph into smugness. An overconfident teen may lose his capacity to maintain a balanced perspective of the world. This problem often arises when teens cling to their personal fables. Their sense that they are special leads them to conclude that they are invulnerable and invincible. Other people have to wear seat belts or bicycle helmets, or not drink and drive—but not them. They're exempt from the laws that apply to everyone else. If they feel this way, they may believe that there's no danger if they speed down a country road at ninety miles an hour, holding their cell phone in one hand and a burger in the other and steering with their knees.

That's why teens need to be brought back down to earth. They need to de-center. They need to be told that accidents can happen to everyone—no one is immune. Teens also need to be reminded that no one is entitled to be smug. As good as your son may be on the tennis court or in class, there's always room for improvement. Professionals in every field, you can tell him, whether it's sports, the arts, or technology, are always striving to outdo themselves, to get better, to try for more. There's not much room for self-satisfaction. As the great pitcher Satchel Paige said, "Don't look back; someone may be gaining on you."

Another important tactic is to keep the conversation focused on your teen. That is, don't compare her to others. Comparisons breed competition and anxiety about not measuring up. You may hate it when people do this to you, and so will your teen. Instead, emphasize that you think she's special—that you and others value her attributes, and that she should, too. If your daughter comes home with a terrific report card, for example, you may have the impulse to ask her how her friends did, or if anyone said anything to her about her good grades. Instead, talk about her achievement on its own terms, and leave everyone else out of it.

LOOKING AHEAD

What happens to teens suffering from a lack of confidence? It's a tough question. All we can say for sure is that they won't perform up to their potential. Your son who loves to write for his high school newspaper may not turn out to be the next Bob Woodward no matter how much confidence he has . . . but he has no chance of becoming a star journalist if his confidence is low. Even the most competent teen can fail if he doesn't have confidence.

That's why it's imperative for parents to foster confidence. We need to remember, as Bandura reminds us in the epigraph to this chapter, that we can't afford to be complete and total realists when it comes to our own behavior and performance—we have to be idealistic, to dream, and to have faith in our abilities.

But neither competence nor confidence is enough on its own to ensure that teens have a smooth and successful transition to adulthood. By the time kids reach adolescence, they're old enough to appreciate that the world is a complex place and that no one can negotiate it alone. To succeed requires collaboration. Confident people are able to overcome their egocentrism by saying to themselves, "It's not just about me." They know that their contribution is important, but it will be even more effective if it's part of a team effort. So in the next chapter, we'll discuss this important link, connection.

Connection

A candle loses nothing by lighting another candle.

—Erin Majors

A few years ago, a colleague of mine told me a story that made such an impression that I haven't forgotten it.

"When my children were younger," he said, "we lived in State College, Pennsylvania. It's a big town because it's the home of Penn State University, but in many ways it's also a very small town. Though we lived less than two miles from a major road, we were still out in the middle of nowhere. At that time, Stephanie, who was about eleven, became passionate about gymnastics. It was all she wanted to do. We found a school for her—the town had several—and she spent almost every waking hour when she wasn't in school practicing her cartwheels, headstands, and other contortions I can barely describe. For three seasons of the year, she thought nothing of practicing in our yard, where the other kids from the neighborhood could watch her. They were drawn to her, amazed at her ability, and often surprised by how friendly she was, even toward the youngest children. She'd take time out of her practicing to talk to those who came out to watch her; she'd think nothing of patiently explaining and demonstrating all the steps she had to master before executing a cartwheel. Because it was such a small neighborhood, everyone knew about Stephanie's hobby, and they also knew how kind and generous she was with her time.

"In the early spring, her gymnastics school sponsored a show for the parents and community in which all the students would compete for prizes. Stephanie was tremendously excited about this, and told not only us but also her 'fan club' about the event. Everyone on the block was rooting for her.

"The night before the competition, I listened to the weather report before going to sleep and heard that six to eight inches of snow was predicted—no big deal in rural Pennsylvania. But when I woke up, the only thing I could say was, 'Oh my God.' Nearly twenty inches of snow had fallen overnight, drifting higher than two feet in some places. I quickly did the math and my heart sank: even if my wife and I woke up immediately and began shoveling the heavy, wet snow off our 200-foot driveway, we'd never make it to the gymnastics school in time for the event. And even if we could have accomplished this superhuman feat, there was no way of knowing if the small road we'd have to travel to get to the main road would be clear. The four miles to the gymnastics school seemed an insurmountable distance.

"My heart breaking for my daughter, I got out of bed figuring that I had to give it a try. After all, she'd worked so hard that I had to work hard, too. I put on my parka and gloves and went into my garage to open the door from the inside so I could get started.

"I'll never forget what I saw. I can still see it to this day: my driveway was perfectly clear. Not a speck of snow on it.

"As it turned out, a neighbor who knew about Stephanie's event— because his children had been among those Stephanie had befriended—had a small plow that he used to clear our driveway while we slept. Not only that, but he offered to drive with us to make sure that the small local road was cleared of snow so we could make it into town on time. In the end, we were accompanied by a small caravan from the neighborhood.

"My wife and I were grateful beyond words. We couldn't have had better proof of our embeddedness in this small community. That we didn't even have to ask for help—that the strength of our connection to the neighborhood was so strong that others could anticipate our needs and help us out—made us feel terrific. And it made Stephanie feel terrific, too. She'd been generous with the neighborhood children, and in turn the neighborhood was generous with us. We were a mutually supportive unit. In the simplest terms, we were all connected."

UNDERSTANDING CONNECTION

Competence and confidence are qualities we experience individually, within ourselves. Connection, the third C, is the first that extends beyond the boundaries of the self and acknowledges the importance of others. It implicitly draws on the notion that humans are inherently social creatures. No matter how competent or confident we may be, we still need others to create healthy, productive lives. As evolutionary biologists tell us, we're herd animals, embedded in social systems: we travel together, and we recognize that to be productive and succeed, we need to communicate with others so that we can ask for and receive ideas, wisdom, mentorship, guidance, and support. When you think about it, biological life itself is a relational phenomenon: we are born because there was a relationship between two other organisms.

When a young person has positive connections to others—family members, friends, teachers, coaches, mentors, and people in the community—he or she both contributes to their well-being and, in turn, has his or her own well-being enhanced through them. Thus connection is a two-way street. The benefits of being connected flow both ways.

There are many ways parents can foster connection so that teens feel more in touch with themselves, each other, their parents, the adults in their world, and their communities. Again, we'll use the Big Three as a guide.

BIG THREE #1:	MAINTAIN A POSITIVE RELATIONSHIP

- Consider timing and personal space when talking to teens.
- Let shared activities do the talking.
- Support your teen's efforts to connect to people outside the family.
- Support wholesome connections.
- Create and follow family rituals.
- Respect your teen's privacy.

Having Respectful Conversations

Often, the best conversations with teens take place when you respect their needs relating to time and space. Timing, for instance, is a huge variable when talking to teens. Just because you want to talk about something doesn't mean your teen agrees. It's often not wise to pursue a conversation past the point where your teen wants it to go. Rather than press for details, let the discussion rest. Your teen may bring up the subject herself when she feels comfortable. It may be that she simply needs to feel as if she is in charge of the agenda, including when and where to initiate or continue a conversation.

Leann, for example, who was fifteen, mentioned at dinner one night that she was thinking of quitting the chorus she'd worked hard to audition for. Her parents were stunned. When they asked her why she was unhappy, Leann answered with annoyance, "I just hate it. It's boring. And I don't want to talk about it anymore." Biting their tongues, her frustrated parents said nothing. The rest of the meal unfolded in silence.

But the next day, as she helped her mother unload the dishwasher, Leann started talking. "Some people think they're better than everyone else," she said. Her mother didn't answer; she just nodded in agreement. She knew that sometimes silence greases the wheels of conversation better than a verbal response. Sure enough, Leann continued, eventually getting around to explaining that the problem with the chorus wasn't the music or the conductor but the girl sitting next to her, who was a year older. "She's always getting in my face and telling me I'm off-key when I'm not," Leann said. "And she says I mispronounce the words. She gets the other girls to laugh at me."

Ruth felt her heart break for her daughter, and thought for a moment before replying because she wanted to address Leann's situation as accurately as she could. "With kids like that," she began, "you just have to tell yourself that she must have a really bad problem herself if she has to put others down. Some people need to make others feel bad in order to feel good themselves."

"Whatever," Leann said, effectively ending the conversation. Ruth felt hurt but didn't say anything.

A few days later, Ruth was in the kitchen paying bills when Leann, on the phone with a friend, wandered into the room. At first Ruth didn't pay attention to the conversation, but as it drew on, Ruth realized that Leann was advising a friend about a problem the other girl was having. "Some people put others down just to make themselves feel good," she heard Leann say.

Ruth couldn't believe her ears. Leann had heard her every word— and thought enough of the advice to pass it on to a friend. Ruth felt gratified that she had waited to talk to Leann until her daughter was ready to listen, even if Leann hadn't been able to acknowledge her mother's advice at the time.

Positioning and distance are also important. Research on personal space indicates that people communicate their like or dislike of others through the amount of space that exists between them. We naturally seem to give ourselves about three feet when talking to others. Less than that often indicates a more intimate relationship, and more than that often indicates negative feelings.

Teens may experience a conversation in which you're sitting

across from each other, maintaining eye contact, as too intense. Many find it easier to speak freely in the car, for example, with your respective eyes on the road rather than on each other. Some teens open up during shared activities, such as shoveling snow or washing the car, rather than during prescribed "conversational times" such as during dinner or family meetings.

When you do converse, have an open mind. Resolve to listen more than talk. And if you do talk, try to keep your comments personal and specific. Few things turn teens off more than hearing platitudes or stories they've heard before. Above all, let them know that you understand—and if you don't, then that you're trying to understand. You can do this by trying to match their tone of voice—if they sound lighthearted, try to reply in that tone of voice; when they're serious, become serious yourself. This shows them that you're paying attention. When they feel as if you're on the same page, they will be much more likely to continue talking.

In general, try to remain positive. Let everything about your body language and the words you use say, "I believe in you. You have many strengths. You're very resilient. Even if this is a tough time, we'll come through it."

Conversing Through Action

If your teen is more comfortable doing than talking—if confronting feelings and issues head-on makes him squirm—then find ways to connect nonverbally. If your child is not a talker, invite him to do something active with you: doing a chore together, going shopping, playing a sport, or going for a walk. Not only is it a good way to show connection, but it also acknowledges his style of relating, and communicates that you respect it and that you are eager to experience it with him. You'll also model a new way for him to connect with other "nontalkers"—a great life skill.

But again, the way you approach this is crucial. Saying "Let's take a walk together; it's good exercise and it'll give us a chance to spend time together" may not work for every teen. If this is the case, talk about your interest: "I'm taking my after-dinner walk; care to join me?" Your teen may say no the first time you ask and maybe the second or third, but if you persist, gently, she may eventually agree to give it a try.

You can also try to connect through an activity you love. If you're a word or number puzzle fan, for example, make yourself comfortable in a room in your home where your teen can see you and do your puzzles there; one day she just may come over and ask to see what it's all about.

Reaching Out

Adolescence is a time when teens broaden their orbit and reach outside the family for connection. Friends, to say nothing of boyfriends and girlfriends, often become the center of their lives. But even before romance becomes important, friends are vital. According to researcher Brad Brown and many others who have studied peer relationships, it's not the number of friends that counts but rather the quality of the relationships. As long as your child has at least one friend with whom she is genuinely close and engaged, whose support and honesty she can count on, and with whom she can do things, her sense of social connectedness can be strong.

Teens also yearn to belong to a group. Cruise down the street at about three in the afternoon in just about any town in America and you'll spot them: packs of kids walking home from school together or clustered at the local coffee shop or pizza place or ice cream store. Although this pack mentality sometimes works against them—it's hard to convince your child to go to camp or to attend a special program in her area of interest if none of her friends is going—groups are a fact of teen life. Draw on this inclination by encouraging your teen to join committees, clubs, and athletic teams whether they're at school, through religious institutions, or in the community. If none of this appeals, and if you have the resources, you can enroll your child in a specialized program according to his passion—perhaps your son wants to join a dojo not only to learn martial arts but also to find others who love it as much as he does. Or perhaps your teen would enjoy volunteering weekends at the local hospital, where she could meet other like-minded girls. Teens may be more willing to extend themselves in these ways if they see their parents involved in groups as well. Parents can also help facilitate group "dates"—opportunities for young people to spend time together in public settings such as malls and movie theaters. Or maybe your teen is more of a loner and enjoys the company of just one or two others. In this case, don't press too hard. Your child may be temperamentally more comfortable moving in smaller social circles.

Don't be surprised if your teen starts reaching out to adults outside the immediate family, such as teachers, coaches, or in some cases religious leaders. This is developmentally appropriate, and as long as these relationships stay within acceptable boundaries, they should be encouraged. Many teachers, for example, are both willing and eager to establish close relationships with students and will make themselves available after school or for special projects. A friend of mine, now in her forties, recalls that a seventh-grade English teacher, who made an indelible mark on her but who was dismissed for suggesting that students might want to think about the words they were reciting in the Pledge of Allegiance rather than repeating them by rote—wrote his address on the board on the last day of class and said he'd welcome a letter from anyone who cared to stay in touch. My friend took him up on his offer. Throughout high school, college, and graduate school, the two corresponded; he served as a kind of literary guide, suggesting what she might want to read, discussing the books with her, and sending her critical essays to broaden her perspective. Twenty-five years later, they are still in touch. "I wouldn't be the person I am without his influence on me," she tells me.

Making the Right Connections

At the same time that you encourage connection between your teen and her peers as well as other adults, be vigilant. Make sure your teen is well aware of your family values and knows how to behave and conduct herself at all times. Not all peers or groups with whom your teen wants to associate will be equally beneficial to her. *Do not unquestioningly accept relations among your child and his peers.* If you don't approve of a friend, don't be afraid to say so. Likewise, if you don't think a friend's parents provide enough supervision, speak up. Don't shrink from taking the heat: it's your responsibility to be authoritative about this. You're trying to help your teen develop in positive ways, not befriend her.

Suppose your thirteen-year-old daughter asks if she can sleep over at her friend Janis' house on a Friday night. When you ask about supervision, she says that Janis' older brother, who is eighteen, will be there; her parents are away. Your immediate answer is, "No way."

Your daughter begs you. She pleads with you. She tells you that everyone else is going—no other parents mind except you. Her best friend, Eva, whom you like, is allowed to go.

Quick response: I don't care what Eva is doing. What if she were jumping off the Brooklyn Bridge—would you follow her? You are *not* sleeping over at Janis'.

More thoughtful response: Janis' older brother is not old enough to be responsible for a houseful of teenage girls.

Positive development response: It isn't that I don't trust you or your friends. And I understand that Janis' brother will be there, but he's not an adult. It's that unexpected things happen that could need an experienced parent to handle, and I care about your safety too much to let you sleep over without such supervision. So no, you can't go, not this time.

Keeping your teens well connected means that you have to connect as well—to the parents of your teen's friends. This way, you can help ensure that your standards are being maintained even when your kids are in other people's homes.

Luckily for us, research by University of Michigan psychologists Elizabeth Douvan and Joseph Adelson indicates that adolescents, both boys and girls, tend to select friends whose values correspond to those maintained in their own homes. In other words, your teen is likely to find friends from families who value the importance of a good education, the role of faith in a person's life, or the significance of family in the same way your family does. Therefore, the best way to ensure that the connections your child is making with peers are wholesome and reflect the values you hold in life is for you to be closely connected with your child about these values. Let her know what you believe and why you believe it. By being authoritative you can elicit her opinions and work to integrate her take on these topics into the "culture" of the family, resting assured that in the vast majority of the cases, when the apple does fall, it won't land far from the tree. By then being an authority about positive development you can help link your child to those social connections that will reinforce the values you hold dear, which in turn will help your child internalize these values.

Try to create a home that becomes a "hangout" in which your teen's friends—those you feel comfortable with—feel welcome. For instance, create a space in your home where your teen and her friends can watch DVDs or listen to CDs. And keep a supply of (nutritious) snacks handy for them. Having kids congregate at your house is a great way to stay connected. "I realized that I often learn some of the most intimate details about my daughter's life when there are others around," explained Lorraine, mother of fifteen-year-old Zoe. "When her friends are over and they come into the kitchen for a snack, they sit around the table and chat as if I'm not there. No one seems to mind, even though they know I'm listening. In fact, they often bring me into the conversation. They talk about things Zoe would never talk to me about if we were alone. And if I ask a question or venture a comment, they're generally OK with that. Sometimes one of Zoe's friends will stop just to talk to me if we meet in the hallway or in the yard, and she's often very chatty about things that are happening. It's a kind of window into my daughter's life."

You also have to be especially vigilant about new forms of communication through the Internet. Although some of the new technology teens seem to prefer can seem fairly innocuous—cell phones and instant and text messaging—other venues, such as Facebook and MySpace, may not be totally safe, as we'll discuss later in the chapter.

What's Right About Rituals

Thanksgivings spent gathered around the table with friends and family, a Fourth of July picnic and softball game, Labor Day at the beach, birthday celebrations that always feature the same special cake, Arrival Days for kids who were adopted (during which the entire family commemorates the day you began life as a family): rituals such as these have always existed because they are a kind of glue connecting us to one another, and to generations both past and future. If you ask many adolescents to name their most pleasant memories, many will recall holidays and vacations spent together. It's often not easy to plan to celebrate holidays with the extended family, but it's effort well spent.

To support connection, give teens the opportunity to help plan the holiday or to create a new family tradition. Ask them, for example, to make place cards for the meal, to organize an after-dinner treasure hunt for the younger children, or to be responsible for staging and snapping the family photo. In some families, teens take an even more active role. As Cindy explains, "The Fourth of July has always been a very special tradition in our family. We live in a small town, and there's a huge parade, and afterward my whole family comes back to our house for a barbecue. One year, my husband's sister, who's unmarried and always lived around the corner, took a new job and moved about four hours away. About a month before the holiday, Peter, who's fourteen, said, 'Aunt Rhoda's going to miss the parade and barbecue this year. Maybe we should go to her instead.' When he first mentioned it, I was against the idea. I hated the thought of not celebrating as we usually did. But we talked it over as a family and decided that he was right: this year we wanted to support Rhoda. So we went to her new house and watched the parade in her town, and then went out for burgers and hot dogs at a roadside stand near her new house. And we all had a great time." What made it special for Cindy was acknowledging that it was her son's connection to his aunt that set the whole event in motion.

Rituals don't have to be followed slavishly; you aren't bound to do the same thing every year. In fact, adding new touches can enliven age-old celebrations that may be growing stale over the years. Even small changes can make a big difference. Leah, for example, used to plan dinners for the first night of Hanukkah exactly as her parents had—a traditional meal of potato latkes, applesauce, and jelly donuts, then the candle lighting, and finally presents. And each year her children would tease her about having to wait to receive their gifts. So one year she stunned them by placing the gifts on the table when they came down for dinner. "Go ahead, open them," she said. As it turns out, it was one of the best holidays they'd ever celebrated as a family. "With the suspense of what they were getting out of the way," Leah explained, "they were all much more relaxed during the meal and candle lighting. I felt as if they were actually enjoying and soaking in the meaning of the holiday for the first time. It made me wish I'd been more innovative years earlier."

The Family Dinner

Perhaps the most important family ritual can unfold every day: eating dinner together as a family. Gathering around the table, sharing impressions about the day, complaining or praising the meal, shouts of "No dessert if you don't finish your peas"—this used to be a given of family life. And in many parts of the country it still is. But for many families, particularly those in which both parents work and commute, getting everyone together for a meal can prove challenging. And it's probably never as challenging as when children reach adolescence and their busy lives complicate family commitments: if they don't have to leave at 6:00 P.M. for play practice, they have a study group or a class meeting, or their closest friend is having a crisis and needs an immediate visit. Or they swear they're not hungry and promise to grab something later, on the way home.

Yet sharing dinner together shouldn't be sacrificed: it's one of the key developmental resources. In fact, my research and that of others shows that this may be the single most important change you can make in family life to give your children a good start. A study by the National Center on Addiction and Substance Abuse found that those teens who regularly eat with their families are less likely to get into fights, think about suicide, smoke, drink, and use drugs; are more likely to initiate sexual activity later in life; and are more likely to perform better academically than teens who do not.

Stella, a home health care worker who lives in Manhattan, and her husband, Simon, who owns his own computer consulting business, can vouch for this. Ever since their son Ernesto was a baby, Stella insisted that the family eat dinner together. It was a tradition her family had observed when she was growing up in Puerto Rico. As it turned out, both she and her husband returned home from work later than they'd like, sometimes as late as eight o'clock. When Ernesto was young, he never questioned having to wait. But when he became a teenager, he began to gripe endlessly about it. "What's the big deal about sitting down together?" he asked. "There's only three of us; it's no big deal." But Stella was adamant. When Ernesto complained that he was going to keel over and die from starvation if he didn't eat "now," and that "normal" people ate dinner earlier, Stella told him to have a snack but, come eight o'clock, he was expected at the table with the family. A few years later, when Ernesto had to write his essay for his college application, he ended up describing why he wanted to become a doctor: "I decided to become a doctor at my kitchen table," he wrote. "It's the heartbeat of my family. It's the place where our bodies, minds, and souls find nourishment. I hope to have such a gathering ground someday, too—although dinner at my house will surely be served no later than six-thirty!"

If your family has trouble establishing a family meal, you may have to get creative. As suggested in the chapter on competence, if your teen has any interest in food, ask her to plan a couple of menus each week. You can use the Premack Principle, explained in the confidence chapter, and say, "Tomorrow night at dinner is the only time we'll get to talk about our family vacation. So if you want to have a voice in what we do, I suggest you show up."

You may have to become flexible about day and time. It may be that the family can gather as a group only two or three times a week. Your schedule may be so changeable that you can't plan more than a week in advance; if this is the case, you might decide to meet together on Sundays to block out those nights during the upcoming week when you all meet around the dinner table. One of my friends has a ritual Saturday brunch with her family. No single recipe will work for each family, but each family needs to find a way to sit down together and break bread. Remember, quality time isn't enough. You need big quantities of quality time.

By remaining close to your child in all these ways, you support her need to reach out and connect to others.

Respect Your Teen's Privacy

Teenagers may seem obsessed with privacy: they often love closing the doors to their rooms and spending hours inside. This behavior is not atypical, according to Reed Larson of the University of Illinois. His studies have shown that teens like to spend time alone, and it's healthy for them to do that. To appreciate oneself, to feel engaged in one's own company, is one of life's pleasures. You should afford your teen her privacy without inducing guilt. She likes it, and it's good for her.

At the same time, privacy can be perilous. Teens left to their own devices with no monitoring can find themselves in hot water pretty quickly. One of the challenges of parenting teenagers is finding ways to negotiate a privacy policy with your child that's flexible but responsible enough so that you both feel comfortable.

"I walked into my fourteen-year-old son's room the other day to leave a letter that came for him on his desk, and I saw a hard-core porn magazine lying on his pillow," said Frances. "I knew that sooner or later something like this would happen, but I was still shocked to see it. What do I do? Did he leave it there for me to see so that I'd say something about it? If I did bring it up with him, would he be mortified? And how would I begin?"

Here's how *not* to begin: by getting angry at him. Let's say you were putting away some laundry and found pot in your son's dresser drawer. You may be furious at him, feel betrayed by him, and despair about his stupidity—but it's best to not go ballistic when you approach him. Otherwise, if you come out swinging, your teen will simply say, "This is exactly why I can't tell you anything." And that's a conversational dead end. If you demean your child, he'll end up thinking that you don't—and now never will—trust him to make good choices, which is your ultimate goal as a parent. That's why the first step is to have a conversation about what you found that is respectful and positive, but also in line with your viewpoint on drugs.

Your goal during this talk is to get information. "Look," you can begin, "I found this. Do you think it's right to hide things from me? Do you think it's OK to be using drugs? I don't." You should then start talking about values: "I'm very concerned about your experimenting with drugs. You know my position; I think it's terribly unhealthy, and it's also illegal. Let's talk about the implications for you and for the family. How can we deal with this situation together?" If you begin the conversation with respect, most likely the conversation will stay respectful. And even if you end up imposing sanctions on your teen, which you're entitled to do, your son will feel as if he was heard and as if he collaborated with you in finding a workable solution to the problem.

But what happens if you walk into your child's room and find a gun, or evidence that your child is heavily into drugs? Or notice that your teen is visiting the Web site of a neo-Nazi or anti-Muslim group? In these cases, it's best if you stay calm, let your teen know your position on these issues, and ask what he thinks—but be firm in your conviction that this activity is not acceptable. When you feel that the values you hold most dear are being violated or that your child is in danger, you have to be a parent and insist that the behavior stop immediately. Impose sanctions if the behavior continues and a monitoring system to ensure that it doesn't, explaining to your teen why this is necessary. But remain resolute. We'll return to situations like this in Chapter 9, "When Real Trouble Brews."

It's also important to remember that sometimes teens leave private things, such as sexy magazines and diaries, lying around because they want you to see them. Whether you want to take them up on their opening gambit or not say a word depends on what you feel would be best for your child. Always keep in mind, though, that privacy is a balancing act. You constantly have to weigh your rights as an authority against your teen's need to express herself. However, the value of respecting her right to privacy always must take second place to keeping her safe.

The issue gets more serious these days with the ubiquity of Web sites such as Facebook and MySpace. As hard as it is to monitor teens as they live their actual lives, it gets even harder to monitor their virtual lives. And we all know that there are bad people out there, who mean to do harm; there are also crazy, hurtful ideas circulating every minute. But many teens don't realize this. "My daughter is a bright sixteen-year-old," said Helen, "and I showed her how with a couple of clicks I was able to get to her site by accessing the site of one of her classmates, and clicking on a photo. Yet she refuses to acknowledge the potential dangers."

This is a perfect opportunity for parents to be authoritative and authorities in positive development. You need to explain the dangers to your teens. Let them know what behavior you consider safe and what crosses the line. Teens may protest the limits you place on their online activity, or the need to monitor them, but many teens actually appreciate knowing that their parents are behind them, that they're not "out there" on their own.

Keep in mind the dangers of becoming too punitive, however. A recent news story reported that 90 percent of teens admitted that they feared that a predator had tried to contact them online. Not a single one of these teens ever told his or her parents. Why? They were afraid if they did, their parents would take away their computer time and privacy.

This chilling story underscores the importance of keeping the lines of communication open, of staying connected to your child as you negotiate a privacy policy that works for both of you. Work with your teen to develop guidelines that make you both feel comfortable and help your teen feel simultaneously autonomous and protected. There's no single answer—but you need to know the complexity of the issues before drawing any conclusions.

BIG THREE #2:	BUILD LIFE SKILLS

- Make connection part of the conversation.
- Be active in your community.
- Promote social and emotional competence.
- Help your shy child.

Talking About Connection

There's no mystery to supplying your teen with the life skills he needs to develop his sense of connection. Mostly, it's a question of talking about what we tend to take for granted, of making explicit what we normally keep to ourselves.

For example, most of us, in our work as parents and in our careers, have to maintain healthy connections to others in order to succeed and grow. In two-parent families, adult partners need to work in synergy to foster a healthy and positive family life. In one-parent families, support from other relatives and friends often is vital for success. Similarly, in our employment or our community work we need the partnership of others to succeed. Yet many people don't talk about how these connections are made and kept up.

To highlight the importance of connection, talk to your teen about the people you work with, your friends, your support system, and your extended family. Make a point of letting your child know about these people so that when they call on the phone or come to your home, your teen can say hello and perhaps have a brief conversation with them. Reflect on why and how you value these people, how the relationships meet your expectations, and where they have fallen short.

If you're having a particular problem with a colleague or friend, ask your child for her reaction and suggestions. By soliciting her advice, you're showing her that you value your relationships with people outside the family, as well as her help in solving your problem. You're also letting her know that it's good to talk about and reflect on our connections with others.

You can also be proactive by suggesting how your teen can forge peer connections. Sometimes the simplest strategy works wonders. During middle school, for example, Shannon didn't have many friends. She felt overly self-conscious about her weight, and this probably isolated her more than it should have. Her parents kept after her to join an after-school activity or club, hoping that this would help her make friends. She always resisted. But when she entered high school, she decided to try out for the basketball team

Despite her nervousness, she made a series of foul shots, and an assistant coach noticed her ability and drafted her onto the team. But she still hung back from making friends. Whenever her parents would ask her about this, she'd say, "Look, you wanted me to join a team, and I did, so now just leave me alone."

One day her mother was driving her home from a team practice and began telling Shannon a story about how she met a friend at work just by noticing that the other woman liked to use the same kind of pen. "You can strike up a conversation about the silliest things," the older woman said—and left it at that. The next day, after practice, Shannon noticed that a teammate whose locker was nearby used the same shampoo as she did. Shannon mentioned this, and the girls started chatting. After a week of worrying that she'd be rejected, Shannon asked her new friend if she wanted to hang out after school, and the girl said yes.

Swinging into Action Yourself

Nothing proves to teens that you value connection like getting out of your living room and participating in civic, social, and community activities. Volunteer to serve on committees at school and in religious institutions; become active in events. Let your teen know when you're going out in the evening to sing with the community chorus or attend a PTA meeting. You don't have to be a coach if that level of involvement is too much for you—you can coordinate the refreshments at each game, or coordinate buying the gift for the coach. Show that you care about other kids as well as adults with whom you interact in the family, at work, and in the community. Volunteer at your child's school, coach a sports team, become an adult leader of a 4-H club, or become a Big Brother or a Big Sister. Follow up by talking about what you're doing in these groups as part of the family conversation. When you reach out and support the positive development of youth in your community you are showing your child the value of connections. Equally important, you are becoming a model for your child.

Peter Benson, president of Minneapolis' Search Institute, an independent applied research organization specializing in child and adolescent development, often challenges the parents in the groups to which he talks across the nation to learn the names of at least six kids in their communities who are not family members or members of their children's immediate social group, as well as something about them. They, in turn, should learn who you are. Benson notes that many youth go to school and walk through their communities as if they were strangers, without any personal connection to bus drivers, cafeteria personnel, school administrators, librarians, or other adults with whom they come into contact.

Because teens may seemingly dress alike and listen to the same music and use the same vocabulary, it's easy to assume that they are happy to take refuge in anonymity. But in fact this is a developmental stage during which teens are seeking to establish their identities, their specific definition of self. They crave recognition—to be seen as individuals distinct from their friends and families, to define themselves on their own terms and claim their journeys in life.

If you accompany them to the library or corner store when they're younger and strike up a relationship with the reference librarian or the man in the convenience store who sells breath mints, then your child will know these people by name when he's old enough to frequent these places on his own. He'll be recognized and called by name, and he'll be able to reciprocate. He'll be making connections. He'll have the sense that others are looking out for him. As much as teens want to be on their own and responsible for themselves, they also want to know that they're being watched over, protected from harm. The connections they weave in their communities form their safety net, their convoy of social support. They also can serve as his conscience, preventing him from giving in to temptation and acting out in ways that he perhaps knows he shouldn't. When children feel that no one cares who they are or that no one notices them, they may be more likely to do things that do not serve or further the public good.

By connecting to the diverse young people in our community we can foster in them a conviction that they matter, that they are important to and valued by their community. In such a context, young people are likely to thrive.

Emotional Education

Ultimately, a person who is connected with others is connected with herself. She has an awareness of her own thoughts and feelings as they relate both to her and to others. In our "just do it," product-driven culture, we often tend to give short shrift to the process of emotions—why we feel as we do, what we can change. Keeping a "feelings" or "connections" diary is an excellent way to manage one's emotions and social relations; it allows us to reflect on what we're feeling rather than focusing only on action. You can suggest to your teen that she write in her diary either the first thing in the morning or before bed. You can keep one, too. The very nature of writing down one's reflections helps us understand ourselves more fully.

This is an especially helpful tool for those teens who may have trouble reading the nonverbal cues of others or managing their own behavior. Some teens simply don't know that they're standing too close, talking too loudly, or standing in a way that communicates menace and threat rather than welcoming approach. JT, for example, a star on his basketball team, had few friends on the team because of his propensity to interrupt when others were talking. It was a terribly annoying habit, and one he was unaware of . . . until his dad noticed it after a game. "The kids want to talk to you," he told his son on the way home, "but they get frustrated because you always start talking before they're finished."

"I just get so excited," JT said. "If I think the same thing, well, I just want them to know, right away."

"All you have to do is wait until they're finished talking," his dad said. "Maybe when someone's talking to you you can do something to remind yourself to wait."

"I could look at my hands," JT said, spreading his fingers the way the coach did when he wanted the team to slow down. That gesture seemed to work.

Besides talking about issues such as personal space, tone of voice, facial expressions, physical gestures, and posture with your teen, you can encourage him to note and keep track of other people's nonverbal communication and their responses to his. In this way, he'll learn how he can best communicate and connect with others.

The Shy Child

Some teens may never seem to master the skills discussed above. Whereas some children plunge into social situations and never look back, others remain on the sidelines. In class they never raise their hand, at parties they never seem to know how to mingle, in large groups they clam up. Shyness isn't a pathological condition or even a problem but rather a matter of temperament, a normal variation of behavior. Shy children may experience what most of us would consider as a small amount of sensory input as overwhelming. About 10 percent of the children Thomas and Chess studied during their groundbreaking work on temperament were shy, which they described simply as being slow to warm up.

If the time it takes for your child to loosen up with new people is measured in hours rather than seconds, there are ways you can help her make and sustain connections. Shy children can be encouraged to rely on the friends they have—since even the shyest child probably has one friend—to help them acclimate to stressful situations. As a parent, you can ask your child's friend to accompany your daughter to the homecoming game and stay with her until she feels comfortable. Putting the buddy system in place during transitional periods is a good idea whenever your shy child enters a new situation, whether it's a basketball game or a party.

You can also help your teen to adjust his expectations concerning how long it will take for him to feel connected to or comfortable with others by encouraging him to use his imagination and memory. Ask him to imagine the social situation he will be entering. Whom does he think will be there? What will they be like? What might they say to him? What would he like to say or do? How would he feel if the person says what he expects? How would he react if something unexpected is said? In short, work with your child to rehearse how he might behave and feel in the situation. Role-play with him to help him feel he has the skills he needs in the situation.

You can also ask your child to recall social situations that worked out well and ones that did not. What does he remember about these situations? Ask why he thinks some went well, whereas others did not. What new strategies will allow him to re-create the conditions that led him to succeed? Did he approach a new person with a trusted friend by his side? Did he volunteer to work on a class project with people he knew? Again, role playing will help your child increase his repertoire of skills.

Finally, shy teens can also use e-mail, instant messaging, and list-servs to meet new people in less stressful conditions before meeting them face-to-face. Once shy teens get past the intensity of the initial encounter, often they may do pretty well.

BIG THREE #3:	LEADERSHIP OPPORTUNITIES

· Create opportunities to collaborate with teens.
· Encourage cross-generational relations.
· Make teens know that they matter.

We often complain about teens who seem alienated—withdrawn, quiet, sullen, uninvolved. If only we bothered to ask why they felt that way. All too often, teens who act this way are really feeling silenced, unappreciated, and unvalued. It's no wonder that teens just give up when they feel their voices aren't being heard, or when their energy isn't appreciated or accepted in the spirit in which it was given. Yes, teens don't have as much experience as we do, so it's easy to assume that their contributions will be slim. In truth, though, teens may offer a fresh perspective, and in any case they deserve to be heard. They need opportunities to feel valued and welcome—not just at home but in schools and in their communities as well.

The Importance of Being Included

Once you start thinking through my positive development perspective, you'll find countless opportunities to allow your teens to practice leadership. The point isn't to give them more responsibility than they can handle, but rather to exercise their decision-making abilities by starting small and increasing the load as they grow. Within certain parameters, and while retaining your authority, you can provide teens with many leadership opportunities. For example, you may not be ready to ask your twelve-year-old to assume complete care of the family dog, but you can ask him to be responsible for walking her on weeknights or making sure that she has dinner each night.

As mentioned earlier, teens can also help plan family activities, such as how to spend weekends, birthdays, anniversaries, and holidays. Solicit your child's input on vacations, starting from when she's young. She may not get to determine by herself whether you go to the seaside or to the mountains, but once the decision is made to go to the shore, ask her help on planning some day excursions. By the time she's a little older, she can be put in charge of researching information about the area you're visiting—sending away for brochures, planning the itinerary, mapping the route.

It may seem simpler to plan family vacations without your teen's input, but you may end up paying for it later on. For example, every year Pat and her husband, Leo, rented a house on the shore for a month. Both their sons, Wallace and Eddie, had always loved spending August at the beach. But one spring, when Pat and Leo announced their plans, only Wallace, who was ten, was gleeful. Eddie, sixteen, wanted to spend August at home, hanging out with his friends, especially since he'd be away at camp for July. "I'm not going," he announced. "No way."

That's when Pat and Leo realized they should have talked to Eddie beforehand. Now they were in a bind. They'd already paid a substantial deposit and didn't want to risk losing it. More than that, they didn't want to give Eddie control of their vacation schedule. But clearly they needed to find some way to rescue the situation—and Eddie's feelings.

One evening, after Wallace was in bed, Pat and Leo sat down with Eddie. First they apologized for not taking Eddie's desires into account, and then they asked how they could make him feel better. At first, Eddie stuck to his original contention: he wanted to spend four weeks at home. Pat and Leo were adamant that it couldn't happen, and asked if he had any other suggestions. He didn't, and the family meeting ended on a sour note.

But the next morning, at breakfast, Eddie said that if he could have even a week at home after getting back from camp, he'd spend the rest of the time with the family at the beach. He suggested staying over at the home of his aunt and uncle, who lived nearby. Eventually, his parents agreed. Eddie felt as if his parents respected his wishes, and Pat and Leo realized the need to talk to their children before making decisions that involved them.

Though compromises such as this can often be worked out, they aren't guaranteed. Kyle and his wife, Deirdre, wanted their eighth-grade daughter, Lily, to transfer from the private school she'd been attending to a public high school where she could get more services for her learning disability. They involved Lily in the process from the beginning—sitting down with her to talk about the situation, involving her when they made appointments to visit the high schools in her area, touring them with her. But when it was time to make a decision, Lily had a meltdown. "I don't want to go to a new school," she said. "All my friends will be at my old school. I'm not going to transfer." Her parents were at a loss—up until the last moment, Lily had been on board and seemed to understand both the necessity for and the implications of changing schools. But it may be that teens won't realize what's really at stake until the moment of truth approaches. And then all the weeks and months of careful collaboration may be forgotten.

Kyle and Deirdre knew that Lily wasn't equipped to determine her educational future; they had to do what was best for their daughter. The bottom line was that Lily couldn't decide whether or not to transfer, but she could make the final decision as to which of two possible public schools, each with different strengths and liabilities, to attend. She still wasn't happy about it—"She pouted all summer and barely spoke to us," Kyle remembers—but in September she attended the new school, and soon found her own niche.

Reaching for More Responsibility

If you begin the collaborative process early, it will be in place as teens grow and as more important family decisions are at stake. Because Randy had always helped plan his family's annual backpacking trip, he and his parents had a blueprint to follow when it was time to talk about which colleges Randy should apply to. "We sat around the living room one afternoon and they asked me what I wanted in a college, and I asked them about their college experiences and what they could afford to spend," Randy recalled. "I felt a very positive energy, as if we really were all working together toward a common goal. I guess our time planning those camping trips paid off."

It's always a good idea to hone teens' sense of responsibility because emergencies always crop up. Carl, nineteen, had just returned from college after his sophomore year. One evening at home, he was talking to his mom when she began to feel dizzy. Within a few minutes, her speech became slurred, and she couldn't stand up.

Scared, Carl called for his father, who sized up the situation and said that he had to take his wife to the emergency room—he was afraid she was having a stroke. "You come with me," he told his son.

Carl seemed shaken. He'd never been asked to do something like this before. Taking people to the hospital was something adults did. "Why do I have to come?" he asked. "Mom needs you, not me."

"I need you," his father said. "I'm a little scared, too, and I'd appreciate having you there for support."

"I was a little freaked out," Carl admitted afterward. "Neither of my parents had ever let me know that they needed me in that way. At first I wanted to say 'No, thanks—I'll stay home.' But then I realized that my father really wanted me there for him in case Mom's diagnosis was bad." As it turned out, Carl was very helpful: he was able to answer some of the doctor's questions more lucidly than his dad, and his presence helped calm his mom down. As it turned out, his mom was suffering from an unusually acute migraine and was released within a few hours. But the momentous impact of the evening stayed with Carl. "It was the first time I felt like a full-fledged member of the team," he said. "I never before felt that they really needed me the way they would need another adult." An experience like this boosts a teen's confidence and competence as well as connection.

Connecting Across the Generations

Helping teens connect to older members of their families and communities gives them a key developmental resource. Some kids easily connect to adults such as teachers, coaches, or uncles, and older cousins. Others may need some guidance. You can highlight the importance of intergenerational connection by making this sort of connection a priority in your own life. Stay close to your extended family if at all possible. Make every effort to have your teens know their grandparents, great-aunts and -uncles, and older family friends.

Similarly, teens of all ages can work collaboratively with school teachers and administrators, or with the community members. For instance, young adolescents can help plan assembly programs and suggest ways to make community programs more accessible to those who don't yet drive. At religious institutions, they can serve on youth advisory committees. When a local synagogue, for example, planned a holiday program at the local veterans' hospital, several teens served as the liaison between the rabbi and the Veterans Administration official arranging the visit. Not only that, but their suggestion to begin the program at eleven o'clock Sunday morning rather than at nine-thirty, as originally planned—to ensure that more teens would be awake enough to attend—helped ensure the success of the program.

In fact, both in school and in the community, within- and between-generation connections can and should be established simultaneously. We need not just token teen representation but a critical mass of young people on any school or community group. The actual number may vary, of course, but a good starting point is the number three. When the National 4-H Council decided to act on their belief about the importance of youth participation and leadership in the constitution of their board of directors, they increased the membership of the board by 50 percent (twelve people), and all the new members were young people between the ages of twelve and eighteen.

BREAKING BAD CONNECTIONS

Sometimes connections that start out healthy take a wrong turn. Jenny, age seventeen, began going out with Gary, a slightly older boy who became increasingly moody and withdrawn over time. Although he came into the house to get Jenny on their first dates, talking with her parents and having a soda, he now waited in the car. He also no longer asked her what she wanted to do, assuming instead that he could make plans and she'd acquiesce. Her parents noticed these changes and were growing concerned.

Finally one day they asked Jenny about him, and she welled up, admitting that things weren't going well. But she was reluctant to break it off. That's when her parents suggested that Jenny draw up a "plus and minus" sheet. This would help her separate what she was gaining from maintaining the relationship and what she was losing. It wasn't hard for Jenny to do this. On the plus side, she said, she really enjoyed having a boyfriend. She was afraid that if she broke up with Gary, she wouldn't meet anyone else for a long time. In addition, by this point, all of her good friends had boyfriends. She feared being excluded from many social events if she wasn't part of a couple. And part of her still liked him. He was very good-looking, and he took her to nice places where he made her feel special—when he was in the mood.

But on the minus side, he made her feel bad about herself. When he failed to take her wishes into account, she felt as if she didn't matter to him. And if she did break up with him, maybe she'd meet someone who would treat her better.

After compiling her list, the choice was clear: she'd rather be on her own than feel demeaned. But then she had another choice to make—how to let Gary know about her change of heart. Should she rip the Band-Aid off quickly by calling him up and ending it, which would be hard on both of them but quick and honest, or should she pull it off slowly by turning down his request for dates, a strategy that would take longer but would spare her a potentially ugly confrontation? This decision was almost as hard as deciding what to do. In the end, she asked her parents for advice. "Honesty's the best policy," they told her. She agreed. They also assured her that they'd support her if the conversation with Gary turned ugly.

Sometimes parents need to take an even more active role, difficult as that may be. Suppose, for example, you hear your son's best friend boast about a fake ID he just purchased, and how he's going to use it that night to buy some beer. What do you do?

Responsible adults are true to their values and speak up. Make sure your child and his friends know that you don't condone illegal activity and that you don't allow it in your home. You can also let the boy know that either he tells his parents about his fake

ID and illicit drinking or you'll have no choice but to tell them yourselves.

Behavior such as this can't be ignored. If the situation was reversed—if your son was contemplating behavior you know is wrong and his friend's parents found out about it—you'd want the parents to call you. This is part of the contract we make as parents—that we'll look out for each other's children. It takes time and effort to get to know the parents of those teens in your child's social network, but it's your responsibility. You have to know which parents can be trusted to maintain the same standards of behavior in their home as you do in yours; otherwise, you can't trust your child to spend time there. When parents establish these standards collaboratively, teens don't feel as if they're singled out. And they also can't say, "But everyone else is doing it!"

WHEN TEENS DON'T CONNECT

What happens if parents aren't able to help their teens master this crucial C? Parents, after all, aren't always around. Some parents are called to military service—sometimes two parents in the same family are called. We also know about high divorce rates. And it's very hard to help children to forge connections if their parents are incarcerated. In 1999, for instance, the Justice Department's Bureau of Statistics reported that 2 percent of American children—more than 1.5 million kids—had a parent in prison. A majority of both fathers and mothers said that their children had never visited them in prison (more than 60 percent of incarcerated parents are held more than a hundred miles from their families).

In truth, we don't know too much about the long-term effects of a severed parent-child connection. What we do know tends to be negative. As a rule, children and teens don't do well when they're separated from their parents for long periods of time. Some of the specific pitfalls are well documented. The older the child when a divorce occurs, the better she'll do, generally speaking. The longitudinal research of E. M. Hetherington, professor emeritus of psychology at the University of Virginia, indicates that young girls in divorced families tend to act out sexually more than boys. This period rarely lasts longer than a couple of years, however. In addition, children of single-parent families often don't do as well in school as those who come from two-parent families. Children with a parent in prison are more likely to end up in prison themselves. Children of parents in the military live with constant anxiety. And children go through all the stages of grief that adults go through, as outlined by Elisabeth Kübler-Ross, when a parent dies. And the stages of grief aren't like developmental stages—that is, you don't pass through them once and complete them. Instead, we cycle through them many times over.

But we need to remember that children are remarkably resilient, and many do well even when facing the obstacles of poor connections. It's also the case that because divorce and separation have become so commonplace, these children can find a great deal of social support to help them as they navigate their lives. Again, the stronger a child's convoy of social support, the better he will do.

LOOKING AHEAD

The importance of making connections can't be overstated. As we all know, it's not what you know, it's whom you know—a cliché that couldn't be more true. From a deficit perspective, or through the lens of cynicism, this may sound like cronyism or exploitation. But from the positive development perspective, having good, reciprocal connections can help you get into the right school for you, help you find the best job for you, and perhaps even help you meet your spouse. Having a reliable convoy of support helps teens travel safely along the road of life despite all the bumps and jolts.

To recognize and support reciprocity and the two-way nature

of connections, we need a moral compass. We need to believe that supporting those who support us is the right thing to do. Another way of saying this is that to be truly connected in positive ways we need to have character, which we'll explore in the next chapter.

Character

Our character is what we do when we think
no one is looking.

—H. Jackson Brown Jr., author of
Life's Little Instruction Book

As an eighth grader, our older son Justin was appointed student manager of the middle school's girls' volleyball team. During one of the games, two kids sitting in the bleachers began throwing candy from the stands onto the court. Justin asked them to stop.

When they refused, Justin consulted a coach, and the boys were escorted out of the gym. After the game, as Justin was leaving the building, the boys confronted him. One held him as the other shoved him to the ground and began to punch him. Soon blood was flowing from Justin's nose and the back of his head where his skull had hit the floor. Frightened, the boys ran off.

By the time I arrived at school—I'll never forget how I felt following the trail of Justin's blood—police officers were talking to him. They asked him to identify his attackers, which he did, and if he wanted to press charges, which he didn't. "If you don't press charges, I will," I told him, and he acquiesced.

Later that evening an officer came to our home to tell us some unwelcome news. It seems that as Justin's attackers were forcing him to the ground, he grabbed one boy's shirt, which then ripped. If we pressed charges against the boy who had beaten him, the police officer reluctantly told us, that boy's father would press charges against Justin for vandalism, malicious mischief, and assault—all because of the ripped shirt. He also explained that if Justin was charged, he'd be treated in the same way as his attacker until the matter was fully adjudicated.

Justin, his face swollen and painful, was stunned. "What should I do?" he asked my wife, Jackie, and me.

My son was facing a moral dilemma. He had to make a difficult choice, one where neither option was desirable: if he went ahead with his suit, he would himself be charged with a crime. If he dropped it, he'd allow his attackers to walk away from their attack without consequence. There was no one clear answer, one that would address all of his concerns.

Unfortunately, teens face decisions like this all the time. As I emphasized earlier, part of growing up is moving from a black-and-white world to one that is dominated by shades of gray. For many adolescents, every aspect of their lives—their relationships within the family, with friends, at school, at work, and in the world at large—seems riddled with increasingly complicated and difficult choices. Sometimes they have to choose between the lesser of two evils; sometimes they feel as if they have no choice at all. Navigating their way through complex situations is how teens develop character.

DEFINING CHARACTER

Character is easy to recognize but resists succinct definition. It's not simply about how we feel and think but also about how we act. It derives from our belief in the social contract—the implicit agreement between citizens and society. When we behave in ways that support society and its institutions, society in turn supports and protects us. Actions are moral if they reinforce this reciprocal relationship between the person and a just society. At the same time, we develop character through our interactions with other individuals and institutions.

People who have character understand the importance of respecting the delicate balance between serving oneself and acting selflessly for the good of other individuals or society. They appreciate the importance of investing themselves—in both word and deed—to improve not simply their own lives but the lives of others, the lives of their children, their country, and the world. Importantly, they are able to empathize with those in different circumstances so that they can include in their circle of care those who are less fortunate. In other words, people with character carry out what developmental psychologists Howard Gardner, Mihaly Csikszentmihalyi, and William Damon call "good works."

According to my positive development framework, people we recognize as having character usually display three attributes.

- They have a clear sense of right and wrong, a moral compass that guides them in all situations, no matter how murky. They do the right thing, and help others do the right thing.
- This sense of right and wrong is also very consistent and reliable. There are certain lines they won't cross. Others count on them to make the difficult decisions. They show integrity.
- This sense of right and wrong treats everyone with equal consideration. In other words, there's one set of rules: what's right for one person can't be right unless it's equally right for everyone else. For people with character, everyone has an equal opportunity. (I derived this perspective on character from the concept of "distributive justice," which I will discuss soon.)

None of these three attributes is present at birth. In fact, in the earliest stages of our lives, we follow scripts that lead us in the opposite direction: babies and toddlers are guided by their own narcissistic needs and desires for immediate gratification, two motivations we need to tame in order to become people of character. We're often guided by anger, as my family nearly was when we learned about the double bind in which Justin was placed—Justin, who'd done nothing wrong yet was being punished twice! Like any other parents, we were furious.

Yet if we'd held on to our anger, we wouldn't have been able to help Justin respond in a moral way. To become a person of character, we need to rely not on our snap judgments or our most inflammatory emotions, but rather on the "moral emotions," which we'll read about soon. Ultimately, we had to experience our anger, acknowledge it, and let it go so that we could move on and help Justin.

By using ideas derived from the Big Three, you can help your child develop character in the face of difficult challenges to his well-being.

BIG THREE #1:	MAINTAIN A CLOSE RELATIONSHIP

- Make sure what you believe and how you act are in alignment.
- Explore conflicts rather than make assumptions.

Aligning Your Beliefs and Actions

A fundamental aspect of character is that it unites moral feelings and action. When we act on our beliefs, when there's no separation between what we feel is right and what we do, we have character. Parents can model such integration of belief and action by behaving in a manner that's true to their word. They can do this by coupling feelings of or statements about unconditional love with behavior that conveys devotion, commitment, and constancy.

For example, Lucie, sixteen, stayed home with a good friend one weekend when her parents went to visit her older brother at college during Homecoming Weekend. Her parents, Chet and Jamie, were wary of leaving Lucie at home but rationalized that it was only for one night and that they'd be only three hours away. Sure enough, at about three o'clock on Saturday afternoon, in the middle of the college's family picnic, Jamie's cell phone rang. "This is the emergency room," a voice said. "Your daughter, Lucie, just came in; she has some injuries that need immediate attention." Jamie blanched. She learned that Lucie and her friend had gone inline skating, and Lucie had fallen and apparently suffered compound fractures. When Jamie finally reached Lucie on the phone, she promised her daughter that she and Chet would be at her bedside as soon as they could—they were leaving within minutes.

"I was able to stay pretty calm until my parents arrived at the hospital," Lucie reports. "I mean, the emergency room was creepy and I was in pain. But I knew that I could rely on my parents to get to me as fast as they possibly could—I could imagine my dad speeding the entire way—and knowing that they'd soon be with me helped me get through the next few hours."

Exploring Before Making Assumptions

We don't always know when our teens are wrestling with questions of conscience. Sometimes they act in ways that seem strange or suspicious, and we resort to the deficit model to explain their behavior— "She's just being obstinate, like a typical teenager." It's important to find out all the facts you can before drawing conclusions.

For example, during an annual holiday party held by Nick and Ann, their daughter, thirteen-year-old Janet, found herself spending a lot of time with one particular girl. While the other kids huddled in front of video game consoles and watched TV, Janet and Colette hung out in Janet's room.

A month later, Nick, Ann, and Janet were invited to a party at the home of Colette's parents. Janet, however, blurted out, "I'm not going and you can't make me!"

Nick and Ann were flummoxed. It wasn't like Janet to be so obstinate. Normally, she was a compliant girl, eager to please and easygoing. "We can't *not* go," Ann told her daughter. "It would be terribly rude to not accept, especially since Colette's father works for Dad."

"Fine," Janet said—which meant it wasn't fine at all. Nick and Ann threw up their hands. They assumed that Janet had picked this moment to morph into a teenager—that is, she'd become selfish, oppositional, and uncommunicative. But they were wrong.

The next morning, Janet showed up for breakfast visibly upset. "I don't want you to be angry at me," she said to her mother. "It's just that I don't want to spend time with that girl, Colette. I don't like her. She's not a good person."

Ann's antennae went up. "Did something happen when you spent time together during our party?" Had Colette pulled out a pack of cigarettes? Were drugs involved?

"Nothing like that," Janet said. "It's just that . . . she said nasty things about the other kids who were here—that she didn't want to hang out with the black and Asian kids. . . ."

In an instant, Ann realized what had happened. Her daughter was facing a genuine moral crossroads. She didn't want to spend time with a girl who was racist, but she also knew that telling on this girl amounted to squealing. Neither option was satisfactory, and as a result, Janet had simply shut down.

If Janet's parents had used my positive adolescence perspective, if they had rejected the "discontinuity" thesis—that Janet had suddenly changed into a teenager, a person they no longer knew—they could have helped Janet resolve her moral dilemma by saying, when Janet refused to visit Colette, "This isn't like you. Usually you're very friendly. Why don't you want to go?" That way, Janet's parents could have affirmed their ties to their daughter and the strength of their relationship rather than disavowing it. And in this context of trust, it's more likely that Janet would have opened up sooner about what was troubling her.

Maintaining Perspective on Infractions

It's also important not to get too upset about minor incidents in which your teen may not acquit herself with good character. Let's be realistic: even teenagers with an acutely sensitive moral compass do things they come to regret. An honor student who was just accepted to an Ivy League college decides to take her father's car for a joy ride around the neighborhood with a few friends. The president of the student council runs a stop sign and mouths off to the police officer who pulls him over. Stuff happens.

This is not to say that teens shouldn't have to face the consequences of their actions. But it does mean that not every infraction has equal weight—and you don't have to become concerned about your teen embarking on a life of crime after one stupid decision.

If you think the worst of your teen, if you view every minor infraction as evidence of her incompetence or inadequacy, then you may create a self-fulfilling prophecy: your teen will most likely continue to disappoint you. If, however, you view kids as I do, and think the best of them, they'll thrive. Sure, you may be disappointed once in a while when they don't rise to the occasion. But when this happens, they may feel moral emotions such as shame and guilt, which will help them behave differently next time. And the fact that you trust and respect them will help shore up their competence, confidence, connection, and character.

> **BIG THREE #2:** **DEVELOP LIFE SKILLS**
>
> · Expect teens to perform chores around the house.
> · Model and talk about all the moral emotions.
> · Work together to build trust.

Work in the Home

Few things build character like having a job to do. Working, whether around the house or outside the home, teaches teens many valuable lessons: the importance of being dependable, punctual, responsible, adaptable, and efficient.

But not all jobs are created equal. According to Lawrence Steinberg, psychology professor at Temple University, and Ellen Greenberger, professor of psychology at the University of California, Irvine, when teens toil at boring, repetitive jobs for minimum wage, they end up with a cynical view of work. They come to view work as extrinsically rewarding (as something they do to get money to spend on what they really enjoy), as opposed to realizing that work offers intrinsic rewards—that it can be enjoyed as an end in itself.

Keep this in mind when you and your teen talk about what jobs around the house he can assume. Chores that build character are those that teens understand are important, that are essential to the family's functioning. Rely on the concept of distributive justice to explain why they're getting chores—that what's fair for one person has to be fair for another, and that everyone should shoulder his share, no more and no less.

Remember as well, as discussed in Chapter 3, that job competence doesn't become an area of self-perceived confidence until teens are about fourteen years old. Even so, young teens have the capacity to take on many jobs and chores around the house. Then, as they get older, their roles and responsibilities can increase and become more complex. For example, young teens can:

- Mow the lawn
- Clean their plates after dinner
- Take out the garbage
- Update the family shopping list
- Babysit for younger siblings

"I'll Do It Later"

As many of us know, the reality of getting your teen involved in chores is often complicated. Many households find themselves engaged in unpleasant "chore wars."

"I haven't given my teenagers many jobs around the house," says Louise, "because, frankly, I can't stand to nag them. My younger son said he'd be responsible for putting out the trash twice a week. He thinks this is an important and fair contribution to family life. But he either forgets or he has too much homework, and I end up reminding him from the moment we finish dinner until he goes to bed. I can't stand to hear myself—I sound like a broken record. But if I don't keep at him, the garbage would never go out."

If you find yourself nagging your teens more than you'd like, stop. It doesn't work! Here's a more constructive alternative: give your teen what psychologists call a "limited hold." That is, Louise should say to her son, "The trash has to be collected by nine o'clock tonight because that's when I'll put it out on the street. I'll remind you once after dinner about this. If it's not done by nine, then you won't be able to do something important to you, such as go out after school tomorrow." Then, of course, you have to follow through with this consequence. I'm the first to admit this is easier to do when our kids are seven rather than seventeen, but the strategy is worth a try.

As teens grow, they can look for work in the other two environments in which they live—school and community. But taking a job without understanding the responsibilities involved is like trying to drive a car without fuel: you won't get very far. You need to talk to your kids about the qualities that are important for getting and keeping a job, such as being punctual and presentable; having good hygiene; being respectful, diligent, and reliable. And because very few kids perform flawlessly at their first jobs, teens also need to be coached in how to deal with criticism. They need to practice not being defensive when confronted with their shortcomings, and to learn how to incorporate feedback so they can become more successful. Teens also need to work at getting along with co-workers so that friction doesn't arise.

Mastering the Moral Emotions

Our ability to act with character depends on developing what William Damon, a developmental psychologist at Stanford University, calls

the seven moral emotions, which we call upon when we try to understand and resolve moral issues:

> *Empathy*—the ability to feel another's pain
> *Sympathy*—feeling bad that another person is suffering
> *Admiration*—having positive regard for someone who has
> acted morally
> *Self-esteem*—feeling good about oneself when one acts morally
> *Shame*—feeling badly for oneself for having done something
> wrong
> *Guilt*—feeling regret for having done something wrong
> *Outrage and anger*—a strong, negative feeling when one
> encounters or witnesses social injustices

Some of these emotions are present early in life—empathy, for
instance, and shame. Others, including sympathy and admiration,
take time to develop.

I advise parents to help their children make moral decisions by
asking them to experience these emotions. For example, when Justin
seemed unable to reach a decision on how to proceed, I evoked his
sense of sympathy by asking him how he thought he'd feel if he were
the boy who had attacked him.

I could almost see Justin trying to imagine how it would feel to
be brought up in the other boy's family. "I think I'd feel ashamed
that my parents didn't know right from wrong," he said. He went
on to explain that he felt as if this boy was "disadvantaged" because
his family equated a violent assault with a ripped shirt. This realization helped Justin see that he felt sorry for his attacker, a
fact that became important as Justin tried to reason out what he
should do.

Guilt is also a powerful emotion in the shaping of character. Ken,
for example, a tenth grader in a small rural junior high school, was
summoned to the principal's office along with three of his techno-
savvy friends. Together, they'd discovered a free program on the Web
that enabled them to get the passwords to the e-mail and personal

files of every student in the school. The principal accused them of violating the community's trust. He also told them that school-based consequences would be forthcoming; meanwhile, they were to go home and tell their parents what happened.

Not all the boys did—but Ken couldn't keep the news to himself. "The moment he came in the door that afternoon, he told me he had to talk to me," said Noriko, Ken's mother. "He confessed to everything. At first, I was nearly beside myself. How could he do something so stupid! When I told him how upset I was, he first grew defensive: 'No one got hurt,' he said. 'All we did was read people's e-mail. It's not like we sent them spam or anything like that.'

"'That's not the point!' I wanted to say to him. But I held my tongue. I could see that he looked miserable, and that the hardest part probably was the fact that he knew he'd disappointed me. So I thought for a minute and then said, 'Remember the day I walked into your room when you were IM-ing a friend, and you thought I read what you had written? Remember how upset you got?' He nodded. So then I said, 'I wonder how you would feel if one of your friends sat down at your computer while you were having a snack and read your e-mail. How do you think you'd react?'

"It was an 'aha' moment for him," Noriko said. "I could see the light dawning in his eyes. He immediately realized how important and basic a right to privacy was." Ken also realized how bad his judgment had been. In a moment, he went from defensively saying, "It's no big deal," to acknowledging that he'd betrayed his friends in a way that would have made him furious if it had happened to him.

At that point, he was ready to accept responsibility and consider how he could make up for his transgression. Ultimately, in a meeting with his mom and the school principal, Ken agreed to stay after school for a month and work in the school's computer lab, helping fellow students solve their computer problems, to make up for his mistake.

Talk About Your Own Moral Dilemmas

Once Ken realized that he'd breached the trust of his classmates and his mother, he was filled with remorse. To help him gain perspective, Noriko confided in her son. She told him that in 1967, when she was a college student, she went to Washington, D.C., to protest the war in Vietnam. A small group of protestors broke off from the main march and ended up at the Pentagon, where they tried to force their way inside. The situation turned violent—protestors linked arms and started forcing their way through the line of U.S. marshals guarding the entrance. Those who made it into the building were then dragged out bodily and arrested. Although Noriko did not enter the building herself, she was there, urging the protestors on.

"At the time it seemed like the right thing to do," Noriko explained to her son, "because I was so adamantly opposed to the war. But I've always regretted going to the Pentagon. Even though I never threw a rock or forced my way in, I felt as if my presence tacitly condoned violence. We thought we were right at the time," she said, "but if I had to do it again, I'd commit myself to non-violence."

Noriko had trouble talking about this, and Ken had trouble accepting that his mother had made a decision that she later came to regret. This gave Noriko the opportunity to talk to her son about the fact that in a democracy we have the right to take unpopular decisions, but at the same time we need to uphold the rights of others with as much conviction as we do our own. She also told Ken that she found a way to live with the regret, and felt that she atoned for her youthful insensitivity by supporting various organizations devoted to good works, such as Doctors Without Borders (medical humanitarian aid) and UNICEF (child welfare). "Ken's at the age when he usually tunes me out," Noriko concluded, "but I could see that he was fascinated to learn that I had made what I considered a grave mistake. And he was comforted to know that he wasn't the only one who had to wrestle with remorse."

Or take this situation I recently heard about: a friend of mine went out to dinner with one of her closest friends from work, a

Korean woman who'd moved here from Seoul when she was in her teens. After a lovely meal, they went to the coat check to retrieve their coats. That's when my friend heard the coat check girl make a racial slur about Koreans. Her friend didn't hear; only she did. In the moment, she felt so upset that she couldn't do or say anything—she just left the restaurant vowing never to go back.

But the incident gnawed at her. The next morning, she called the restaurant, relating the incident to the manager. He said that he'd take care of it, and asked for my friend's number. My friend never expected to hear from him. But a few days later, he phoned to say that he'd fired the coat check girl. My friend had very mixed feelings upon hearing the news. On the one hand, she was glad to know that the girl learned that intolerance won't be tolerated. On the other hand, she felt terribly guilty that she'd caused the girl to lose her job. This eventuality hadn't crossed her mind. What if she had a baby to support? What if losing her job meant she couldn't pay her rent?

I listened to my friend's story and urged her to tell her teenage children what had happened. Our teens need to know that we struggle with moral issues, too. They need us to realize that we don't have all the answers, that the process of growing up is one of learning to distinguish among shades of gray. Because of this, we also need to cultivate humility, not hubris, and help our teens to do the same.

Building Trust Together

Trust is the glue of relationships. All parents want to trust their teens. Yet no matter how well intentioned, teens don't always live up to their word. How should you handle a situation in which your teen is caught in a lie? Can broken trust be repaired?

Joe, sixteen, was invited to a Saturday night party with his girlfriend, Marie. After the party, he told his parents, he wanted to sleep over at his friend Vic's house. Joe's parents knew Vic's parents and had no qualms about the sleepover. When they asked about Marie's plans, Joe said that her brother would pick her up and take her home.

The next morning, Joe came home at eleven o'clock, as agreed. Ten minutes after he walked in, the phone rang. It was Marie's parents wanting to know if Joe knew what time Marie would be getting home because they wanted to go to church. As it turned out, Marie and a group of girls also had slept over at Vic's the previous night.

"Why did you lie to us about Marie sleeping over?" Joe's parents asked him.

"Because I knew you wouldn't let me sleep over at Vic's if you knew the girls would be there, too," Joe said.

"It's possible that we would have said no," his father said, "but we also might have said yes. The problem now is that you've violated our trust in you and I'm not sure how we'll be able to trust you again."

Joe and his family worked out a plan according to which Joe would regain credibility in small steps. That is, the next time he went out, he had to phone his parents—not from a cell phone but from a land-line—so they would know where he was. Slowly and incrementally, he earned back his parents' trust.

BIG THREE #3:   **LEADERSHIP OPPORTUNITIES**

- Allow teens to reach moral decisions—and to live with the consequences.
- Encourage teens to take active roles in giving to charity.
- Encourage teens to find models to emulate.
- Let teens make their own decisions—even when you disagree.
- Learn about the power of peer pressure, acknowledge it, and let your child deal with it.
- Help your teen stand up to peer pressure.

Making Moral Decisions

No matter how old your teen is, it's your job not to make a moral decision for your child. Rather, your role is to give him the opportunity to reach a decision on his own. Justin, for example, asked Jackie and me to help him decide whether to press charges against the boy who assaulted him or to let the boy escape with no consequences. We told him that we couldn't decide *for* him, that the final decision was his. But we'd help him think it through.

First, we encouraged Justin to weigh the pros and cons of each choice. If he pressed charges, the other boy would suffer—but so would he. If he didn't press charges, the other boy would feel as if he got away with his actions, and Justin would suffer alone. In this case, he reasoned, the cost-benefit ratio of pressing charges might not work out in his favor. On the other hand, he knew that everyone in school would know the true story. He guessed that both of the boys who attacked him would suffer at school; if not held legally responsible, they'd be reprimanded, possibly suspended from school, and prohibited from attending any other school sporting events.

He still seemed uncertain, however, about whether to press charges. He'd counted on society's institutions to protect him; he'd been assured that he had access to a legal system that would acknowledge the wrong he suffered and attempt to redress it. When he found out that his attacker had equal access to the legal system, even though the boy's claim wasn't honest, Justin felt as if the system was abandoning him. He recognized that the other family wasn't being honest in their attempt to manipulate the situation. He also knew that his "crime" wasn't intentional and therefore wasn't as grave as the attack against him.

It's often not possible to think your way out of a moral dilemma; you also have to feel your way. That's where the moral emotions come in. When Justin seemed unable to reach a decision on how to proceed, I asked him again to think how he'd feel if he were in the other boy's shoes.

He remembered what he'd discovered earlier—that he felt sorry for the other boy because he'd been brought up in a household that didn't know right from wrong. Having tapped into this well of feelings, Justin ultimately decided not to press charges.

Janet also was aware that she was facing a dilemma: she had to decide what to do about the invitation. As she explained, "When

Colette was at my house, I could walk out on her when she started saying nasty things. But if I'm at her house, I won't be able to do that without appearing rude. If she says something objectionable, though, I'll need to tell her off, and that's rude, too. What do I do?"

Ann, Janet's mother, didn't answer her daughter directly. Instead, she thought of Young Mi, one of Janet's Asian friends. "How do you think you'd feel if you heard Colette saying prejudiced things about Asians when Young Mi was in the room with you?" Ann asked Janet.

"That would be just terrible!" Janet exclaimed. "I'd be so pissed at Colette. And I'd want to protect Young Mi. I guess I'd feel terrible that I even knew someone like Colette."

Here, Janet was drawing on her sense of outrage and anger. During the ensuing discussion, her parents remarked that Janet's attitude reminded them of Rosa Parks, who defied the conventions of her day, insisting that she could sit in the front of the bus even though the segregated society in which she lived demanded that she move to the back. This enabled Janet to tap into her feelings of admiration for someone else who had done the right thing in difficult times, and to acknowledge her own sense of self-esteem—she was willing to risk being perceived as antisocial or ungrateful in order to feel good about herself.

In the end, Janet's parents phoned their friends and said that Janet wouldn't be coming with them.

Justin and Janet were old enough to recognize that they faced a moral dilemma and had to come to a decision. But sometimes teens, especially younger teens, need help framing dilemmas as moral. Suppose, for instance, your thirteen-year-old finds a $50 bill in the parking lot after getting his hair cut. To him, it's a huge amount of money. Although he's eager to simply pocket the money, something nags at him. He turns to you and asks, "What should I do?"

You can begin by asking him how he thinks the money ended up there. Next, ask, "How would you feel if you were the person who lost it?" Your son will probably be able to acknowledge that he'd feel terribly disappointed.

But your son could also take another tack: "Maybe I'd be so rich that I wouldn't even miss it," your son could respond. You can then ask, "What if he's your age, and after his haircut, he planned on buying a video game with that money? What if he got the money for his birthday? How would you feel then?"

These questions help your son focus on the reality that his gain is someone else's loss, someone who may be just like him. This establishes the moral framework. By this point in the discussion, your son will probably see that the only honest course of action is to ask if anyone in the barbershop lost some money, or to ask the barber to hold on to the money in case the person comes back to claim it. What began as a stroke of good luck ended as a lesson. With practice, your son will be able not only to recognize these situations in the future but also to act appropriately.

When to Step In and When to Hang Back

As teens grow and encounter more thorny dilemmas, the stakes rise as well. In some cases, you may begin a discussion with your teen intending to let him assume a leadership role only to realize that he may not be mature enough to handle the situation and its consequences.

For example, Tisha had a sterling record after she got her license, but when she turned eighteen she began to accumulate traffic tickets. Not that she told anyone she was being ticketed. On the contrary, her mother didn't know about the tickets until the day she got into Janine's car to move it and discovered a stash in the glove compartment. When she confronted her daughter, Tisha said, "I never got a moving violation. Those are all parking tickets."

"You still have to pay attention to them," her mother said, "or you'll lose your license." But Tisha didn't. And soon she lost her license.

Another family made a different choice. Ray, eighteen, and some of his friends liked to go to a town park on a summer's evening. One night, a police officer approached the group. "It's eleven," he said. "According to that sign posted over there, the park is now officially closed."

"That's funny," Ray said. "It doesn't look closed to me."

For his lip, the officer presented him with a ticket, a fine, and a date to appear in court. Unlike Tisha, Ray told his parents what had happened and said that he wasn't going to appear as summoned. His parents tried to reason with him, but he kept blowing it off. In desperation, they consulted an attorney friend, who told them that if Ray didn't appear as summoned, the violation could become a misdemeanor on his permanent record. Under pressure, Ray agreed to appear at court when scheduled with his parents. But he wasn't done fighting. He insisted that he could wear shorts, a T-shirt, and flip-flops—until his parents insisted otherwise.

"The moment we set foot in the courtroom," his mother said, "Ray's demeanor changed. It was just a local courthouse, but it had its own severity, and Ray realized that this wasn't something to take lightly. I could see it in the way he stood up and answered questions. He was no longer a sassy, wiseacre kid, but a young man who understood that he had to pay the price for his actions."

In the end, the judge dismissed the charges after hearing Ray's heartfelt apology. On their way home, Ray's parents asked him what he had learned from this incident. "I learned not to joke around with police officers," he said, "and that sometimes I have to swallow things I don't necessarily agree with."

As you can see, the hardest part for parents is knowing when to hang back and let teens suffer the consequences, as Tisha's did, and when to intervene. You have to make a judgment: which consequences can your child cope with and learn from, and which are so unnecessarily harsh that they will overwhelm him? The overarching goal is for teens to learn to monitor and assess:

· The decisions they make
· The process by which they reach these decisions
· The outcome of these decisions

Taking the Lead in the Family Philanthropy

We often think of teens as being on the receiving end of family life. That is, they're often passive—they get invited to parties and celebrations, they receive gifts, they follow along instead of initiating. But all teenagers are old enough to take a more active role. They can, for example, demonstrate leadership in the area of family philanthropy. If your family donates $100 a year to charity, ask your teen where she thinks half of this donation should go. If she doesn't know of any worthy charities, ask her how she can learn about some. One family I know sits down together each year just before the December holidays to decide which organizations to support and how to apportion their charitable funds. Each child is asked to prepare a pitch for his or her favorite charity and to be prepared to explain why this particular cause deserves support.

Finding Heroes

Character doesn't develop in a vacuum—we all need people to look up to. In Janet's family, her mother and father referred to Rosa Parks during their discussion with their daughter as a woman who had the strength of her convictions.

There are many people in the public eye today who serve as role models for teens. Think of Bono, or of Angelina Jolie, whose work on behalf of African children has made headlines, or of Bill Gates, who has resigned his position at Microsoft to devote himself full time to his philanthropic foundation.

You can also find heroes close to home—in your own family and circle of friends and neighbors. We all know people who faced daunting challenges—who lost their jobs, suffered through illnesses and bereavements, who were the victims of crimes—and yet survived stronger than ever. Refer to them in conversations with your teen, and encourage your teen to get to know them better. Talking to someone face-to-face is perhaps the strongest prescription of all for developing character.

What you're doing is encouraging the moral emotion of admiration. Seeing how others negotiate adversity and persevere can only inspire us to live up to our ideals.

WHEN YOU AND YOUR TEEN DISAGREE

Character ultimately means acting according to what you think is right, and the reality is that parents and teens don't always agree. In fact, one of the biggest tests of character occurs when a teen takes a position that goes against his parents' beliefs.

Fourteen-year-old Emily thought Mr. Simon was the best teacher she'd had. He made history come alive. One day, Emily went to see Mr. Simon before school began—she had a guidance appointment during his class and wanted to hand in the paper that was due. Mr. Simon thanked her for being so conscientious and told her to put her paper on a pile of papers on his desk. Emily hesitated—as much as she loved him, she knew how disorganized he was, always misplacing papers and running late to class. But she did as she was told and turned to leave.

Mr. Simon followed right behind her, rushing past her down the hall. Emily watched as a paper flew out of the pile he was carrying. Thinking it was her report, she picked it up. To her surprise, she found herself holding a copy of the final exam that she and her classmates would be taking in a few days.

Emily froze. What should she do? She knew that Mr. Simon would never know that he dropped a copy of the exam, and since there was no one else in the corridor at that moment, no one else would ever know that Emily had found it. What if she just stuck it in her backpack? With a high mark on the final, she was sure to get an A for the year.

It would be so easy.

On the other hand, she could catch up with Mr. Simon and give him the paper, explaining that he dropped it. But what if he suspected her of looking at it and memorizing some of the questions? To avoid that unpleasant circumstance, she could simply destroy the page, realizing that Mr. Simon would never know that he had lost it.

In the end, she walked into an empty classroom and ripped the paper to shreds without even looking at it. Then she called her father to tell him what happened. "Why didn't you give it back to the teacher?" her dad asked. According to his way of thinking, that would have been the most honest decision.

Emily felt flustered. To her, destroying the page was not only honest but also the easiest decision. She wished that her father could have seen the situation from her point of view. I agree: Emily acted with great character. But her father felt otherwise.

In cases like this, families need to talk so that they can understand one another's perspective on the situation. Sometimes there's more than one way to act with character.

Some teens learn all too quickly that making a principled decision doesn't always end well for them. Tito, the father of fourteen-year-old Pedro, established a rule that Pedro had to come home right after school to start his homework. One afternoon after school, Tito called home expecting to reach his son, but Pedro wasn't there. He didn't show up until dinnertime. It turns out that he'd gone to his friend's house. "You know the rule," Tito said. "You're going to have to accept the consequences"—which meant that Pedro was grounded for two days.

Pedro objected, saying, "I know about the rule, but I had a good reason for going over to my friend's house. His father is sick, and my friend didn't want to be alone. He asked me to come."

"You know the rule," Tito said. Pedro insisted that he'd done the right thing—the moral thing. He'd thought things through, and this was his conclusion, based on compassion and sympathy.

But Tito was equally insistent. "You could have called to explain the situation to me," he said. "But you can't just break the rule like that. If you do, there are consequences."

Optimally, what Pedro will take away from this discussion is an understanding that he should have asked his father about breaking the rule before he did it. Because he didn't, he has to accept that he and his father disagree, and he'll have to face the penalty.

Often, conflicts between parents and teens elude easy resolution. Ali, for example, was an exemplary student all through high school. His parents, who had emigrated from Turkey and opened a small restaurant that only minimally supported the family, believed that having a good education was the key to success. "If I got a 97 on a test," Ali said, "they'd ask me what happened to the other three points. All they cared about was that I get the best grades so I could get a scholarship to a top-notch college."

Ali achieved all these goals, securing a spot at an Ivy League university, where he declared a double major in math and economics. But after a month, Ali found himself disillusioned. "Everyone there was just as smart as I was," he said. "No matter how hard I studied, I didn't stand out the way I did in high school. Here I was at seventeen, having reached the pinnacle of success. Now what? I was feeling burned out."

Ali ended up pledging a fraternity, which his parents considered a huge waste of time. They let Ali know how disappointed they were in him that he was pursuing something so frivolous. But to Ali the fraternity was a lifeline. "I learned to value working with people, not competing against them," Ali says. "I learned to value my people skills, which I'd always put down. I also realized that there was life beyond good grades. We're all going to get good grades and go on to find good jobs. Suddenly it didn't matter if I was valedictorian. I knew I'd get a good job whether my GPA was 4.0 or 3.3. The point is to be personable, to get along with others. My parents would kill me if they heard me say this, but I cheated in high school—everyone does. I didn't outright copy answers or buy term papers, nothing like that. But if I saw that someone had a different answer than I did on a test, I'd rethink what I'd put down. It's cheating, but in a way I could justify. But now I realize I don't want to cheat at all. I guess I just disagree with my parents: grades aren't the be all and end all of life. Life's not a rat race—there's not one winner. I have to act on my own beliefs."

Slipping on the Veil of Ignorance

In this case, Ali was establishing his own set of values, which differed from his parents'. But what if your teen takes a position that goes against *everything* you hold dear? Suppose your daughter decides to join a protest against a gay/lesbian club that's being formed in her high school. How can you handle this?

Try going back to the moral emotions—to empathy and sympathy, for example. First, ask her to take the perspective of the other person. You could say, "How would you feel if you weren't allowed to form a club at school for people who love ballet?" The goal is to try to get your child to see how it feels to step outside herself.

There's another concept you could use at a juncture like this—the "veil of ignorance." This concept was developed by philosopher John Rawls, considered one of the most important philosophers of the twentieth century. In his 1971 book, *A Theory of Justice,* he espoused a theory of individual rights arguing, among other points, that punishment is just only if we agree that it's just from every perspective, whether we are the one doing the punishing or the one being punished. According to Rawls, we have to consider every moral decision as if we were shrouded in a "veil of ignorance"—as if we couldn't know whether we were the victims or the perpetrators of a misdeed. That is, if we would make the same judgment as to what is right even though we were ignorant about whether the sanctions for bad behavior applied to us or not, then our decisions are just. Only those beliefs that hold up in every case, for every person, are moral.

Suppose your daughter believes in the death penalty for murderers. "What about in cases of self-defense?" you can ask her. She may then argue that self-defense is a special case, at which time you can suggest that she slip on the veil of ignorance and pretend she doesn't know whether she's the person who just murdered someone who was trying to kill her parents, or the judge handing down the sentence. Does she still think the death penalty is always the right punishment?

In the end, you may not be able to change her mind. But you can urge her to articulate her position so that it's based on the "right" reasons. That is, you wouldn't want her to make decisions based on transient feelings such as anger, or on blind prejudice, or because she feels pressure from her peers. Instead, you want to ensure that she's thoughtfully acting out of deeply felt, legitimate ethical and moral principles. Toward this end, you can talk about how you arrived at the positions you hold dear; perhaps you didn't always believe as you do today. How did your feelings change? What influenced you to change? Maybe at one point you thought differently about homosexuality, but reading and talking to others about the issue caused you to modify your position.

Discussions like this are important not only for moral development but also for positive development in general. Psychologist James Marcia warned of the dangers that occur when teens latch on to an ideology without fully understanding the consequences of that ideology—as in the case of those German youths who ended up embracing Nazism. In Marcia's term, these teens are "foreclosing on their identity"– that is, they are prematurely abandoning the quest for self-definition in order to adopt a prescribed societal role and the matching ideology.

But teens can also foreclose on their identities when they take on roles without believing in their value. A teen who decides very early on that he wants to identify himself as a jock, for example, may find out after enduring a grueling season on the football field or wrestling mat that he's not really as gung-ho or competitive as his teammates—he actually feels bad for his opponent and has trouble delivering the knockout punch. If he clings to this identity without embracing its belief system, he's in effect opting out of the steps needed to adequately define himself. By settling too early, he's depriving himself of an opportunity to grow. Only by grappling with his true feelings and by trying to understand the forces in his life, by trying to think through his decisions and by placing his beliefs and actions in alignment, can he achieve the self-understanding that leads to positive development.

Standing Up to Peer Pressure

The pressure to conform to the crowd bears down on many teens. If there's strength in numbers, then peer pressure can often prove very powerful. It seems to kick in when teens reach middle school and build throughout high school. As teens' social networks begin to expand. they feel the need to "fit" with one or more groups, fueling the impetus to conform.

There is some good news, however. As mentioned earlier, studies indicate that teens tend to pick friends who share their values and the values of their families. So while peer pressure exerts some influence, it's unlikely to change a basically good kid into a troubled one.

It's also true that teens are aware that they have a private and a public self. While they may feel compelled to go along with the group when they are in school or with others during various activities, they are able to access their more private selves when they need to, and can stand up to injustice when it is necessary. If parents have done their job and have helped their teens understand which lines of behavior cannot be crossed, then it's likely that these teens will be able to stick to their principles. Then the private self can influence how the public self behaves and buck the tide of peer pressure.

WHAT HAPPENS WHEN PARENTS DON'T INSTILL CHARACTER

If you are remiss or laissez-faire about inculcating character, if you expect others—teachers, authors, religious leaders—to develop your child's moral compass for you, you're taking an extraordinarily big risk. Teens who grow up *not* understanding that they need to be true to themselves and others, or who think it's acceptable to cut ethical corners, often end up with a cynical view of human nature. They care only about results, not about the process. They also earn a name for themselves as people who can't be trusted, and may find themselves pushed to life's margins because they've alienated and harmed the very society they need to protect them. In short, parents who ignore character development place their teen's eventual well-being and adjustment at risk.

LOOKING AHEAD

On the other hand, teens with character become adults who are capable of going beyond the self. That is, they can marshal their energies and emotions in the service of things that are not in their own self-interest. They are committed—behaviorally, emotionally, and morally—to enhancing other people and the world beyond themselves. They care about doing the right thing. Such concern is part of the social contract we make with each other—that we care about those who care about us. We'll explore caring in the next chapter.

Caring

The true measure of a man is how he treats
someone who can do him absolutely no good.

—Ann Landers

M y thirteen-year-old daughter, Amanda, found
me in the yard one day and told me that she wanted her own cell
phone," Delia said. "I launched into a lecture about how she was too
young, about how she didn't have to have something just because
everyone else had it, that it was a luxury, not a necessity, and that I
wasn't going to pay for it. When I finished, she just stared at me. 'Are
you done now?' she asked, in that condescending way I hate."

Rolling her eyes and taking a deep breath, Amanda proceeded to
tell her mother that she wanted the phone so she could be in touch
with her mother more easily throughout the day. "It's true that my
schedule is unpredictable," Delia admitted. "Some days I have to
work late, but I often don't know this until the last minute. Amanda

wanted to know as soon as she got out of school what time she could expect me home. No way I could argue with that."

Delia's assumption should be familiar by now—she ascribed a less than noble motive to her daughter because she expected Amanda to behave like a "typical" teenager. In truth, Amanda was expressing an important reality, one that is more widespread than we realize— kids actually *like* being in touch with their parents. They *like* feeling watched over, worried about, and protected, even from afar. What Delia needed to realize was that Amanda wasn't concerned about being "cool" or "in." Sure, in part the cell phone was another piece of high-tech glitz, but more importantly, it also was the vehicle through which she both expressed her love for her mother and acknowledged her mother's love for her.

DEFINING CARING

Caring wasn't an original C. In fact, it is my specific contribution to the set of five characteristics constituting Positive Youth Development. In 1995, I attended a meeting in Aspen, Colorado, that brought together many of the key researchers and practitioners who had been working in the field of Positive Youth Development, as well as representatives from several of the foundations funding our research. The attendees were very impressive, and I was in awe of them. Through their foresight and insight, they had not only realized that we needed a new paradigm to talk about children but also gone on to pioneer the positive development movement and put it on the map. After years of painstaking work studying and serving thousands of teens, they had formulated a new, positive vocabulary to talk about adolescents—a list of four Cs.

However, I had the nagging sense that the list of the four Cs, wonderful and helpful though it was, was incomplete. "I think we're missing something," I said.

I acknowledged that kids needed competence and confidence in order to do well and to believe they could in fact succeed in life. I also acknowledged that connection was what linked them to others, and enabled them to use their skills optimally. But connection could also be used selfishly, I argued. "Think of a lobbyist," I said. "That's a person who's extremely well connected, who understands and values the fact that people need each other to succeed in the world. Yet he may use his competence and confidence to work the system, to manipulate his connections for cynical, self-serving ends. Is that the kind of connection we want to promote?"

"Well," my colleagues replied, "that's why teens also need character."

"Character implies integrity," I said. "Kids with character are true to their word. Being honest is necessary but not sufficient. You can be well connected and honest, yet think only of yourself. Character alone isn't enough."

And that's when my grandmother's words came back to me. When I was in grade school, and I'd show my grandmother my report card, she'd say, "This is very nice. Getting good grades is important. But what's really important is being a mensch!"

Though I had no idea what the word meant, I soon learned that it was Yiddish and referred to a good person, someone who thinks not only of himself but of others, too. To be a mensch is to care about issues and people outside of your own orbit.

Remembering this conversation with my grandmother, I was able to put my finger on what was missing. If we left the list of Cs as it was, I argued, we'd be raising kids who could adequately address the business of America but not its heart. In order to behave like a mensch, we had to care about others.

"Caring is what's missing," I told my colleagues. "Without caring, without understanding that we have to think beyond ourselves, we have no sense of social justice. Caring reminds us of the need for a level playing field, for working to ensure that others are as well-off as we are. Teens don't just need competence, confidence, connection, and character—they need to *care*."

This time I received no argument. Everyone agreed and thanked me for my addition to the Cs. I thanked my grandmother.

What does it mean to be a caring person? Most often, we speak of someone who is kind, who listens, who always seems to know the right thing to say or to offer, who seems genuinely interested in us, with whom we feel at home. Describing a person like this, we often say that she has a "big heart," a figure of speech that reminds us that caring is about feelings.

Although we tend to think of feelings as intangible, in fact, we experience them in our bodies. When we say, "My heart goes out to him," we mean that we feel something in our chests, perhaps a kind of physical expansion. Sadness, anticipation, disappointment, anxiety, grief—all these feelings have physical and physiological components.

Caring may be thought of as being composed of two specific feelings, which are among the moral emotions that we explored in Chapter 6:

· Empathy—the ability to feel another's pain
· Sympathy—feeling bad that another person is suffering

These feelings can occur independently and also simultaneously.

Understanding Empathy and Sympathy

Empathy is an emotion strongly rooted in our biological heritage. If we see another member of our species frightened by the advance of a predator, we become afraid as well, which motivates us to protect ourselves. Through this lens, empathy is a self-defense mechanism helping to ensure the perpetuation of the species. That's why a parent who sees his or her child being harmed will experience actual pain—tightness in the chest, abdominal pain—that mimics the pain the child is feeling. This mimicking response applies to all close relationships. Research suggests that infants will cry if they see or hear another baby crying. Empathy needs to be reinforced by parents, however, or it may atrophy and disappear.

Sympathy is a more complex emotion because it's not just about how we feel but how we think. For example, how do we determine what social issues and people we should care about? Why do we feel the pain of others? Why do we feel sorry for a person undergoing bad experiences?

Because of our capacity for sympathy, we can think beyond our immediate physical needs and creature comforts. A caring person isn't content to say, "I have mine, so now it's every man for himself." He looks beyond his own situation and is concerned with the welfare of others, often to the extent that he can't be happy with what he has if he knows others have less. He wants everyone to have what they need and deserve. He knows that everyone should expect to receive a fair chance, equal opportunity, freedom from discrimination, and a full measure of equality and dignity under the law.

Both sympathy and empathy can be nurtured and enhanced, using the Big Three.

BIG THREE #1:   MAINTAINING A CLOSE RELATIONSHIP

· Empathize with your teen.
· Understand idealism as an expression of caring.

Empathizing with Your Teen

Sometimes it's difficult, perhaps even painful, to recall how we felt when we were teens. But when we do, we end up having more empathy for what our kids are going through. We also need to find ways to express our caring for them even as they pull away.

When my kids were little, I read them the Hugh Lofting books about Dr. Doolittle, a doctor who traveled the world to meet and talk to animals, including the exotic pushmi-pullyu—a creature that faced in two opposite directions at once. Mr. Lofting may have been writing to entertain young readers, but he certainly knew a lot about teenagers. They, too, often seem to be traveling in opposite directions at the same time, simultaneously reaching out to us and shutting us out.

In truth, one of our most challenging tasks is to maintain the close, intimate relationship we've created with our children over the years. It's easy to love a young child who looks up to you, likes to snuggle, looks forward to a goodnight kiss, says "I love you" for no reason, and thinks you're the best cook, the best athlete, and the most beautiful and intelligent creature on earth. But what happens when all that changes?

"I remember the precise moment my son became a teenager in my mind," a friend told me, referring to her twelve-year-old. "He was out one evening, bowling with some friends, and when I came to pick him up, I made the mistake of walking into the bowling alley to let him know I was there instead of waiting in the car. Well, did he let me have it! When he got in the car, he shot me a look that would have frozen water and wouldn't say a word until we pulled up to our house. 'How could you embarrass me like that?' he asked with a pained expression on his face. I sat there in disbelief. When I'd driven him to the bowling alley, he'd given me a kiss goodbye. Now I was persona non grata—all in a matter of hours!"

Just as you don't have to make peace with your friends, only with your enemies, you have to work a lot harder to love an ungrateful, moody, overly sensitive, inconsiderate, demanding teenager who sneers at you instead of saying, "Thanks, Mom, for picking me up." The caring, loving child is still in there; he just can't come out to play—and probably won't for a few years. It's human nature for a parent to want to get angry or to shut down at junctures like this. Every cell in our body wants to say, "Oh, yeah? Well, if you want to treat me like dirt, that's how I'll treat you."

When our teens treat us as if we're disposable is often when they need us the most. It's not so much that they're rejecting us or that they've stopped caring about us; what they're rejecting is the old way of staying close. Teens don't outgrow the need for sustained and close interaction with their parents; they simply express the need in different ways. Many don't appreciate hovering—it may make them feel claustrophobic, and it may actually undercut their competence and confidence. We need to find new ways of maintaining our ties while allowing them room to breathe and grow. Yet there's no reason to abandon hugs and kisses entirely. You may just need to wait for the right time, like on a birthday or during a graduation party. Many teens still expect to be hugged when they return home or leave in the morning, especially after a weekend or a few days away. As Jackie and I have discovered with our own kids, if we're patient, they'll come back to us with open arms.

For many parents, physical expressions of closeness need to become more spontaneous. In the past, you may have relied on certain rituals to keep you close, like making breakfast together on Sunday mornings. Now your teenager sleeps till all hours and shows no signs of wanting to cook with you, much less be in any room with you at the same time. But she may approach you one day as you're reading the newspaper and start asking you about a difficult situation at school. You may not be in the mood to talk just then, but *she* is. Seize the moment. It's her way of reaching out to you.

It may also involve your becoming more sensitive to his nonverbal cues. Years ago, your son may have thought nothing of sitting down on your lap and throwing his arms around your neck. Now he generally averts his eyes on his way from the kitchen to his room. But on certain days he may catch your eye and wink, or shoot you a smile when you serve his favorite dessert. Learn to translate these minimal gestures for what they are: expressions of his feelings for you.

Coping with "I Hate You"

Few parents and teens make it through adolescence without sweating out at least a couple of heated exchanges. The first time your child hurls an "I hate you!" your way, you may be so stunned that you're not even sure what to say.

It's a provocative statement designed to hurt and to provoke an equally heated response. That's why the best strategy is to try to hang back. "When my daughter says, 'I hate you' to me," says Maryanne, mother of fourteen-year-old Gina, "I try to be calm but honest. 'Wow, that hurts!' is what I try to say."

You can also say something like, "I'm sorry you feel that way right now," underscoring the fact that intense feelings are transient. Add, "However, I still love you!" Your teen may not acknowledge it, but she will feel reassured that despite her tantrum, you still feel close to her.

Understanding Teens' Idealism

The way children think changes during adolescence. They begin to reason more abstractly. Many love to debate deep philosophical issues, taking into account people and situations outside their own experience. Ideals such as justice and truth may now matter to them deeply. They may want to know why—and not just as the question relates to their own lives, but to all human beings.

Sometimes, their commitment to idealistic goals seems to eclipse their caring for the people they're closest to. Shannon, the basketball player we met in Chapter 5, eventually became so involved with her teammates that she neglected someone closer to home. "Shannon was notified late one afternoon that she needed to attend a special team meeting that night to plan for a charity event the team was sponsoring," explains Josie, Shannon's mom. "I reminded Shannon that she had agreed to come with us to watch her younger sister play in a championship soccer game, and so she'd have to skip the meeting. Shannon just about exploded. She said that her commitment to her team was much more important than her sister's game, and why couldn't I see that? I told her that maybe she should start saving the world by paying attention to her sister."

Josie was right: Shannon was being insensitive to her sister. But Shannon's fervent commitment to her team and its charitable activities is an expression of her capacity to care, which in time may expand to include her sister as well.

BIG THREE #2:	BUILDING LIFE SKILLS

· Make your home a caring laboratory.
· Model sympathy and empathy, and actions that display caring.

Exploring Caring at Home

Caring is contagious: caring parents raise caring teens. Perhaps no C benefits from parental modeling and support more than caring. A child who comes from a compassionate home will be sensitive to others. He'll notice and absorb the values evinced by his friends and other adults with whom he comes into contact; as he grows, he'll also be influenced by the media and by society at large.

If your family has an ongoing discussion about the evils of racial injustice and false accusation, for example, your daughter will probably be especially moved when she reads *To Kill a Mockingbird* in tenth grade. She may even add to the family conversation by relating what her teachers and her friends think of the book and what she knows about injustice from the media. In turn, her parents will have the opportunity to reinforce these values, the very ones they instilled in her.

Caring can be reinforced more casually, as part of your everyday conversation. For example, don't hesitate to let your teens know how you're feeling. Let them know how *they* influence your feelings. When what they do makes you happy, angry, sad, frustrated, or inspired, tell them. But don't stop there: feel free to talk about how you're feeling in general—how you react to other people, events, and situations in your life. At the dinner table and around the house, for example, you can become as opinionated as a talk show host about those issues close to your heart. Explain *why* you care. Read newspapers and newsmagazines. Discuss the state of the world. Make it acceptable to have and share an emotional life with your children.

It's become a cultural cliché to ridicule the "touchy-feely," "I feel your pain" type, which can of course be carried to the extreme, as any stereotype. But there's nothing inappropriate or even atypical about attending to your feelings. Emotions are part of our essential landscape: we all need to be able to recognize, acknowledge, and label them accurately. No feelings are off-limits.

Are Girls Gushy and Boys Buttoned Up?

In our culture, it's often considered a given that girls acknowledge and express their feelings more easily than boys. But such categorical thinking needs to be attacked head-on. Resorting to stereotypes ignores the rich diversity that exists in each gender.

You can counter these misguided statements by disputing those supposed truisms that impede caring. To say "Boys will be boys" lets an entire gender off the hook. Let your children know that you don't buy into this. Talk about your beliefs about sexual stereotypes and what's expected of both males and females.

If your son tends to be tight-lipped, try to find a safe conduit to his emotions. "I see that your team lost in the play-offs this year," you can say to him. "I wonder how the guys feel about that. What do you think they're going to talk about in the clubhouse? What do they say to their families when they get home?"

Some teens may feel comfortable expressing only their negative emotions, such as anger or frustration, while eschewing their softer sides. In this situation, it's helpful to teach them to draw the important distinction between feelings, thoughts, and actions. Thirteen-year-old José, for example, came home boiling mad, and although he didn't at first want to talk about it, he finally broke down and told his mother that he got into a fight with his music teacher in the middle of class. "We were going over homework," José explained, "and I wrote my answers in the workbook instead of on a separate sheet of paper. When I tried to hand it in, he said he wouldn't accept it. I said I'd write my answers on a separate sheet and give it to him after next period, when I had a study hall. He said if I did that it would be marked late. That's so unfair!"

"So what happened next?" his mom asked, holding her breath, fearing the worst.

José didn't answer at first. His eyes darted around the room, as if he were desperate to escape. "I said, 'Screw you.'"

"Oh, my goodness," his mother said. "How could you say that? What happened next?"

"I got sent to the principal's office. I have in-school detention tomorrow."

José needs to learn that while it's OK for him to feel angry at the teacher over the blatant unfairness and to think angry thoughts, it's not always acceptable to act on these feelings. If this distinction isn't made clear, some teens may continue to labor under the assumption that they need to act out every feeling.

Conversely, suppose your fifteen-year-old son tells you that a girl on his bus was being picked on by a certain clique of girls, and he wanted to stand up for her but was afraid that if he did, everyone would think that he liked her—which in fact he did, but he didn't want to show it. In this situation, your son would benefit from being able to separate out his feelings, thoughts, and actions. That is, he can see that he feels sympathy and perhaps even empathy for the girl who is being abused, which leads him to feel angry about the abuse and frustrated that he doesn't know what to do. At the same time, he's also thinking, "They shouldn't act that way! I want them to stop!" In terms of actions, he needs to see that it's incumbent on him to act appropriately—to rally to the girl's defense if he thinks that's the right thing to do. He can do this by directly intervening with the bullying girls, asking them to cease and desist. If this action seems too scary for him, he can appeal to the bus driver or speak with a teacher or school administrator. In addition, he should tell the bullied girl that he is concerned and ask if she'd like help.

Caring Actions

Talk, however, can be cheap—when it's not followed up by action. Your son may not be likely to take any actions to help the bullied girl unless he has a good model. Teens learn to be caring by watching. You probably already do many things in the course of the day that express your caring without realizing all of them.

A good place to start is within your immediate and extended family. Do you routinely call and visit elderly parents and relatives? Do you include cousins and in-laws in family celebrations? Do you extend your caring to the neighborhood by participating in block parties and holiday parades? Do you water your neighbor's flowers while she's away, or make soup for a family down the block when a parent is in the hospital? Do you follow up a visit or a gift by writing a thank-you note?

What's your caring quotient in the larger community? For example, if you read a story in the paper that piques your sense of moral outrage, do you write or e-mail a letter to the editor? Perhaps you contribute to various causes or sign petitions that support your political and social agenda. Does your teen know about your activities?

If you're moved to write a letter to your congressional representative or senator, you could involve your teen by asking her to help you find the contact information. All governmental officials have Web sites where your teen can retrieve the information you need. Urge your teen to write as well. You can also volunteer at a local homeless shelter, or buy a package of greeting cards produced by children from developing nations.

There is some chance that your teens may react with a "ho-hum." They may very well appear not to notice and to not be interested. "Yeah, sure, Mom," they may say, "I heard you—you wrote a letter to the editor, big deal. What's for dinner?" I suggest that you keep going, however, having faith that your actions are being noticed and registered.

Lori, for instance, seemed to sail through her adolescence in a sea of self-absorption. Her only destination was the mall, shopping magazines her only reading material. Her mother, a professor of political science at a prestigious university, was tearing her hair out. Here she'd devoted her life to studying ways in which to enrich democratic institutions, and all her daughter cared about was Paris Hilton. When she first went to college, Lori had no idea what to major in. By junior year, having run through business, English, psychology, and art history, she decided that she wanted to major in education. In her senior year, she student-taught in a public middle school in an area of Manhattan that many people chose to avoid. When she graduated, she took a job in the same school. The neighborhood was so unsafe that her mother was worried about her. But Lori was adamant about wanting to teach there. She even asked her mother how she might arrange the chairs in her classroom so that the principles of democracy could be better enacted. Lori had assimilated her mom's values—not immediately, and not apparently, but thoroughly.

This doesn't happen all the time. I know another family in which both parents devoted themselves to nonprofit work—Jim was an attorney who represented those seeking political asylum, often pro bono; his wife, Elaine, founded an organization devoted to improving women's health. One of their daughters decided to go to medical school, and left to work in India as soon as she was done with her residency. Another daughter, just two years younger, couldn't find herself. She shuttled between interests and professions, occasionally dabbled in drugs and alcohol, and went through periods of unemployment. The last I heard of her, she was a telemarketer.

Despite our best intentions, individual differences and events beyond our control can conspire to take kids in different directions. Not every child who grows up in a caring environment will become a caring person. And some children raised in stark, hostile conditions can overcome their upbringing to show great compassion. But in the end, you'll increase your child's chances of being a caring adult if you build her compassion skills as she grows.

BIG THREE #3:	PROVIDE LEADERSHIP OPPORTUNITIES

· Encourage teens to hone their caring skills close to home.
· Encourage teens to speak out for social justice.

Caring Begins at Home

Caring, like charity, starts at home—and it ends at home, too, as long as you expand the definition of home to include not only your house but your community, nation, and planet. There are opportunities for teens to take the lead in caring at every stop along the way.

Caring can be expressed in many ways around the house. In addition to requesting that your teen pitch in with household chores and taking care of pets, you can also let him know that you expect him to act with kindness and good manners on a daily basis. Some children grow up feeling as if they can take for granted those closest to them: although they know enough to say "Excuse me" when they're with other people, they forget their manners once they cross the threshold of their homes. Let them know that there's only one standard of behavior that applies both within and outside of the family, and that practicing etiquette and respect in the living room and kitchen will help them in the world at large. You can also point out, yet again, the difference between feelings, thoughts, and actions. No matter how they feel or what they think in a particular situation, they can still act in ways that express caring. Instead of telling his little brother that he hates him for messing up the stuff in his room, your son can find a way to express his quite legitimate annoyance with the violation of his space without overdoing it by condemning his brother.

You can also sensitize your teen by helping her care for those who are sick or indisposed. Strengthen her caring by asking pointed questions like, "What do you think Grandma would most appreciate since she's not feeling well—some cookies? A good book? Or just some company?"

Toward the same end, you can help your teen remember what he most appreciates when he's not feeling well. Maybe his girlfriend brought over some chicken soup when he had the flu, or perhaps his best friend dropped off a DVD he had been wanting to see. Discussions like this, which encourage your teen to reflect on his own emotional experience, enhance his empathy and underscore the connection between how he feels and how others may feel.

Encouraging Teens to Promote Social Justice

Teens can also be encouraged to speak out about larger political and social issues they care about. For example, in 2006, the Archdiocese of Boston decided that Catholic Charities, the Church's basic social services organization, could no longer support adoption by gay or lesbian parents. This meant that the archdiocese was in violation of Massachusetts antidiscrimination laws and therefore that Catholic Charities could not receive public funds for any of their work. The governor of Massachusetts, however, believed that the archdiocese was correct to discriminate against gays and lesbians who wanted to adopt children, and tried to introduce legislation to exempt it from the penalties of violating the antidiscrimination laws.

Needless to say, the issues involved in this situation elicited debate on several sides of this issue. Letters poured in to the *Boston Globe,* most written by adults. But one of the most eloquent letters was written by Steve, the adopted son of two lesbians. He was born crack-addicted to a mother who died giving birth to him. Several physical anomalies required surgery. Feared blind and brain-damaged, he seemed bound for an institution and a future bleak beyond words.

But he caught the eye and heart of a nurse on the neonatal ward where he was being treated, a lesbian, who soon urged her partner to adopt him. Since both women were Catholics, they did so under the auspices of Catholic Charities. Steve thrived under their love and care. At the time he wrote the letter, he was about to graduate from high school and go on to college, he had a part-time job that enabled him to help pay for a car, and he had a girlfriend whom he had been seeing for two years and with whom he was in love. Although medically fragile, he considered himself to be leading a great life. But none of this would have been possible, he wrote, if not for the love and courage of the two women who saved his life. How, he argued, could other children be deprived of the love and opportunities for a happy life that he had been given just because the only people who were willing to adopt them were homosexual? Where, he questioned, was the social justice in such deprivation? Would it be better to let children like him live in a loveless institutional setting rather than allowing them to have a chance of a happy life within a nontraditional family? Clearly, Steve was moved to make an appeal for social justice based on issues about which he cared deeply, issues that reflected the caring he had received and the caring he felt other young people like him deserved.

We can only imagine how important it was for Steve to write this letter, how cathartic and meaningful it was to him. But think how many people his letter may have reached. More than six hundred thousand people receive the Sunday edition of *The Boston Globe*. In addition, on that particular Sunday, Steve's letter was featured in a special section of letters about gay and lesbian adoption. Over the next few days, Steve's moms received countless e-mails, phone calls, and expressions of support from friends, family, and colleagues. Steve found a similar reaction at school: people came up to him all day to say how the much the letter had impressed them and how proud they were of him. Clearly this heartfelt testimonial had an impact on others, changing more than a few hearts and minds.

There are many places to hone one's caring skills through institutions: churches, mosques, and synagogues; schools; and community organizations. Teens can also create their own opportunities, organizing toy drives during the holiday season, for example. Volunteering promotes teamwork and perseverance, two skills vital for success in a job or career.

A terrific example comes from Northport, a New York City suburb on Long Island. In the early 1980s, a social studies teacher at the high school became frustrated with the urban studies class he was teaching: it seemed all talk and no action. All the students got very fired up during class discussion, and then when the bell rang they'd get up and leave to attend to their relatively privileged lives. One semester, he assigned each student to find an opportunity to volunteer in the community. One boy took the train to New York City, where he worked at a homeless shelter for a day. That day turned into several. He asked a few friends to join him. Within a few months, they'd formed the Committee on the Homeless.

This committee continued to grow after the founding students graduated; another teacher joined the effort, attracting a new group of teens. Together, they organized clothing drives, which included monthly visits to New York City homeless shelters where they delivered the needed clothes. They began calling themselves Students for 60,000 because, during the 1980s, it was estimated that sixty thousand people in New York City were homeless. But more than the number was significant: rather than conceive of themselves as being "against" homelessness or hunger, they thought of themselves in a positive way, as a force *for* good in the world. Today, the organization that modestly began with a single student claims 200 members. Its presence in the community is very strong: twice a year, during its fund-raising drives, every Northport resident who enters a supermarket sees a few representatives stationed at the door, soliciting support. In 2005, they raised a total of $150,000. At school, the group meets weekly in the school auditorium, one of the few rooms that can accommodate such a large organization. Perhaps most impressively, it sponsors an annual trip to two villages in Nicaragua that the committee has adopted.

Finding New Ways to Care

Caring can be as old-fashioned as ministering to those who are sick and raising money for those in need, but it also has never been so cutting-edge as it can be today. If your child regards writing a letter to the editor as too twentieth-century, she may be more inclined to e-mail her response to an article to a newspaper's Web site, or reply to a blog, or start her own blog. Innumerable Internet sites are devoted to political, social, and economic causes, and there she can meet others who care about these issues, sign petitions, plan meetings and rallies, and answer opinion polls. This sort of effort may be especially appealing to computer-savvy kids: since they're already more familiar with the technology, they get to feel as if they're contributing to the enterprise instead of following your lead. It may feel to them like a true collaboration.

WHAT HAPPENS WHEN TEENS DON'T LEARN TO CARE?

Not all teens are brought up to learn to care. Because no one helped them to see beyond themselves, they are locked in self-interest.

Because no one fostered their empathy, they can think of no one but themselves. Because no one schooled them in the rudiments of justice, they don't think about what's fair, only of what's coming to them. And the sad reality is that, as adults, they are ill-equipped to nurture caring in their own children. Many adages allude to this repetitive pattern: "What goes around comes around," "As ye sow, so shall ye reap." Parents who take the time to nurture caring in their own children ensure a better life for their grandchildren—and for themselves, in their old age—as well as for society as a whole.

LOOKING AHEAD

Competence, confidence, connection, character, and caring: these are the characteristics that we've identified as being essential components of a healthy teen. In this and the previous four chapters, we've considered the Cs one by one to understand how we can nurture them in our teenagers. The ultimate goal, as we've discussed, is to raise kids who become engaged, responsible, productive members of society, who are able to contribute to their own lives, those whose lives they touch, and society at large.

We've also seen how the Five Cs are interrelated. For example, competent teens are able to make sensible choices that are consonant with their interests, aspirations, talents, and abilities. They will be able to identify the means to pursue their goals. If they want to achieve good grades, for instance, they may need to do an extra-credit report, or show up for extra-help sessions with the teacher. When competence is coupled with confidence, not only are teens able to make the right choices, but they also are able to act on their choices in a timely way. If they have character, they won't be deterred when facing life's inevitable disappointments and failure. Character will also enable them to take responsibility for their actions and to calculate the costs and benefits of staying on course or developing alternate plans. If they have good social connections, they will be able to consult with parents, peers, teachers, coaches, mentors, and faith leaders for guidance. Finally, if they care about others, they will develop plans that take the feelings of others into account; thanks to their compassion, they will always stop to consider their impact upon others.

When all these come together, the sixth C, contribution, emerges. We'll explore this in the next chapter.

Contribution

We make a living by what we get. We make a life
by what we give.

—Winston Churchill

It was Friday afternoon and Ryan wasn't looking to save the world. A high school sophomore, he spent most of his days feeling mildly bored, on the lookout for something to take him away from his drab routine—school during the week, weekends lost in a haze of sleep and late-night video games. But one Friday afternoon, on the way out of school, he noticed a poster near his locker. Some club at school was sponsoring a sleep-out on the football field. "Bring a sleeping bag," it read, "and find out what it means to be homeless."

He didn't know much about the club except that it was some kind of service, do-good organization. Sleeping out sounded pretty cool, though. He decided he'd try it.

He had no way of knowing what was in store for him. Through-out the long night and into the next day, the other kids and the teachers who had joined them talked about homelessness from all angles. It was a subject Ryan hadn't thought much about, but by the end of the event, he couldn't stop thinking about being his age and not having his own bedroom to go back to, a bathroom, a hot meal. The next week, a member of the club asked Ryan if he'd like to "Tootsie Roll," which meant soliciting money from shoppers at a busy supermarket to raise money for the homeless. (Anyone who donated received a Tootsie Roll as a thank-you.) Ryan agreed. "I still wasn't supercommitted," he remembers. "It was just that everyone who did it looked like they were having such a good time."

By the end of the semester, Ryan became a member of that club. Two years later, he spent a couple of weeks in a tiny village in Costa Rica, building a one-room schoolhouse and teaching kids how to use a compass, in a program he'd devised and financed himself. No one was more surprised to find himself there than he was.

I'm not surprised to hear Ryan's story. There are millions of teenagers like him who are discovering the sixth C, contribution.

DEFINING CONTRIBUTION

I define contribution as the desire and the capacity to give back to those people and institutions that give to us. It's the concept closest to my heart. I've spent my life trying to understand how individual development fits into the larger landscape of human development.

To me, contribution to others and to society is the glue that creates healthy human development. If we contribute to a world that supports the rights and welfare of all individuals, then we are simul-taneously building a better life for ourselves by enhancing the lives of others.

Contribution helps each of us by helping all of us. Think of a teenager who is growing in positive ways, who possesses all of the Five Cs we've discussed in the previous chapters. He's developing pos-itively, and he'll probably have an easy transition to adulthood and become a healthy and productive adult, who will in turn raise healthy children and contribute to society in many other ways as well.

Being strong in the Five Cs feels good! We enjoy feeling competent and confident, connected to others. We appreciate knowing that we're trustworthy, and that we can create and sustain caring relationships. It's a rewarding way to exist in the world.

But is that enough?

I don't think so. All the characteristics of positive development we've talked about so far are necessary but not sufficient. We have to take it one step further.

In the chapter on connection, I pointed out that our very existence is predicated on social relationships—we come into being because we connect with others. Ultimately, we depend on each other. This doesn't mean that we can't be independent-minded. I like to make up my own mind and to act on my beliefs. But in other aspects of life, interdependence underlies all we do. We need people and communities to support us so that we can continue to flourish in our daily lives. I can't fix a computer or a clogged sink. I don't want to become a fund-raiser. Yet our society needs computer repairers, plumbers, fund-raisers, and a whole host of workers in other occupations. If I'm going to avail myself of the services that my community offers me, it's only fair that I give something back. I do this in my research and teaching. We don't take without giving. If we do, there will be nothing left!

If we only think of our own self-interest, we become a nation of self-absorbed egoists. Such a society is a house of cards that will easily fall. To survive and prosper, people and society must be inextricably linked in mutually beneficial ways; their fates need to be bound together. Unless both the individual and society flourish together, both fail.

OUR TEENS' VOICES

Teens who contribute have a special kind of vision, the kind that allows them to see beyond—beyond themselves so they can think of others, beyond today so they can consider what happens tomorrow.

This thinking is reflected in a speech I read that was given by a high school valedictorian. His words impressed me: "As all of us go into the world, we're going to be forced to start questioning and exploring why we're here. My life is a search for meaning. Why do I do what I do? Why do any of us? What will any of it accomplish in the end? The best answer I have found may lie in a quote from the movie *Kingdom of Heaven*, which I was watching yesterday: 'What man is a man who does not make the world better?'"

The long journey to making the world better begins with one step, and often that step is taken close to home. As I discussed in earlier chapters, teens contribute to their family when they help out with chores, help plan events, care for those who are sick, or help solve a problem. They see themselves as having something valuable to offer rather than simply being the recipient of love and care. "My dad was in the hospital for about two weeks," said Carlo, age nineteen, "and my mom was with him just about every day. When he finally came home with a good prognosis, we were all so happy—as if this great load was lifted off us. But later that evening, I saw my mother's face when she noticed all the mail that had piled up all those days she spent in the hospital—all the bills and bank statements. Some of the notices said that there were packages at the post office that we had to sign for, that the cat needed a checkup, and that the car needed to be inspected. When I told her that I'd take care of the post office and the car, she was so unbelievably relieved. And she told me that what was most important to her was the fact that she didn't have to ask me to do it; I volunteered. I never thought of it that way before—that it was time for me to take the initiative."

Teens can also contribute to their schools by participating in school arts and athletic events, clubs, or school government— perhaps even by serving on the school board. But you don't have to be the president of the class or the captain of the soccer team to contribute. Teens contribute by being a member of the foreign-language club, being on the tech squad of the radio station, or playing piccolo in the marching band.

Teens can contribute to their communities by serving on town councils and planning commissions or by volunteering at local charities. During the summer of 2006, I read in the *New York Times* about a group of teens in western Connecticut who regularly volunteer for a local ambulance corps. The Darien volunteer ambulance corps has "58 young members, ranging from 14-year-old candidates to 17- and 18-year-old crew chiefs." These young men and women are certified by the state as emergency medical technicians, and work 365 days a year. Charles Hannon, sixteen, who volunteers, explains that he initially became involved because he was born with a clubfoot, requiring seven surgeries. But his service quickly evolved into something much more. "You learn responsibility. You learn trust. You learn so many things that maybe you start with a specific motivation—medical school, something to do—but soon you're so caught up in it that you really don't need a specific motivation. It becomes so much a part of your life that you just do it without thinking why."

Teens who get involved in their community experience a lot more than they bargained for. As Barrett Brown, for example, who has been volunteering for four years with his town's ambulance corps and local fire department, said, "I'm only 19, so I haven't experienced most things in life. But not too many things can compare with being that person walking into someone's house during the worst part of their life and being there for someone when no one else is. It's an indescribable feeling."

Other teens relish the fact that they feel valued. Garrett Deutsch, seventeen, who lives in Chappaqua, New York, volunteers with a local fire department and ambulance corps. He remembers a fire at a nearby arboretum that happened during a time when most of the adult members of the corps were unavailable, so that teens outnumbered the adults on the call. "And I was thinking," Garrett recalled, "'We're only in high school but we're playing such a big part in this.' I don't know what they would have done without us. It was really enjoyable and really rewarding."

Teens can also bask in the glow that results from volunteering for innovative programs that are being developed around the country, such as Common Cents. This is a truly astonishing program that began about fifteen years ago in New York City schools (elementary through high school). It is built on the idea of affording students rich leadership opportunities. First, the students stage an annual Penny Harvest during which they knock on doors and ask for people's left-over pennies. Last year, 195 tons of pennies were collected—more than $700,000!

That's impressive enough—but the program doesn't stop there. Once their fund-raising role is finished, the students become philan-thropists, participating in roundtable discussions during which they decide how to allocate the money they raised. To help them decide, they may make site visits—to homeless shelters, day care centers, and senior citizens' centers—and invite potential grantees to make pitches for funds. After they've made their grants, the students revisit the sites to see how their gift has helped. "I used to think I was only a little penny," one fifth-grade philanthropist said, "but now I know I'm bigger than a penny." Or, as one of her classmates put it, "When you see things fixed in your neighborhood and you say to yourself, 'We did that,' it's like you create a mayhem of happiness. It's like God is entering your heart."

In addition to volunteering, the majority of American teens work part time while attending school. If you've imbued your child with good decision-making skills and a sense of responsibility, then this work experience can be a huge benefit to her. She'll learn about the nature of the world outside of academics, she'll have the opportunity to engage with people of different ages and walks of life, and she'll gain valuable experience handling money.

Mandating Contribution

Many high schools have begun requiring that students complete a mandated number of community service hours in order to graduate. I have problems with this. Requiring youth to do service may get them out in the community, but it is not a sound approach. When service is required, teens come to regard it as a means to an end—graduation—and are deprived of the opportunity to see the task as intrinsically rewarding. In this sense, such service may foster a cynical attitude, which is not what we want. When it comes to meaningful contribution, fewer but more intense experiences of longer duration are more important than many shallow, short-term, drop-in experiences. It's only over time that teens come to understand what is necessary to make a significant contribution, one that has a real impact on those being served.

True, one-day events such as Global Youth Service Day, which is organized by Youth Service America and the Global Youth Action Network, are very visible and important. But their importance comes from their ability to let people know about how ready and willing teens are to serve. Involvement that lasts but a day does not really help communities or create durable, sustainable, and effective changes.

Finding Meaning in Mandatory Service

It's also true, however, that in some cases what begins as extrinsic motivation—racking up enough community service hours to graduate—can turn into something much more genuine and intrinsically rewarding.

Jonathan, the duct tape expert we met in Chapter 3, had to complete fifteen hours of community service each year that he was in high school. Many of his classmates chose to volunteer at religious institutions to which their family belonged, but Jonathan chose to become a "buddy" in his town's Special Athletes League, a sports program for children with physical and emotional disabilities. It was a very difficult placement—many of the children were paralyzed and in wheelchairs, several had Down syndrome, and others had significant hearing impairments.

But what began as the fulfillment of a requirement morphed into something much more profound. Although he was required to devote fifteen hours a year to community service, he logged more than four hundred hours during his four years of high school. He also rose through the ranks to become one of the Special Athletes head coaches. And Jonathan chose to write about his experience in his college essay. Specifically, he focused on Rubin, an eight-year old boy who was paralyzed on his left side, deaf in his left ear, and blind in his left eye. "For the past year, I not only have been Rubin's coach but also his pal every Tuesday while his mom works," Jonathan wrote. "I meet him at the bus stop, sometimes drive him to his doctor's appointments, and usually cook him a simple dinner. Then he becomes *my* coach, teaching *me* to play some tricky one-handed video games and how to race remote-control cars with one eye shut. Rubin is realistic about his capabilities. I admire the ease with which he constantly redefines the meaning of success. I prize his ability to ask for help without shame and secretly wish I could be as trusting of people as he is. Rubin's enthusiasm for life is infectious and his positive attitude and determination uplifts me, too."

By acknowledging the mutuality of his relationship with Rubin (that they affected each other), Jonathan was acknowledging his capacity for connection. But the reason he was drawn to Rubin—and to the placement itself—was because Jonathan had a medical condition that required daily monitoring. As a result, he felt a special sense of empathy with teens who were coping with physical problems, and was able to respond with more empathy, and with gratitude. Jonathan's essay continues, "As I reflect on my experiences with Special Athletes, I see that I learn from all my kids just as much as they have learned from me. They inspire me to take challenges, no matter what obstacles are placed in my path. They push me to be more creative, adaptive, compassionate, and patient. They help me appreciate that I am blessed and that I often take all I have for granted. They remind me to take pleasure in little things, like a brand-new baseball, and not to take everyday problems so seriously. Above all, they enrich my life by allowing me to be part of theirs." Clearly, although he wouldn't have met Rubin if not for the school requirement, Jonathan counts this as one of his most important high school experiences.

NURTURING CONTRIBUTION

How can we encourage teens to contribute? How can we ensure that they will gain and practice the skills they'll need in the future, when they become the adults upon whom the future of our families, communities, and civil society will rest?

- The way to launch your teen on the path to contribution is to put into practice all the Big Three suggestions I discussed in the preceding chapters. Remember to pay particular attention to the first facet of the Big Three—maintaining a close relationship. This is the linchpin of all the others.
- You can also help, using the second facet of the Big Three, by modeling a very specific life skill—contributing to yourself. That is, parents need to show their teens how to take care of themselves, physically, mentally, and emotionally.

You're probably asking yourself what in the world I mean. Here I am, talking at length about how it's essential for us to think beyond ourselves, and all of a sudden I contradict myself. Isn't contributing to oneself the height of selfishness?

Not really. Think about it for a moment. In order to help others, we have to be in a position to offer help. We have to be fit and healthy. If we're not, we'll end up drawing on the resources of others rather than adding to that pool. In this framework, an adult who is generous to herself—who takes time to relax, to nourish, pursue, and enjoy her own interests, attend to her diet and health, to recharge her own batteries, to be fit mentally and physically— is not being selfish. Instead, she is contributing to herself so that she enhances her capacity to contribute to others. In fact, we're obliged to take care of ourselves under the social contract: if we don't assume responsibility for ourselves, we'll end up as a drag on others; instead of helping them, they will have to help us. This is what our teens learn from us when we give generously to ourselves.

THREE WAYS TO ENCOURAGE CONTRIBUTION

That's not enough, of course. Parents need to enact the third facet of the Big Three, and provide their teens with leadership opportunities.

Keep in mind, though, that taking that first step is often scary. To volunteer to make a contribution can be risky. You may meet with success, but you may also face failure, rejection, and misinterpretation. I've seen what happens when teens commit to participating in a community activity only to have the experience turn sour. Sometimes the projects aren't well supervised; sometimes kids have unrealistic expectations. What you don't want is for kids to end up so turned off that they won't think about volunteering or contributing again for years.

Of course, there's no way to guarantee success. But there are some steps you can take to minimize failure, to help your child's contributions be more effective. You can, for example, help them to select the activity that's right for them, optimize their chances for success, and help them compensate when things don't work out as planned, a three-step approach I adapted from psychologists Paul and Margaret Baltes' model of adult adaptation.

Selecting the Right Activity

When it comes to contribution, teens need to find the venue that's right for them. Some find themselves drawn to a particular cause for any number of reasons. Charles Hannon, for example, the Connecticut EMT who was born with a clubfoot, empathized with those who had medical conditions.

Not all teens can find their way to contribution on their own, however. That's when you have to help. In some communities teens face a full menu of choices, while in others there are very few. In either case, it's important to choose wisely.

• Help your child discriminate which choices would be best according to his or her goals, the same way you'd help her decide whether to take French over Spanish depending on her interests. If your daughter is passionate about science, perhaps she'd be interested in joining the fight against global warming, or toward eradicating a particular disease (such as cholera, due to drinking contaminated water). If she's more people-oriented, perhaps she'd volunteer time in a shelter for homeless families or staff a suicide-prevention hotline. In all these cases, she's contributing to people, places, or events beyond her own self-interest. (For help aligning your teen's interests and activities, refer back to your teen's competence and confidence inventories that you compiled in Chapters 3 and 4.)

· If your teen doesn't gravitate toward these activities, you can help by seeking out people or institutions in the community that are looking for teen participation and point your teen in that direction. Perhaps you know someone who wants to hire summer interns, or someone who runs a volunteer program in your town.

· You can also help steer your child toward contributing by stressing the element of surprise, of the unknown. Talk about the fact that we often don't know what we're signing on for and that we can't always anticipate what we'll discover through participation. As Ryan, whom we met earlier in this chapter, said, "What surprised me the most about joining this club was seeing how little effort it took for each of us. I mean, everyone just gave a little bit, but when we added it up, the results were huge. We raised about $10,000 to spend on the Costa Rican village. That's a huge about of money—it blew my mind. But it wasn't hard to do. We each gave what we could, but it made such a difference. It's so much more efficient to work with others. And when you see how much your efforts are appreciated, it's the best. I feel as if I gave a little, but I got back so much."

Optimizing the Outcome

Having good intentions and noble goals isn't enough. Teens have to have a plan to achieve those goals. They have to be able to identify and marshal the people and material resources that will help them be effective. In other words, they have to be able to maximize or optimize the chances that they can meet their goals.

Suppose your child looks in her closet, notices that she has a couple of old winter jackets and other clothes she has outgrown, and realizes that these could be donated to those who need them. She tells a couple of friends, who share her enthusiasm, and they meet to plan a campaign. Very quickly they realize that the task is more complicated than cleaning out a closet and telling a few friends. If they really want it to be successful, they have to answer a number of questions:

- How can they publicize the clothes drive?
- What date will it begin and end?
- Where should the clothes be collected?
- How can they raise money for expenses?
- To which town agency will they donate the clothes?

As your daughter learns how to answer these and other questions, she'll develop the capacity to accomplish what she sets out to do, to make the contributions or reach the goals she sets. Help her see that she'll be drawing on her social competence when she negotiates with town officials as to where and when the clothes drive can take place, on her vocational competence when she talks to shopkeepers to enlist their help (maybe they'll let her put up posters in their stores), and on her cognitive competence to plan the logistics of the drive. Taken together, these skills will help her get the job done.

Coping with Complications

Even the best-planned event can fail, and the best intentions can go awry. This is why your teen needs to learn a final skill—to deal with, or compensate for, failure.

Some adults who get involved with children's sports feel that the score shouldn't be kept—that kids need to learn about participating without having to worry about winning or losing. I couldn't disagree more! Winning *and* losing are part of life. I strongly believe that our role as parents isn't to protect kids from failure—because such an attempt itself will always ultimately fail. Despite our best efforts, life is filled with disappointment.

Take what happened to Jonathan, whom we met earlier in the chapter. After leaving for college, Jonathan kept in touch with Rubin's mother only to learn that Rubin's father had had a heart attack and died. A few months later, Rubin's mother was injured in a car accident and was forced to place Rubin in a special school to live and learn while she went through rehabilitation. He is still there. Jonathan wonders if he isn't somewhat responsible, asking himself, "I wonder what would have happened if I hadn't gone away to school." Sadly, there are limits to what empathy can accomplish, and this is perhaps the hardest lesson Jonathan had to learn.

We cannot serve our children by protecting them from these realities; instead, we need to help them understand that real contributions, the ones that are often the most important or even the most heroic, are born amid adversity. We don't always get the part in the play, have the date we want, or win the election we've pinned our hopes on. Instead, we need to teach kids how to cope with failure so it doesn't emotionally devastate them. Part of being a successful and productive adult is to bounce back from such experiences, to set new goals or to try to find other pathways to reach our intended objective. As Sir Winston Churchill said, "Success is not final, failure is not fatal: it is the courage to continue that counts." There's another Winston Churchill quote that applies here as well: "Success is the ability to go from failure to failure without losing your enthusiasm."

To help the bitter medicine go down, you can do several things:

- Express unconditional affection and pride in your teen.
- Legitimize your teen's anger, frustration, and disappointment.
- Be open about your own experiences with success and failure.
- Partner with your teen to find other routes to meeting the goal.
- Model the skills needed to negotiate these new routes.
- Help your teen redefine his goal or select another goal that may be more realistic.

LOOKING AHEAD

When we're able to set the stage for contributions for our teens, we're helping to ensure that they will become adults who continue to contribute to themselves, their families, and their communities. They will thrive and flourish, maximizing their potential, developing as positively as they can, and using their skills to become engaged in their world.

The good news from my most recent research is that this can actually happen. My original research goal, as I talked about early in the book, was to prove that the Five Cs really existed and that they could be measured. Now that we've shown this, and followed a group of more than four thousand adolescents, we've discovered something else that's incredibly exciting: as the fifth graders showed an increase in positive development, they also showed an increase in contribution in sixth grade. This relation was true of all children regardless of socioeconomic status or ethnicity. Fifth graders who had high positive development became sixth graders who contributed more.

Think of the ramifications! If this trend continues, and we have no reason to think it won't, imagine how much more strongly the idea of contribution will take root in these kids over the course of adolescence. By the time they reach young adulthood, contributing will seem like second nature. The important fact is that when we promote positive development by fostering the Five Cs, we raise teens who will want to give back, who will want to nurture the society that nurtures them.

I am 100 percent confident that these are the kids who will turn our country and world around. If we are able to extend our longitudinal study through the high school years and perhaps beyond, following them into young adulthood, I bet we'll see their drive to contribute continue and grow. Teens who are developing the Five Cs know that the world isn't a zero-sum game: that is, that the only way I can win is if you lose. Instead, they believe that they win by helping others win. That's why they want to see a level playing field for everyone—so that each person has an opportunity to succeed in life. They know that when you have character and when you care, you start thinking about giving back. These teens are truly thriving.

THE Cs AT A GLANCE

Here's a recap of some useful ways to build teens' strengths and maximize their opportunities to develop the Cs.

Competence
- Find things your child likes, and support these passions and activities without taking over.
- Help your child see that the skills she has are portable, that they can be generalized into other areas where she feels not so skilled.
- Actively involve your teen in making decisions that will have an impact on family life.
- Turn mistakes—whether trivial or serious—into teachable moments.

Confidence
- Make sure your child has a convoy of support so he feels loved and valued every day and everywhere.
- Share you own life woes and lapses in confidence and ask your teen for help when you can.
- Find things that your teen does well and encourage him to pursue interests, activities, or hobbies that emphasize these skills.
- Be especially attentive to challenges to your daughter's confidence: Confidence is likely to dip more for girls than for boys during early and middle adolescence.

Connection
- Foster family dinners no matter how busy everyone is.
- Respect your teen's privacy but appreciate that privacy can be perilous. Be respectful but vigilant.
- If you don't approve of a friend, relationship, or activity, speak out. Let your teen know your values, and explain why some behavior can't be tolerated.

- Create opportunities in your family or community so your child feels her voice is being heard. All teens want to feel that they matter.

Character

- Make sure *your* actions align with *your* words—after all, you are the primary model for your child.
- Keep a sense of perspective—and sometimes a sense of humor—about minor infractions.
- Provide opportunities for your teen to make his own decisions—and when you give him this opportunity, live with the decisions he makes.

Caring

- Times when our teens treat us as if we're disposable may be when they need us the most. Hang back, wait for an opening to talk, and respond.
- When your child hurls an "I hate you," step aside and be honest: "Wow, that hurts!"
- Caring is contagious: caring parents raise caring teens. Model caring in your homes and communities.
- Encourage teens to join school boards, civic organizations, or faith-based institutions to promote caring and social justice in the world around them.

Contribution

- Encourage your teen to participate in causes that align with her interests.
- Encourage people and institutions to welcome teen participation.
- Help teens marshal the resources they need so their contributing efforts have a good chance of succeeding.
- Don't overprotect your kids from failure; they need to understand that even the most worthwhile efforts sometimes meet with disappointment.

But what if your child isn't thriving? What if she's encountering more than her share of problems, problems that threaten to derail her healthy development? It's time to take a look at these teens and discuss some strategies to get them back on track, which we will do in the next chapter.

When Real Trouble Brews

The line of demarcation between mental health and illness cannot be drawn as sharply as had been thought before.

— Anna Freud

Try as we might, no one is perfect. There are no perfect parents, no perfect children. We all encounter problems at some time in our lives. There are problems particular to every age. The teenage years are no exception.

Be assured, though, that some problems are normal. This may sound like an oxymoron—how can something be a normal problem? What I mean is that there are problems we all can expect to face. When our kids were little, they may have cried when they cut teeth, or had a difficult time coping when we left them at kindergarten. We hated to see them in pain and we worried about them when we left them.

But these were normal, predictable problems. Most teenage problems fall into this category as well. Their faces break out, they gain weight, they grow too tall too fast and become clumsy. These too are normal (to-be-expected) problems. Some teens test the limits of your forbearance; they sometimes lie, play hooky, possess what I call "low-level contraband" (the *Playboy* magazine artfully concealed underneath the mattress), and experiment with illicit substances. We've already talked about some of the ways to handle these issues when they arise, and about the importance of maintaining perspective when they do.

But there are larger, more ominous problems as well.

Tanya, fifteen, had been sneaking out of her house for months to meet her boyfriend, returning just before dawn. She wasn't discovered until she inadvertently broke a glass bowl climbing in through a window.

Ned, sixteen, was on the verge of being expelled from his high school—for the past three months, he'd been showing up to class drunk and ultimately revealed that he kept a bottle of vodka in his locker.

Denny, fourteen, had become involved with a white-supremacist group online and was distributing hate literature at school.

These are just a few of the serious problems that can plague our teens. Others I would add to the "When Trouble Brews" list include:

- Aberrant behaviors (torturing or murdering animals)
- Antisocial behaviors (hate crimes, racist attacks)
- Behaviors resulting in school suspension (fighting, destruction of school property, bringing banned materials to school)
- Chronic truancy
- Drug or alcohol abuse/addiction
- Engaging in crimes (stealing, arson, drug sales, teen prostitution)
- Externalizing disorders (aggression)
- Internalizing disorders (depression, anxiety, eating disorders, suicidal ideation, suicide attempts)
- Joining a gang or a cult

- Possession of illegal weapons
- Risk behaviors (engaging in unsafe sex, driving while intoxicated)
- Running away from home

Many of these problems will sound familiar. Others may seem remote. They aren't. According to a 2005 study by the Children's Defense Fund:

- Every second a public school student is suspended.
- Every nine seconds a high school student drops out.
- Every twenty seconds a child is arrested.
- Every minute a baby is born to a teen mother.
- Every four minutes a child is arrested for drug abuse.
- Every eight minutes a child is arrested for violent crimes.
- Every three hours a child or teen is killed by a firearm.
- Every five hours a child or teen commits suicide.

All of these are what I consider "drawing the line" behaviors. That is, these behaviors must end. Some of these behaviors cut into your child's chances in life; others decrease his or her chances even to have a life.

A BLUEPRINT FOR COPING WITH SERIOUS PROBLEMS

What should you do if you were Tanya's parents, or Ned's? If you are, I know you're desperate for advice, for a way out of the frightening situation in which you find yourself.

Here are the two pointers to keep in mind, first and foremost:

- *Lay down the law.* You have to let your teen know that certain behaviors won't be tolerated, that certain lines cannot be crossed. Your teen has to know that your stance on certain issues is unequivocal. Distributing hate literature is wrong.

Worshiping violence is not acceptable. Drinking in school is out of bounds. Stealing cannot be condoned.

· *Don't demonize your child.* If your child is in trouble, she needs your attention, your compassion, your concern, and your competence, not your condemnation. Don't simply assume that she's fundamentally flawed, that "the devil made her do it," or that she was driven to act this way because of her genes. Any of these approaches is nothing more than a way of avoiding confronting the situation that led to the problem and finding a real solution. Your goal is to deal with the problem in an honest, comprehensive way, not sweep it under the rug or make false attributions.

Remember the concept of plasticity I discussed in Chapter 2. By focusing on your child's strengths as a strategy for redemption, you can find a way to change the relations your child has with his social world, and you can expect at least some improvement in even the most egregious behavior. To illustrate the potential for positive change even in the face of really negative behaviors, let's examine one of these problems in more depth.

CAUGHT IN THE ACT

Your sixteen-year-old daughter recently got a job at a donut shop and is delighted to be earning some extra money. You notice many new additions to her wardrobe—new shoes, new pocketbooks—and talk to her about the possibility of opening a savings account so that she doesn't immediately spend all of her earnings. She assures you that she is saving money.

But one day you get a call from a man who identifies himself as a security guard at a clothing shop in your neighborhood. Your daughter was caught shoplifting: she tried to leave the store with two tank tops stuffed into her waistband. Her actions are recorded on the store's security camera—there's no mistaking her intention. The security guard asks you to come there immediately. To your knowledge, this is the first time something like this has happened.

This situation is never easy, but you need to keep several points in mind.

First, when you arrive at the store, make sure that everyone is calm, no one's yelling or screaming, and your child is safe. Remember that even in this situation your daughter has a right to be treated with dignity. The store personnel have an equal right to be treated with respect.

At the same time, be respectful of the seriousness of the situation. You don't want to come off as the kind of reactive parent who just assumes that her teen is an angel whom everyone else is out to get. But you also want your child to understand that she's in real trouble.

What you'll want to do next is talk to your child. Say, "Can you please tell me what happened? Would you like to talk here" (if others are present), "or do you want to talk to me privately?"

At this point, she may break down, or she may tell a disjointed story claiming her innocence. Your job is to try to get the true story. Push her to tell the truth. You can say, "If I'm going to help you, you really need to tell me absolutely everything that happened. This is a serious charge. What you did in the dressing room is on videotape—they can see you trying to hide those tops. Honey, this is not like you forgot to take out the trash. I'm not in control of what happens from this point on. You took someone else's property, and it's up to them what happens next. The store owners can ask you to apologize and that will be that; they could ask you to make restitution, or they could go to the police, and this could go on your record and affect your future in all kinds of ways you can't anticipate. You could end up in juvenile court, you could be reported to your school—I don't know where this will lead. That's why you need to be honest. And that is why you need to explain to them you understand the seriousness of what you did. I'll stick with you through this. I love you. But now it is up to you to take this seriously, to show respect to these people whose property you've violated, and let them know you are truly sorry. This may not be enough to get you out of this situation. But it is how you *must* start."

At this point, your daughter may confess. You'll have to urge her to not only apologize to the store owners but also acknowledge that she made a mistake and that she knows that she'll have to suffer the penalty, whatever that is. Your role is to help your teen to stand up and face the consequences of her actions.

This isn't easy. For most of us, our natural inclination is to act as an agent of our child, to explain our child to the world, to advocate on her behalf. But when your child does something grievously wrong, you have to shift your role: you have to become an agent of society and become the representative of society to your child. Otherwise, teens persist in thinking that they can get away with things, and that their parents will always serve as a buffer between them and the world and *real* consequences of their behaviors. Becoming the voice of society isn't the same as "tough love," as I mentioned in the first chapter. You're not abandoning your child, leaving her to get out of the hole she dug for herself. Instead, as I have just explained, you're standing by her as she stands up for what she did.

Maybe this really isn't the first time your child has landed in serious trouble. Or maybe it's the first time she's been caught shoplifting, but there have been other instances of serious problem behaviors—truancy, vandalism, fighting, breaking curfew. If this is the case, you need to recognize that your child may have to face even more serious consequences. He may need professional help that is beyond anything you can provide. He may even need to be institutionalized so that he can be rehabilitated.

For example, the sixteen-year-old son of a well-off family I know stole a neighbor's car and totaled it. The boy's father worked out a deal with his neighbors whereby his son would be responsible for paying all the car replacement costs that were not covered by insurance. The boy was also grounded. "I hope you learned your lesson," his father declared, and the son responded that he had. No stronger steps were taken by his family. That was the end of it—or so the boy's parents thought.

Within a year of the car incident, the teen began breaking into stores. It didn't take long for the boy to be caught. And this time his father wasn't nearly so lenient. He let charges be filed against his son, and accompanied the boy to court, where he told the judge that he realized that his son was going to be punished. But he added that he hoped his son would also be rehabilitated. He asked the judge to place his son in a facility with rehabilitation programs available for young, first-time perpetrators of a felony. The judge agreed. He sentenced the then seventeen-year-old to prison for eighteen months, but placed him in a state prison that separated youthful offenders from the general, hard-core prison population and had a rehabilitation program. The father believed—or at least hoped—that this mandatory program would instill in his son the personal discipline and motivation to follow society's rules that he and his wife had not been successful in fostering.

Here, trouble had brewed beyond the point where the father could fix it. He could have gotten lawyers to argue his child's case, and more than likely a much less severe punishment would have been meted out. However, with the advice of friends and adolescent development experts, the dad recognized that to intervene in this way would not be in his son's best interest. He realized that his son wasn't just flirting with lawlessness over the past year—this was an escalating series of incidents. He understood that this situation required dramatic interventions. He had to accede to more drastic steps to salvage his son's future.

In the remainder of this chapter, I will not offer you a step-by-step solution to all of the problems listed earlier. It's not only a question of space; it's simply not possible to address all the different scenarios in all their complexity. No one can. Each family, each individual, is different. When problems arise, they often stem from situations deeply embedded in the family structure. The root causes of these problems are so diverse—ranging from personality issues to social and cultural factors such as racism and sexism—that specific solutions require an in-depth understanding of each family member.

But I can offer you something perhaps more important: I can give you a blueprint for how to proceed *no matter what problem you're facing.*

COPING WITH DIFFICULT PROBLEMS: THREE KEY STEPS

1. *Understand your teen's problem within the context of your family history and your current situation.* As we discussed in the chapter on connection, we are social beings; we exist in relationships. For that reason, the problems kids experience, no matter how severe or life-disrupting, develop in the context of the family relationship. Problems, in other words, are a product of an individual's relationships. When a teen encounters a problem, there's always a history of social relationships accompanying that problem. We can't rewrite the past, but we can acknowledge the things in the past that still hurt or concern your child.

In addition, all problems unfold in the context of the current family situation. All issues that come up in daily life—family discord; marital separation due to divorce, death, or military assignment; or the stress of moving to a new community—affect your child.

For these reasons, parents need to take into account the history and current status of their relationship with their child. It's not that parents are always to blame for their children's problems, but rather that everything in a child's life—past and present—influences how she thinks and feels. Talking honestly with your child can uncover the source of the difficulties. Once the source is uncovered, it's always possible to make changes, especially in the way parents and teens relate to each other.

For example, suppose you or your spouse landed a great new job that required you and your family to relocate to a different part of the country. All your sixteen-year-old daughter knows, however, is that she was yanked out of school during her junior year—the most important year of school she's ever had—and torn away from the best friends she ever had, to say nothing of her boyfriend, and has to start over from scratch with no friends, not even a familiar face to greet her in homeroom. "How could my parents do this to me?" she ruminates in her black mood. "They don't care about me at all! Well, if they don't care about me, then I don't have to care about me, either. I'll show them." Within a month, her self-esteem shot to pieces, she's hanging out with dangerous kids and experimenting with dangerous drugs.

Of course, not all problems have such an identifiable source, and in many cases discussions within the family aren't enough to solve the problem. You may need to go beyond the family. Try talking to your child's teachers or counselors about their views of her behavior. When her best friend visits, try to get a moment with her and ask for her views and advice. The key here is not to lose hope. Remember, thanks to plasticity, we can always hope for a better, more positive outcome.

2. Educate yourself: become an expert about your child's problem. "Get professional help." That's the advice you most often hear if your teen is in serious trouble. I don't disagree with that; I just find it premature. Before you reach out to an expert, become one yourself.

No one knows your child as well as you do. No one is as familiar with your family history, dynamics, and current situation as you are. You are the most expert person in the world about your child and, as such, you are your child's first resource. To help her, you need to educate yourself about your child's problem. There are many ways to do this. Parents networks, advocacy and lobbying groups, and nonprofit organizations in your community that deal with specific issues (such as substance abuse, for example) abound. Ask other parents, call the counseling center at your child's school, or go online to find resources to help you. All too often, parents feel so ashamed of their teen's problem that they fail to reach out, which only isolates them more, shutting them off from the help that's readily available. Don't fall into this trap. If you do, you end up shortchanging your teen—and yourself.

The Web is full of helpful resources, although not all are equally reliable. One of the best is the Child & Family WebGuide (www.cfw.tufts.edu). This comprehensive site functions as a directory linking you to other sites offering advice to parents, all of which are rated by experts associated with Tufts University. You can find information about families, education, development, and mental health for children from birth to age nineteen. You can also ask experts specific questions and find out about the latest research.

Once you've done your homework, you'll be able to consult with a mental health professional or adolescent specialist as an informed consumer. To find a therapist, ask for referrals from friends or from your pediatrician. Therapists who use a strength-based, systems-oriented, and family-centered approach and who work from a positive adolescent perspective are the most helpful. You're looking for someone who will work to enhance your family bond and give you hope, even if it seems things are unraveling. Categorizing your child into a fixed and immutable diagnostic category or labeling your family as "dysfunctional" isn't useful. The best therapists for teenagers are those who support parental efforts and work with teens to make healthy choices rather than assign pathological labels to problems.

Armed with your knowledge and a supportive professional, you'll be able to take a much more active role during the consultation. Instead of passively receiving a diagnosis, you'll be able to ask critical questions. You'll also be in a better position to evaluate the treatment options the specialist suggests, and to ensure that diagnosis and treatment are properly coordinated. If you go to a clinic, for example, a highly trained specialist may make the diagnosis and then send you to other, less advanced practitioners for the actual therapy. These less advanced practitioners may not be sufficiently trained to detect progress in your child's situation, or to suggest that the original treatment plan needs to be revised. This is when you need to take on the role of parent as expert. As an expert/parent, your job is to make sure that nothing is "lost in translation" between identifying the problem and fixing it.

3. *Use my positive development perspective to understand your child's problems and the potential for change.* In times of trouble, it's especially important to remember and rely on the principles underlying the positive development approach:

• *Human behavior is complicated, an intricate interplay of biological and social factors.* When we're in trouble, we often look for and cling to easy solutions. If your son pays so little attention in class that he's on the verge of flunking out, it's easy to ascribe his difficulties to ADHD. But we have to fight the urge to categorize or pigeonhole our teens, to apply a cookie-cutter, one-size-fits-all solution. Instead, we need to understand their situation in all its many dimensions rather than try to reduce it to a single, simple label. For example, a counselor or physician may think that your son is suffering from what he labels depression or your daughter has an eating disorder.

Even when you are faced with such labels presented as "final" diagnoses, keep in mind that such statements are not the whole story. In fact, if you go to a mental health professional and receive a diagnosis from the *Diagnostic and Statistical Manual of Mental Disorders* (DSM-IV), the widely used manual employed to categorize mental and emotional problems, rest assured that these diagnoses are not the last word. The categories in DSM-IV are notoriously subject to the winds of political correctness and to the needs of professional groups to have their pet diagnosis (the diagnosis about which they claim special and, especially, billable expertise) included in the manual. Be sure to research the diagnosis on your own. Speak to other parents to find out what worked for them. The more you know about your child's condition and the variations that exist among kids given an identical diagnosis, the better you'll be able to advocate for what's best for him.

· *People are much more than the sum of their parts.* No matter how overwhelming your child's problem seems, resist the inclination you or others may have to define your child only by her problem. Whatever problematic behavior she's engaging in, or whatever the diagnosis, she's not just a truant, a gang member, or a drug abuser. Her problem is just one facet of her; despite it, she retains her humanity, her wholeness. She is much more than her difficulty. Remember this fact, tell it to your child, *and* tell it to the professionals working with her. Here is when it *is* appropriate and essential to advocate for your child—for the breadth of your child's individuality. When talking about your teen, you can mention the challenges she's facing but resist easy categorization, and put her problem in the context of her other positive attributes. This will help her acknowledge her own complexity; she will then be able to use this knowledge as a lever to help her find a solution to her problem.

· *Plasticity means that change is always possible.* Let me return to the idea of plasticity. Take a developmental perspective when approaching your child's problem. When planning her treatment, make sure to take into account the reality that she will change and mature over time. Thanks to plasticity, we never completely lose our capacity to change and adapt to new circumstances. By taking a longer-range view, you'll be better able to find a solution that will last rather than putting your money on a one-shot, magic-bullet solution, which I believe promises false hope. Resign yourself to the fact that there are *no* magic bullets. Change takes time, and it takes altering the relations between your child and her world.

· *Trust that your teen will be able to take a leadership role in her own life.* Ultimately, your teen needs to be able to handle her problems herself. As I have explained, this is the goal of the Big Three—and it's a practical goal, because it's likely that she will live longer than you will. Rather than regarding her as a patient who needs to be treated, involve her in her own solution to her problem. Help her to understand that she needs to take a leadership role, that she's an active participant in her journey toward health.

The young man who was ultimately sent to prison for breaking and entering eventually understood that his dad was not going to be able to buffer him against the consequences of his illegal behavior. After eighteen long months in prison, painfully separated from his family, he began to mature emotionally. He came to the realization that he was the only one who could get him through life successfully. His dad reports that his son is now taking advantage of educational opportunities while he is incarcerated and that he has made a commitment to himself to attend college when he is released, a decision about which he appears very enthusiastic.

Keeping in mind the idea that your child needs to be the active agent in his own positive change will help him take ownership of his problems—and of their solutions. But my last point is perhaps most important of all, for both you and your teen:

- *Take a community-based perspective.* Problems isolate us: we feel ashamed, singled out, punished. But remember that you and your family are not alone. Reach out to your convoys of support for help. I haven't yet come across a family that hasn't been challenged by difficulties with their kids. And most everyone is grateful and relieved to know that they're not the only ones who have problems. Networking helps you find solutions you may not have thought of on your own. Talking to others also helps normalize what you're going through. It helps us shift our focus. Instead of zeroing in on a single family and a single teen who has a problem, we realize that there may be issues in our society that affect many teens and their families.

Often, collectively, we can advocate in more compelling ways for our children. A state legislator in Michigan once told me that when twelve constituents came to her with a single complaint, she regarded this as a "landslide" sentiment and acted as if she had a mandate from her entire district. Why? Rarely, she reported, did more than one person ever raise an issue with her. If all we need is eleven other neighbors to effect a change in policy, then changing the context for our children may be easier than imagined.

Perhaps, then, there are ways we could—and should—address issues facing our children's development, acting as a collective rather than as individuals. This is what I'll examine in the next chapter.

10

Beyond Our Own Families: A Call to Action

Never doubt that a small group of thoughtful citizens can change the world. Indeed, it is the only thing that ever has.

—Margaret Mead

In the early chapters of this book, I described the personal journey that led me to transform myself from a scientist interested only in the facts of human development to someone interested also in promoting positive change in the world. In subsequent chapters, I explained how you can promote positive change by enhancing the life of your teen and your family.

This is our goal as parents. We want our kids to prosper and thrive. We want to see them grow up safely, meet their challenges, make a smooth transition to adulthood, and become established as productive, contributing members of society who will eventually raise their own children to thrive as they did.

It's a noble goal. But now imagine for a moment that you viewed all teens, not just your own, through the lens of positive development. If all teens are thought of as assets in the making, rather than problems waiting to happen, then not only our own families but also society as a whole could be transformed.

It's not a dream. It could happen. It *is* happening. And I'm inviting you to join those of us who have dedicated ourselves to this call to action. By following the road map this book describes, we will commit ourselves to ensuring that all children have the same opportunities—access to the same resources—that are needed for healthy growth. The principle that guides you is as simple as this: work to give all children the same benefits in life that you provide for your own.

BEYOND YOUR LIVING ROOM

"Why should I?" you may well ask. "Why should I care about children I don't know? It's hard enough focusing on my own kids!"

As a parent, I know that's true. Raising our own kids is nothing short of a full-time job. But as an applied developmental scientist, I know that for many reasons we can't afford to think that narrowly. One of the most fundamental reasons is that it's actually in our own enlightened self-interest: when we take care of other children, our own children benefit. I think of the old adage that a chain is only as strong as its weakest link. This is especially true when it comes to the social fabric of our nation. News reports all too often tell the story of what happens to *our* kids when *other* teens resort to gun violence, crimes resulting from illicit drug use, or involvement in terrorist activities that reflect or express their desperation, hopelessness, anger, or frustration about their lot in life. Bullets kill the innocent as well as the guilty, and therefore we are all linked together in the social web I've described throughout the book.

We need to support, then, the healthy, successful development of every teen to ensure that our own teens will thrive. In our interdependent world, if one "team" loses, we all lose. By serving others, we serve ourselves.

AMERICA NEEDS A NATIONAL YOUTH POLICY

You may not realize it, but America does not have a national youth policy. I know that sounds impossible.

We have violence prevention programs. We have a "war" on drugs. We have programs directed at reducing teenage pregnancy. But these programs, based as they are in the deficit model, don't really add up to a national youth policy. They're about reducing social problems, not advocating for positive growth.

In fact, the United States is the only industrialized country *without* a youth policy. As if that's not bad enough, we're one of only two nations that have not signed the UN Convention on the Rights of Children—a treaty signed by both Iran and Iraq, among others. If the other countries of the world can invest in their children's future, so can we. Until we put promoting the positive among teens on the public policy agenda, our shortsightedness will dramatically short-change our children.

The national youth policy I advocate has a two-pronged focus:

- We need to find the collective will to restructure our society so that all children and teens are valued and supported.
- We need a comprehensive, multigenerational approach to building a caring community around our children and teens so that they can experience a system of seamless support throughout their lives, wherever they are.

Both of these policy initiatives are grounded in positive development in that they address strengths and affirm plasticity—the capacity to change. Let's talk about the points one at a time.

RESTRUCTURING SOCIETY TO INVEST IN TEENS

It's up to parents to take all the resources—the developmental assets listed in Chapter 2, which exist in every community, whether rich or poor, urban or rural—and "grow" them so that teens can become leaders in the ways I have described in the previous chapters. The first step is to reject the deficit, or problem-reduction, approach in favor of advocating for a program of positive development. I did that when the town of Concord, Massachusetts, asked me to consult with it.

Concord, an upscale community, was definitely having problems with its teens. On Saturday nights, for instance, the local hospital swelled with DUI victims. The town elders were concerned enough to create an organization called the Alliance for Teen Safety. It brought together all sectors of the town—parents, school personnel, members of the chamber of commerce, local political leaders, members of the police. The group came up with some ideas, but nothing really worked. That's when they invited me to visit.

I spent some time in the town, talked to various people, and then said to the Alliance, "Your efforts are laudatory. I just have one question: where are the kids? If your goal is to make the town more adolescent-friendly, then you have to include some teens." I went on to explain that if teens were included in the decision-making process, they'd feel valued and appreciated. And under these circumstances, they just might come up with some ideas for activities the town could sponsor on Saturday nights so that they wouldn't feel the need to get drunk and drive around. In other words, by excluding the voices of teens, the Concord town elders were ignoring a key resource.

To their great credit, Concord got it. I know they got it because they eventually changed the name of their organization to The Alliance: Youth and Adults Learning and Growing Together. It's not a sexy name. But it's the right name because its goal is a worthy one—that both teens and adults need to change and learn and grow together. The new Alliance welcomed teens as full partners. Through partnership they created teen ownership of the process. Key developmental assets were tapped: teens had the chance to interact with caring adults and with the town's institutions, and they had access to the community decision-making process. Indeed, they were an integral part of it. These assets proved the key to success.

Here's just one example of the change that took place. A significant bone of contention existed between local shop owners and teenagers who were using the main downtown shopping and historic area as a skateboard park. Their pyrotechnics, to say nothing of their reckless speed, scared shoppers away. Traffic and tourism were affected, and business owners and town officials grew concerned.

When Concord's adults and teens listened to each other, however, they were able to forge a solution. The town created an attractive state-of-the-art skateboard park in another part of town, which got the skateboarders out of pedestrian traffic. But that wasn't the only benefit. The teens who worked toward this solution felt recognized and welcomed in the community: they knew that they mattered and that their contribution was valued.

Transformations like this are happening all over the country. You can be part of it. Change often begins around the kitchen table or in the living room, and with small steps that don't feel very momentous at the time. Maybe you feel strongly that your local high school should create or revive its civics curriculum, which stresses the importance of being a good citizen. After all, when only 60 percent of those who were eligible to vote did so in the last presidential election—a turnout that was regarded as extraordinarily high—a resurgence in the teaching of civics and active citizenship could not be more warranted. Join with other parents in lobbying for the addition of such courses to the curriculum beginning in kindergarten and continuing through high school. Suggest ways to link learning to community service programs. If your teen is especially interested in this area, encourage her to pursue her studies in a college that has programs of this type, such as the Jonathan M. Tisch College of Citizenship and Public Service at Tufts University. This unique program, dedicated to promoting civic engagement, prepares undergraduates to become engaged citizens and community leaders with the goal of creating a more equitable, democratic world for all.

You can also search out and support many organizations and foundations that compose civil society and are working hard to foster positive development. One example is MENTOR (www.mentoring.org), an advocacy organization working to expand mentoring initiatives nationwide. By linking kids who need caring adult relationships with adults willing to give of their time and of themselves, this organization is enacting the Big Three on a societal scale. As the findings of my 4-H Study show, the presence of adult mentors in the community is the most important developmental asset associated with positive development.

CREATING CARING COMMUNITIES

The second prong of creating a national youth policy is to work toward the creation of caring communities. A caring community reaches out and finds ways to anticipate and support the needs and goals of its citizens. It offers its citizens seamless support as they pass from one stage of development to another. A key feature of a caring community is that no one has to ask for help; it's provided. That is, a menu of services and opportunities is already in place for all who need it.

A caring community, for example, might include:

· Parent, continuing education, and ESL classes
· Mental and medical health facilities
· Sports and recreation opportunities for all ages
· A council on aging
· A "healthy families" program (where teenage moms can be given training and support in child care and in understanding their newborn's development)

When programs such as these exist, people understand that they need each other to meet the challenges of daily life, of growing up and growing old. Creating caring communities is a priority for former vice president Al Gore. You've likely heard of his important initiatives on behalf of global climate change, but you may not have heard as much about his ongoing conference series to improve the capacity of communities to support families in their efforts to raise healthy and productive kids. Family Reunion, launched in 1992, has brought together academics, practitioners, philanthropists, politicians, advocates for children, and families—young people and their parents—to discuss ways in which all members of a community can marshal their skills and resources to help families ensure the optimal development of their children and launch them onto a path toward positive adulthood. Gore terms this approach "family-centered community building" and envisions it including child development and family education, parenting and other skill-building activities, and a range of different actions that enhance critical resources for families and that build relationships within and across the community.

In essence, the family-centered community-building approach would help parents attain the understanding and skills needed to promote the Five Cs with their teens. As well, this approach enables parents and teens to become asset builders in their communities so that all teens have a chance to develop positively and grow into healthy and productive citizens.

BUILDING A POSITIVE FUTURE FOR YOUR TEEN

The concept of family-centered community building leads me back to Tom Sawyer and Huckleberry Finn. Huck didn't have the benefit of a caring society or of a positive development perspective. All he had was Aunt Sally, Jim, and Tom Sawyer. When last we read of Huck, he is preparing to "light out for the Territory ahead of the rest," hoping that Aunt Sally doesn't find him and bring him back. He felt ready to take care of himself—to take on the world. We close the book on Huck and wish him well.

Fortunately, when it comes to our own teens, however, we can do much more than simply wish them well. As they grow and get ready to leave our homes for the next stage of their lives, we can provide them with the behavioral skills, values, and attitudes they need to face whatever is ahead. By joining hands and working together, by believing in their strengths and doing all we can to foster these strengths, we can send our teens off into adulthood ready to face the challenges.

It's a noble task, and it may feel daunting. By accepting this call to action, we're affirming that the destiny of our democracy, our aspirations for peace in our world, and our hopes for the very survival of our planet rest on the shoulders of our young people. But for now, these burdens rest on the shoulders of us, their parents. We have to create a society in which all our children will develop in positive ways. If we can make this happen, then my hopes for what our country can accomplish—and for our teens and the teens of the world—are boundless.

Selected Bibliography

1. WHAT WE CAN LEARN FROM TOM AND HUCK

Alberts, A. E., E. D. Christiansen, P. Chase, S. Naudeau, E. Phelps, and R. M. Lerner. 2006. Qualitative and quantitative assessments of thriving and contribution in early adolescence: Findings from the 4-H Study of Positive Youth Development. *Journal of Youth Development* 1(2), http://www.nae4ha.org/directory/jyd/jyd_article.aspx?id=8e826102-f555-4d37-8f5d-41074fd4487c.

Anderson, M. A., J. Kaufman, T. R. Simon, L. Barrios, L. Paulozzi, G. Ryan, et al. 2001. School-associated violent deaths in the United States, 1994–1999. *Journal of the American Medical Association* 286: 2695–702.

Anthony, E. J. 1969. The reactions of adults to adolescents and their behavior. In *Adolescence: Psychosocial perspectives,* ed. G. Caplan and S. Lebovici, 54–78. New York: Basic Books.

Benson, P. L. 2006. *All Kids Are Our Kids: What Communities Must Do to Raise Caring and Responsible Children and Adolescents,* 2nd ed. San Francisco: Jossey-Bass.

Benson, P. L., P. C. Scales, S. F. Hamilton, and A. Sesma Jr. 2006. Positive youth development: Theory, research and applications. In *Theoretical models of human development,* ed. R. M. Lerner, 894–941. Vol. 1 of *Handbook of Child Psychology,* 6th ed., ed. W. Damon and R. M. Lerner. Hoboken, NJ: Wiley.

Centers for Disease Control and Prevention. Youth Violence Fact Sheet, http://www.cdc.gov/ncipc/factsheets/yvfacts.htm.

Damon, W. 2004. What is positive youth development? *Annals of the American Academy of Political and Social Science* 591: 13–24.

Dryfoos, J. 1990. *Adolescents at risk: Prevalence and prevention.* New York: Oxford University Press.

Eccles, J. S., and J. Gootman, eds. 2002. *Community programs to promote youth development.* Washington, DC: National Academy Press.

Federal Interagency Forum on Child and Family Statistics. 2005. *America's children: Key national indicators of well-being, 2005.* Washington, DC: U.S. Government Printing Office.

Fox, M. A., B. A. Connolly, and T. D. Snyder. 2005. *Youth indicators 2005: Trends in the well-being of American youth.* NCES 2005-050. U.S. Department of Education, National Center for Education Statistics. Washington, DC: U.S. Government Printing Office.

Gestsdottir, S., and R. M. Lerner. 2007. Intentional self-regulation and positive youth development in early adolescence: Findings from the 4-H Study of Positive Youth Development. *Developmental Psychology* 43(2): 508–521.

Hall, G. S. 1904. *Adolescence.* New York: Appleton.

Institute for Applied Research in Youth Development Web site, http://ase.tufts.edu/iaryd.

Isaacson, W. 2003. *Benjamin Franklin: An American life.* New York: Simon & Schuster.

Jelicic, H., D. Bobek, E. Phelps, J. V. Lerner, and R. M. Lerner. 2007. Using positive youth development to predict contribution and risk behaviors in early adolescence: Findings from the first two waves of the 4-H Study of Positive Youth Development. *International Journal of Behavioral Development* 31(3): 263–273.

King, P. E., E. M. Dowling, R. A. Mueller, K. White, W. Schultz, P. Osborn, E. Dickerson, D. L. Bobek, R. M. Lerner, P. L. Benson, and P. C. Scales. 2005. Thriving in adolescence: The voices of youth-serving practitioners, parents, and early and late adolescents. *Journal of Early Adolescence* 25(1): 94–112.

Lerner, R. M. 2004. *Liberty: Thriving and civic engagement among America's youth.* Thousand Oaks, CA: Sage Publications.

———. 2005. Promoting positive youth development: Theoretical and empirical bases. Paper prepared for the Workshop on the Science of

Adolescent Health and Development, National Research Council/ Institute of Medicine. Washington, DC, September.

————. 2006. Developmental science, developmental systems, and contemporary theories of human development. In *Theoretical models of human development,* ed. R. M. Lerner, 1–17, Vol. 1 of *Handbook of Child Psychology,* 6th ed., ed. W. Damon and R. M. Lerner. Hoboken, NJ: Wiley.

Lerner, R. M., J. V. Lerner, J. Almerigi, C. Theokas, E. Phelps, S. Gestsdottir, S. Naudeau, H. Jelicic, A. E. Alberts, L. Ma, L. M. Smith, D. L. Bobek, D. Richman-Raphael, I. Simpson, E. D. Christiansen, and A. von Eye. 2005. Positive youth development, participation in community youth development programs, and community contributions of fifth grade adolescents: Findings from the first wave of the 4-H Study of Positive Youth Development. *Journal of Early Adolescence* 25 (1): 17–71.

Lucas, A. R., C. M. Beard, W. M. O'Fallon, and L. T. Kurland. 1991. 50-year trends in the incidence of anorexia nervosa in Rochester, MN: A population-based study. *American Journal of Psychiatry* 148 (7): 917–22.

Mishel, L., and J. Roy. 2006. Rethinking high school graduation rates and trends. Washington, DC: Economic Policy Institute.

Monitoring the Future. 2000. *National survey on drug use, 1975–2000.* Bethesda, MD: National Institute on Drug Abuse.

Nansel, T. R., M. Overpeck, R. S. Pilla, W. J. Ruan, B. Simons-Morton, and P. Scheidt. 2001. Bullying behaviors among US youth: Prevalence and association with psychosocial adjustment. *Journal of the American Medical Association* 285 (16): 2094–100.

Neumark-Sztainer, D., M. Story, P. J. Hannan, C. L. Perry, and L. M. Irving. 2002. Weight-related concerns and behaviors among overweight and non-overweight adolescents: Implications for preventing weight-related disorders. *Archives of Pediatrics and Adolescent Medicine* 156 (2): 171–78.

Perkins, D. F., and L. M. Borden. 2003. Positive behaviors, problem behaviors, and resiliency in adolescence. In *Handbook of psychology,* Vol. 6: *Developmental psychology,* ed. R. M. Lerner, M. A. Easterbrooks, and J. Mistry, 373–94. New York: Wiley.

Phelps, E., A. Balsano, K. Fay, J. Peltz, S. Zimmerman, R. M. Lerner, and J. V. Lerner. 2007. Nuances in early adolescent development trajectories of positive and of problematic/risk behaviors: Findings from the

4-H Study of Positive Youth Development. *Child and Adolescent Clinics of North America* 16 (2): 473–496.

Roth, J. L., and J. Brooks-Gunn. 2003. What exactly is a youth development program? Answers from research and practice. *Applied Developmental Science* 7: 94–111.

———. 2003. Youth development programs: Risk, prevention and policy. *Journal of Adolescent Health* 32 (3): 170–82.

Roth, J., J. Brooks-Gunn, L. Murray, and W. Foster. 1998. Promoting healthy adolescents: Synthesis of youth development program evaluations. *Journal of Research on Adolescence* 8: 423–59.

Silverman, R. J. A. 2005. Body size and image, female attitudes and perceptions about. In *Encyclopedia of applied developmental science,* ed. C. B. Fisher and R. M. Lerner, 155–60. Thousand Oaks, CA: Sage Publications.

———. 2005. Body size, societal views of. In *Encyclopedia of applied developmental science,* ed. C. B. Fisher and R. M. Lerner, 160–65. Thousand Oaks, CA: Sage Publications.

———. 2005. Body types, appraisals of. In *Encyclopedia of applied developmental science,* ed. C. B. Fisher and R. M. Lerner, 165–69. Thousand Oaks, CA: Sage Publications.

Taylor, C. S., R. M. Lerner, A. von Eye, A. B. Balsano, E. M. Dowling, P. M. Anderson, D. L. Bobek, and D. Bjelobrk. 2002. Individual and ecological assets and positive developmental trajectories among gang and community-based organization youth. In *Pathways to positive development among diverse youth,* ed. R. M. Lerner, C. S. Taylor, and A. von Eye, 57–72. Vol. 95 of *New directions for youth development: Theory, practice and research,* ed. G. Noam. San Francisco: Jossey-Bass.

———. 2002. Stability of attributes of positive functioning and of developmental assets among African American adolescent male gang and community-based organization members. In *Pathways to positive development among diverse youth,* ed. R. M. Lerner, C. S. Taylor, and A. von Eye, 35–56. Vol. 95 of *New directions for youth development: Theory, practice and research,* ed. G. Noam. San Francisco: Jossey-Bass.

Taylor, C. S., R. M. Lerner, A. von Eye, D. Bobek, A. B. Balsano, E. Dowling, and P. Anderson. 2003. Positive individual and social behavior among gang and non-gang African American male adolescents. *Journal of Adolescent Research* 18 (6): 547–74.

———. 2004. Internal and external developmental assets among African American male gang members. *Journal of Adolescent Research* 19 (3): 303–22.

Taylor, C. S., P. Smith, V. A. Taylor, A. von Eye, R. M. Lerner, A. Balsano, P. M. Anderson, R. Banik, and J. Almerigi. 2005. Individual and ecological assets and thriving among African American adolescent male gang and community-based organization members: A report from Wave 3 of the "Overcoming the Odds" study. *Journal of Early Adolescence* 25 (1): 72–93.

Theokas, C., J. Almerigi, R. M. Lerner, E. M. Dowling, P. L. Benson, P. C. Scales, and A. von Eye. 2005. Conceptualizing and modeling individual and ecological asset components of thriving in early adolescence. *Journal of Early Adolescence* 25 (1): 113–43.

Theokas, C., and R. M. Lerner. 2006. Observed ecological assets in families, schools, and neighborhoods: Conceptualization, measurement and relations with positive and negative developmental outcomes. *Applied Developmental Science* 10 (2): 61–74.

Twain, M. 1876. *The adventures of Tom Sawyer.*

———. 1885. *The adventures of Huckleberry Finn.*

Yax, L. K. 1999. *Resident population estimates of the United States by age group and sex: April 1, 1990 to October 1, 1999.* Washington, DC: U.S. Census Bureau, Population Estimates Program, Population Division.

2. PROMOTING POSITIVE DEVELOPMENT: FROM THEORY TO PRACTICE

Bandura, A. 1964. The stormy decade: Fact or fiction? *Psychology in the School* 1: 224–31.

Baumrind, D. 1971. Current patterns of parental authority. *Developmental Psychology Monographs* 4 (1, pt. 2).

Benson, P. L. 2003. Developmental assets and asset-building community: Conceptual and empirical foundations. In *Developmental assets and asset-building communities: Implications for research, policy, and practice,* ed. R. M. Lerner and P. L. Benson, 19–43. New York: Kluwer Academic/ Plenum.

Benson, P. L., P. C. Scales, S. F. Hamilton, and A. Sesma Jr. 2006. Positive youth development: Theory, research and applications. In *Theoretical models of human development,* ed. R. M. Lerner, 894–941. Vol. 1 of *Handbook of Child Psychology,* 6th ed., ed. W. Damon and R. M. Lerner. Hoboken, NJ: Wiley.

Block, J. 1971. *Living through time.* Berkeley: Bancroft Books.

Brooks-Gunn, J. 1986. The relationship of maternal beliefs about sex typing to maternal and young children's behavior. *Sex Roles* 14: 21–35.

Chess, S., and A. Thomas. 1999. *Goodness of fit: Clinical applications from infancy through adult life.* Philadelphia: Brunner/Mazel.

deVries, M. W. 1984. Temperament and infant mortality among the Masai of East Africa. *American Journal of Psychiatry* 141: 1189–94.

Douvan, J. D., and J. Adelson. 1966. *The adolescent experience.* New York: Wiley.

Erikson, E. H. 1959. Identity and the life-cycle. *Psychological Issues* 1: 18–164.

———. 1968. *Identity, youth and crisis.* New York: Norton.

Freud, A. M. 1969. Adolescence as a developmental disturbance. In *Adolescence,* ed. G. Caplan and S. Lebovici, 5–10. New York: Basic Books.

Freud, S. 1954. *Collected Works.* London: Hogarth.

Gestsdottir, S., and R. M. Lerner. 2007. Intentional self-regulation and positive youth development in early adolescence: Findings from the 4-H Study of Positive Youth Development. *Developmental Psychology* 43(2), 508–521.

Gottlieb, G. 1997. *Synthesizing nature-nurture: Prenatal roots of instinctive behavior.* Mahwah, NJ: Erlbaum.

———. 2004. Normally occurring environmental and behavioral influences on gene activity: From central dogma to probabilistic epigenesis. In *Nature and nurture: The complex interplay of genetic and environmental influences on human behavior and development,* ed. C. G. Coll, E. L. Bearer, and R. M. Lerner, 85–106. Mahwah, NJ: Erlbaum.

Gottlieb, G., D. Wahlsten, and R. Lickliter. 2006. The significance of biology for human development: A developmental psychobiological systems view. In *Theoretical models of human development,* ed. R. M. Lerner, 210–57. Vol. 1 of *Handbook of Child Psychology,* 6th ed., ed. W. Damon and R. M. Lerner. Hoboken, NJ: Wiley.

Hall, G. S. 1904. *Adolescence.* New York: Appleton.

Hebb, D. O. 1949. *The organization of behavior.* New York: Wiley.

International Youth Foundation Web site, http://www.iyfnet.org.

Jelicic, H., D. Bobek, E. Phelps, J. V. Lerner, and R. M. Lerner. 2007. Using positive youth development to predict contribution and risk behaviors in early adolescence: Findings from the first two waves of the 4-H Study of Positive Youth Development. *International Journal of Behavioral Development* 31(3): 263–273.

Lerner, R. M. 1984. *On the nature of human plasticity.* New York: Cambridge University Press.

———. 1995. *America's youth in crisis: Challenges and options for programs and policies.* Thousand Oaks, CA: Sage Publications.

———. 2000. And a child shall lead you. *Kappa Omicron Nu Forum* 12 (1), http://www.kon.org/forum/12–1/vol12.html.

———. 2002. *Concepts and theories of human development,* 3rd ed. Mahwah, NJ: Lawrence Erlbaum Associates.

———. 2002. Multigenesis: Levels of professional integration in the life-span of a developmental scientist. In *Conceptions of development: Lessons from the laboratory,* ed. R. Lickliter and D. J. Lewkowicz, 313–37. New York: Psychology Press.

———. 2004. Innovative methods for studying lives in context: A view of the issues. *Research in Human Development* 1(1–2): 5–7.

———. 2004. *Liberty: Thriving and civic engagement among America's youth.* Thousand Oaks, CA: Sage Publications.

———. 2005. Promoting positive youth development: Theoretical and empirical bases. Paper prepared for the Workshop on the Science of Adolescent Health and Development, National Research Council/Institute of Medicine, Washington, DC, September.

Lerner, R. M., and S. J. Korn. 1972. The development of body build stereotypes in males. *Child Development* 43: 912–20.

Lerner, R. M., J. V. Lerner, J. Almerigi, C. Theokas, E. Phelps, S. Gestsdottir, S. Naudeau, H. Jelicic, A. E. Alberts, L. Ma, L. M. Smith, D. L. Bobek, D. Richman-Raphael, I. Simpson, E. D. Christiansen, and A. von Eye. 2005. Positive youth development, participation in community youth development programs, and community contributions of fifth grade adolescents: Findings from the first wave of the 4-H Study of Positive Youth Development. *Journal of Early Adolescence* 25 (1): 17–71.

Lerner, R. M., J. V. Lerner, J. Almerigi, C. Theokas, E. Phelps, S. Naudeau, S. Gestsdottir, L. Ma, H. Jelicic, A. Alberts, L. Smith, I. Simpson, E. Christiansen, D. Warren, and A. Von Eye. 2006. Toward a new vision and vocabulary about adolescence: Theoretical and empirical bases of a "positive youth development" perspective. In *Child Psychology: A handbook of contemporary issues,* ed. L. Balter and C. S. Tamis-LeMonda, 445–69. New York: Psychology Press/Taylor and Francis.

Lerner, R. M., and G. B. Spanier, eds. 1978. *Child influences on marital and family interaction: A life span perspective.* New York: Academic Press.

———. 1980. *Adolescent development: A life-span perspective.* New York: McGraw-Hill.

Lerner, R. M., and L. Steinberg. 2004. The scientific study of adolescent development: Past, present, and future. In *Handbook of Adolescent Psychology,* ed. R. M. Lerner and L. Steinberg, 1–12. New York: Wiley.

Lewis, M., and L. A. Rosenblum, eds. 1974. *The effect of the infant on its caregiver.* New York: Wiley.

Linn, M. C. 1991. Scientific reasoning, adolescent. In *Encyclopedia of adolescence,* ed. R. M. Lerner, A. C. Petersen, and J. Brooks-Gunn, 2:981–86. New York: Garland.

Little, R. R. 1993. What's working for today's youth: The issues, the programs, and the learnings. Paper presented at the Institute for Children, Youth, and Families Fellows' Colloquium, Michigan State University, East Lansing.

Magnusson, D., and H. Stattin. 1998. Person context interaction theories. In *Theoretical models of human development,* ed. R. M. Lerner, 685–759. Vol. 1 of *Handbook of Child Psychology,* 5th ed., ed. W. Damon. Hoboken, NJ: Wiley.

Offer, D. 1969. *The psychological world of the teen-ager.* New York: Basic Books.

Overton, W. F. 2006. Developmental psychology: Philosophy, concepts, methodology. In *Theoretical models of human development,* ed. R. M. Lerner, 18–88. Vol. 1 of *Handbook of Child Psychology,* 6th ed., ed. W. Damon and R. M. Lerner. Hoboken, NJ: Wiley.

Phelps, E., A. Balsano, K. Fay, J. Peltz, S. Zimmerman, R. M. Lerner, and J. V. Lerner. In press. Nuances in early adolescent development trajectories of positive and of problematic/risk behaviors: Findings from the 4-H Study of Positive Youth Development. *Child and Adolescent Clinics of North America.*

Piaget, J. 1960. *The child's conception of the world.* Paterson, NJ: Littlefield, Adams.

———. 1970. Piaget's theory. In *Carmichael's Manual of Child Psychology,* ed. P. H. Mussen, 703–732. New York: Wiley.

———. 1972. Intellectual evolution from adolescence to adulthood. *Human Development* 15: 1–12.

Pittman, K., M. Irby, and T. Ferber. 2001. Unfinished business: Further reflections on a decade of promoting youth development. In *Trends in youth development: Visions, realities and challenges,* ed. P. L. Benson and K. J. Pittman, 4–50. Norwell, MA: Kluwer.

Schneirla, T. C. 1956. Interrelationships of the innate and the acquired in instinctive behavior. In *L'instinct dans le comportement des animaux et de l'homme,* ed. P. P. Grassé. Paris: Mason.

———. 1957. The concept of development in comparative psychology. In *The concept of development,* ed. D. B. Harris, 78–108. Minneapolis: University of Minnesota Press.

Steinberg, L. 2004. *The ten basic principles of good parenting.* New York: Simon & Schuster.

———. 2005. *Adolescence,* 7th ed. New York: McGraw-Hill.

Steinberg, L., N. S. Mounts, S. D. Lamborn, and S. M. Dornsbusch. 1991. Authoritative parenting and adolescent adjustment across varied ecological niches. *Journal of Research on Adolescence* 1 (1): 19–36.

Taylor, C. 2003. Youth gangs and community violence. In *Handbook of applied developmental science,* vol. 2: *Enhancing the life chances of youth and families: Contributions of programs, policies, and service systems,* eds. R. M. Lerner, F. Jacobs, and D. Wertlieb, 65–80. Thousand Oaks, CA: Sage Publications.

Taylor, C. S., R. M. Lerner, A. von Eye, A. B. Balsano, E. M. Dowling, P. M. Anderson, D. L. Bobek, and D. Bjelobrk. 2002. Stability of attributes of positive functioning and of developmental assets among African American adolescent male gang and community-based organization members. In *Pathways to positive development among diverse youth,* ed. R. M. Lerner, C. S. Taylor, and A. von Eye, 35–56. Vol. 95 of *New directions for youth development: Theory, practice and research,* ed. G. Noam. San Francisco: Jossey-Bass.

———. 2002. Individual and ecological assets and positive developmental trajectories among gang and community-based organization youth. In *Pathways to positive development among diverse youth,* ed. R. M. Lerner, C. S. Taylor, and A. von Eye, 57–72. Vol. 95 of *New directions for youth development: Theory, practice and research,* ed. G. Noam. San Francisco: Jossey-Bass.

Taylor, C. S., R. M. Lerner, A. von Eye, D. Bobek, A. B. Balsano, E. Dowling, and P. Anderson. 2003. Positive individual and social behavior among gang and non-gang African American male adolescents. *Journal of Adolescent Research* 18 (6): 547–74.

————. 2004. Internal and external developmental assets among African American male gang members. *Journal of Adolescent Research* 19 (3): 303–22.

Taylor, C. S., P. Smith, V. A. Taylor, A. von Eye, R. M. Lerner, A. Balsano, P. M. Anderson, R. Banik, and J. Almerigi. 2005. Individual and ecological assets and thriving among African American adolescent male gang and community-based organization members: A report from Wave 3 of the "Overcoming the Odds" study. *Journal of Early Adolescence* 25 (1): 72–93.

Theokas, C., and R. M. Lerner. 2006. Observed ecological assets in families, schools, and neighborhoods: Conceptualization, measurement and relations with positive and negative developmental outcomes. *Applied Developmental Science* 10 (2): 61–74.

Thomas, A., and S. Chess. 1977. *Temperament and development.* New York: Brunner/Mazel.

Thomas, A., S. Chess, and H. G. Brich. 1970. The origin of personality. *Scientific American* 223: 102–9.

Thomas, A., S. Chess, H. G. Brich, M. E. Hertzip, and S. Korn. 1963. *Behavioral individuality in early childhood.* New York: New York University Press.

Tobach, E., and T. C. Schneira. 1968. The biopsychology of social behavior of animals. In *Biologic basis of pediatric practice,* ed. R. E. Cooke and S. Levin, 68–82. New York: McGraw-Hill.

3. COMPETENCE

Brooks-Gunn, J. 1987. Pubertal processes in girls' psychological adaptation. In *Biological-psychosocial interactions in early adolescence: A life-span perspective,* eds. R. M. Lerner and T. T. Foch, 123–53. Hillsdale, NJ: Erlbaum.

————. 1989. Pubertal processes and the early adolescent transition. In *Child development today and tomorrow,* ed. W. Damon, 155–76. Jossey-Bass social and behavioral science series. San Francisco: Jossey-Bass.

Brooks-Gunn, J., and A. C. Petersen. 1983. *Girls at puberty: Biological and psychosocial perspectives.* New York: Plenum.

Eccles, J. S. 2004. Schools, academic motivation, and stage-environment fit. In *Handbook of Adolescent Psychology,* 2nd ed., ed. R. M. Lerner and L. Steinberg, 125–53. Hoboken, NJ: Wiley.

Floyd, D. T., Jr., and L. McKenna. 2003. National youth organizations in the United States. In *Handbook of applied developmental science*, Vol. 3: *Promoting positive youth and family development: Community systems, citizenship, and civil society*, eds. D. Wertlieb, F. Jacobs, and R. M. Lerner, 11–26. Thousand Oaks, CA: Sage Publications.

Gardner, H. E. 1998. Extraordinary cognitive achievements (ECA): A symbol systems approach. In *Theoretical models of human development*, ed. R. M. Lerner, 415–66. Vol. 1 of *Handbook of Child Psychology*, 5th ed., ed. W. Damon. New York: Wiley.

Gottfried, A. E., J. S. Fleming, and A. W. Gottfried. 2001. Continuity of academic intrinsic motivation from childhood through late adolescence: A longitudinal study. *Journal of Educational Psychology* 93 (1): 3–13.

Lerner, R. M. 2004. *Liberty: Thriving and civic engagement among America's youth*. Thousand Oaks, CA: Sage Publications.

Winner, E. 2006. Development in the arts: Drawing and music. In *Cognition, perception, and language*, ed. D. Kuhn and R. S. Siegler, 859–904. Vol. 2 of *Handbook of Child Psychology*, 6th ed., ed. W. Damon and R. M. Lerner. Hoboken, NJ: Wiley.

Winner, W. 1996. *Gifted children: Myths and reality*. New York: Basic Books.

4. CONFIDENCE

Bandura, A. 1964. The stormy decade: Fact or fiction? *Psychology in the School* 1: 224–31.

———. 1965. Influence of models' reinforcement contingencies on the acquisition of imitative responses. *Journal of Personality and Social Psychology* 1: 589–95.

———. 1977. *Social learning theory*. Englewood Cliffs, N.J.: Prentice-Hall.

———. 1978. The self system in reciprocal determinism. *American Psychologist* 33: 344–58.

———. 1986. *Social foundations of thought and action: A social cognitive theory*. Englewood Cliffs, NJ: Prentice-Hall.

Bandura, A., and Schunk, D. H. 1981. Cultivating competence, self-efficacy, and intrinsic interest through proximal self-motivation. *Journal of Personality and Social Psychology* 41 (3): 586–98.

Bhanot, R., and Jovanovic, J. 2005. Do parents' academic gender stereotypes influence whether they intrude on their children's homework? *Sex Roles* 52 (9–10): 597–607.

Block, J. H. 1973. Conceptions of sex-roles: Some cross-cultural and longitudinal perspectives. *American Psychologist* 28: 512–25.

Bronfenbrenner, U. 2001. The bioecological theory of human development. In *International encyclopedia of the social and behavioral science,* ed. N. J. Smelser and P. B. Baltes, 6963–70. Oxford: Elsevier.

———. 2005. *Making human beings human.* Thousand Oaks, CA: Sage Publications.

Bronfenbrenner, U., and P. A. Morris. 2006. The bioecological model of human development. In *Theoretical models of human development,* ed. R. M. Lerner, 793–828. Vol. 1 of *Handbook of Child Psychology,* 6th ed., ed. W. Damon and R. M. Lerner. Hoboken, NJ: Wiley.

Broverman, I. K., S. R. Vogel, D. M. Broverman, F. E. Clarkson, and P. S. Rosenkrantz. 1972. Sex-role stereotypes: A current appraisal. *Journal of Social Issues* 28: 59–78.

Eccles, J. S. 2004. Schools, academic motivation, and stage-environment fit. In *Handbook of Adolescent Psychology,* 2nd ed., ed. R. M. Lerner and L .Steinberg, 125-153. Hoboken, NJ: Wiley.

Eccles, J. S., A. Wigfield, and U. Schiefele. 1998. Motivation to succeed. In *Social, emotional, and personality development,* ed. N. Eisenberg, 553–617. Vol. 3 of *Handbook of child psychology,* 5th ed., ed. W. Damon. New York: Wiley.

Elkind, D. 1967. Egocentrism in adolescence. *Child Development* 38: 1025–34.

Galambos. N. 2004. Gender and gender role development in adolescence. In *Handbook of Adolescent Psychology,* eds. R. M. Lerner and L. Steinberg, 233–62. New York: Wiley.

Gilligan, C. 1982. *In a different voice: Psychological theory and women's development.* Cambridge, MA: Harvard University Press.

Harter, S. 1983. Developmental perspectives on the self-system. In *Social and personality development,* ed. E. M. Hetherington, 275–385. Vol. 4 of *Handbook of child psychology,* 4th ed., ed. P. H. Mussen. New York: Wiley.

———. 2006. The self. In *Social, emotional, and personality development,* ed. N. Eisenberg 505–70. Vol. 3 of *Handbook of child psychology,* 6th ed., ed. W. Damon and R. M. Lerner. Hoboken, NJ: Wiley.

Kahn, R., and T. Antonucci. 1980. Convoys over the life course: attachment, roles and social support. In *Life-span development and behaviour,* vol. 3, ed. P. B. Baltes and O. Brim. New York: Academic Press.

Lenerz, K., J. S. Kucher, P. L. East, J. V. Lerner, and R. M. Lerner. 1987. Early adolescents' organismic physical characteristics and psychosocial functioning: Findings from the Pennsylvania Early Adolescent Transitions Study (PEATS). In *Biological-psychosocial interactions in early adolescence,* eds. R. M. Lerner, T. T. Foch, 225–47. Hillsdale, NJ: Erlbaum.

Lerner, R. M. 1982. Children and adolescents as producers of their own development. *Developmental Review* 2: 342–70.

Lerner, R. M., and N. A. Busch-Rossnagel. 1981. Individuals as producers of their development: Conceptual and empirical bases. In *Individuals as producers of their development: A life-span perspective,* eds. R. M. Lerner and N. A. Busch-Rossnagel, 1–36. New York: Academic Press.

Lerner, R. M., and S. A. Karabenick. 1974. Physical attractiveness, body attitudes, and self-concept in late adolescents. *Journal of Youth and Adolescence* 3: 307–16.

Lerner, R. M., S. A. Karabenick, and J. L. Stuart. 1973. Relations among physical attractiveness, body attitudes, and self-concept in male and female college students. *Journal of Psychology* 85: 119–29.

Lerner, R. M., and L. Steinberg, eds. 2004. *Handbook of adolescent psychology.* New York: Wiley.

Lerner, R. M., and T. Walls. 1999. Revisiting individuals as producers of their development: From dynamic interactionism to developmental systems. In *Action and self-development: Theory and research through the life-span,* eds. J. Brandtstädter and R. M. Lerner, 3–36. Thousand Oaks, CA: Sage.

Masten, A. S. 2001. Ordinary magic: Resilience processes in development. *American Psychologist* 56: 227–38.

———. 2004. Regulatory processes, risk and resilience in adolescent development. *Annals of the New York Academy of Sciences* 1021: 310–19.

Masten, A. S., and J. Obradovic. 2006. Competence and resilience in development. *Annals of the New York Academy of Sciences* 1094: 1–12.

Pipher, M. 1994. *Reviving Ophelia.* New York: Ballantine Books.

Premack, D. "David Premack." http://www.psych.upenn.edu/-premack/About.html.

Rhodes, J. E. 2002. *Stand by me: Risks and rewards in youth mentoring.* Cambridge, MA: Harvard University Press.

Schunk, D. H. 1981. Modeling and attributional effects on children's achievement: A self-efficacy analysis. *Journal of Educational Psychology* 73 (1): 93–105.

Schunk, D. H., and A. R. Hanson. 1989. Self-modeling and children's cognitive skill learning. *Journal of Educational Psychology* 81(2): 155–63.

Silverman, R. J. A. 2005. Body size and image, female attitudes and perceptions about. In *Encyclopedia of applied developmental science,* ed. C. B. Fisher and R. M. Lerner, 155–60. Thousand Oaks, CA: Sage Publications.

———. 2005. Body size, societal views of. In *Encyclopedia of applied developmental science,* ed. C. B. Fisher and R. M. Lerner, 160–65. Thousand Oaks, CA: Sage Publications.

———. 2005. Body types, appraisals of. In *Encyclopedia of applied developmental science,* ed. C. B. Fisher and R. M. Lerner, 165–69. Thousand Oaks, CA: Sage Publications.

Simmons, R. G., and D. A. Blyth. 1987. *Moving into adolescence: The impact of pubertal change and school context.* Hawthorne, NJ: Aldine.

Simmons, R. G., S. L. Carlton-Ford, and D. A. Blyth. 1987. Predicting how a child will cope with the transition to junior high school. In *Biological-psychosocial interactions in early adolescence,* eds. R. M. Lerner and T. T. Foch, 325–75. Hillsdale, NJ: Erlbaum.

Wigfield, A., J. S. Eccles, U. Schiefele, R. Roeser, and P. Davis-Kean. 2006. Development and achievement motivation. In *Social, emotional, and personality development,* ed. N. Eisenberg, 933–1002. Vol. 3 of *Handbook of child psychology,* 6th ed., ed. W. Damon and R. M. Lerner. Hoboken, NJ: Wiley.

5. CONNECTION

Baumrind, D. 1967. Child care practices anteceding three patterns of the preschool behavior. *Genetic Psychology Monographs* 75: 43–88.

———. 1971. Current patterns of parental authority. *Developmental Psychology Monographs* 4 (1, pt. 2).

———. 1991. The influence of parenting style on adolescent competence and substance use. *Journal of Early Adolescence* 11 (1): 56–95.

Benson, P. L. 2006. *All Kids Are Our Kids: What Communities Must Do to Raise Caring and Responsible Children and Adolescents,* 2nd ed. San Francisco: Jossey-Bass.

Brown, B. B. 2004. Adolescents' relationships with peers. In *Handbook of Adolescent Psychology,* eds. R. M. Lerner, and L. Steinberg, 363–94. New York: Wiley.

Colby, A. 1978. Evolution of a moral-development theory *New Directions for Child Development* 2: 89–104.

————. 1979. Presentation at the Center for Advanced Study in the Behavioral Sciences Summer Institute, July, "Morality and moral development."

————. 1987. Foreword. In *Multiple paths of midlife development,* ed. M. E. Lachman and J. B. James. Chicago: University of Chicago Press.

Damon, W. 1990. *The moral child: Nurturing children's natural moral growth.* New York: Free Press.

Douvan, J. D., and J. Adelson. 1966. *The adolescent experience.* New York: Wiley.

Eisenberg, N. 2006. Introduction. In *Social, emotional, and personality development,* ed. N. Eisenberg, 1–23. Vol. 3 of *Handbook of child psychology,* 6th ed., ed. W. Damon and R. M. Lerner. Hoboken, NJ: Wiley.

Hansen, C. "Dangerous Web," *Dateline NBC,* November 2004.

Hetherington, E. M. 1979. Divorce: a child's perspective. *American Psychologist* 37, 851–858.

Kohlberg, L. 1958. The development of modes of moral thinking and choice in the years ten to sixteen. Doctoral dissertation, University of Chicago.

————. 1963. The development of children's orientations toward a moral order: Sequence in the development of moral thought. *Vita Humana* 6: 11–33.

————. 1963. Moral development and identification. In *Child psychology: 62nd yearbook of the national society of education,* ed. H. Stevenson. Chicago: University of Chicago Press.

————. 1968. Early education: A cognitive-developmental view. *Child Development* 39: 1014–62.

————. 1971. From is to ought: How to commit the naturalistic fallacy and get away with it in the study of moral development. In *Cognitive development and epistemology,* ed. T. Mischel. New York: Academic Press.

————. 1973. Continuities in childhood and adult moral development revisited. In *Life-span development psychology: Personality and socialization,* eds. P. B. Baltes and K. W. Schaie. New York: Academic Press.

————. 1976. Moral stages and moralization: The cognitive developmental approach. In *Moral development and behavior: Theory, research, and social issues,* ed. T. Luckona. New York: Holt, Rinehart, and Winston.

———. 1978. Revisions in the theory and practice of moral development. *New Directions for Child Development* 2: 93–120.

Kübler-Ross, E. 1969. *On Death and Dying.* New York: Simon & Schuster.

Larson, R. W. 1997. The emergence of solitude as a constructive domain of experience in early adolescence. *Child Development* 68 (1): 80–93.

Lerner, R. M., E. M. Dowling, and P. M. Anderson. 2003. Positive youth development: Thriving as a basis of personhood and civil society. *Applied Developmental Science* 7 (3): 172–80.

Lewis, M. 1992. *Shame: The exposed self.* New York: Free Press.

Steinberg, L. 2004. *The ten basic principles of good parenting.* New York: Simon & Schuster.

———. 2005. *Adolescence.* 7th ed. New York: McGraw-Hill.

Steinberg, L., N. S. Mounts, S. D. Lamborn, and S. M. Dornbusch. 1991. Authoritative parenting and adolescent adjustment across varied ecological niches. *Journal of Research on Adolescence* 1 (1): 19–36.

Turiel, E. 2006. The development of morality. In *Social, emotional, and personality development,* ed. N. Eisenberg, 789–857. Vol. 3 of *Handbook of child psychology,* 6th ed., ed. W. Damon and R. M. Lerner. Hoboken, NJ: Wiley.

6. CHARACTER

Adelson, J. 1970. What generation gap? *New York Times Magazine,* January 18, 10–45.

Benson, P. L. 2003. Developmental assets and asset-building community: Conceptual and empirical foundations. In *Developmental assets and asset-building communities: Implications for research, policy, and practice,* ed. R. M. Lerner and P. L. Benson, 19–43. New York: Kluwer Academic/ Plenum.

———. 2006. *All Kids Are Our Kids: What Communities Must Do to Raise Caring and Responsible Children and Adolescents,* 2nd ed. San Francisco: Jossey-Bass.

Brown, B. B. 2004. Adolescents' relationships with peers. In *Handbook of Adolescent Psychology,* eds. R. M. Lerner, and L. Steinberg, 363–94. New York: Wiley.

Chess, S., and A. Thomas. 1999. *Goodness of fit: Clinical applications from infancy through adult life.* Philadelphia: Brunner/Mazel.

Damon, W. 1997. *The youth charter: How communities can work together to raise standards for all our children.* New York: Free Press.

———. 2004. What is positive youth development? *Annals of the American Academy of Political and Social Science* 591: 13–24.

Douvan, J. D., and J. Adelson. 1966. *The adolescent experience*. New York: Wiley.

Gardner, H., M. Csikszentmihalyi, and W. Damon. 2001. *Good work: When excellence and ethics meet*. New York: Basic Books.

Gould, S. J. 1977. *Ontogeny and phylogeny*. Cambridge, MA: Harvard University Press.

Greenberger, E., and L. D. Steinberg. 1986. *When teenagers work: The psychological and social costs of adolescent employment*. New York: Basic Books.

Lerner, R. M. 2002. Multigenesis: Levels of professional integration in the life-span of a developmental scientist. In *Conceptions of development: Lessons from the laboratory*, ed. R. Lickliter and D. J. Lewkowicz, 313–37. New York: Psychology Press.

———. 2004. *Liberty: Thriving and civic engagement among America's youth*. Thousand Oaks, CA: Sage Publications.

Lerner, R. M., J. Pendorf, and A. Emery. 1971. Attitudes of adolescents and adults toward contemporary issues. *Psychological Reports* 28: 139–45.

Lerner, R. M., C. Schroeder, M. Rewitzer, and A. Weinstock. 1972. Attitudes of high school students and their parents toward contemporary issues. *Psychological Reports* 31: 255–58.

Lerner, R. M., and A. Weinstock, A. 1972. Note on the generation gap. *Psychological Reports* 31: 457–58.

Lewis, M. 1987. Social development in infancy and early childhood. In *Handbook of infancy*, ed. J. D. Osofsky, 419–93. New York: Wiley.

Lewontin, R. C. 2000. *The triple helix*. Cambridge, MA: Harvard University Press.

Lewontin, R. C., and R. Levins. 1978. Evolution. *Encyclopedia Einaudi*, Vol. 5. Turin: Einaudi.

Marcia, J. 1964. Determination and construct validity of ego identity status. Doctoral dissertation, Ohio State University.

———. 1966. Development and validations of ego-identity status. *Journal of Personality and Social Psychology* 5: 551–58.

———. 1991. Identity and self-development. In *Encyclopedia of adolescence*, eds. R. M. Lerner, A. C. Petersen, and J. Brooks-Gunn, 529–33. New York: Garland.

———. 1980. Identity in adolescence. In *Handbook of adolescent psychology,* ed. J. Adelson, 000–000. New York: Wiley.

Mumola, C. J. 2000. Incarcerated parents and their children. *Bureau of Justice Statistics Special Report,* U.S. Department of Justice, Washington, DC.

National 4-H Council Web site. http://www.fourhcouncil.edu.

National Center on Addiction and Substance Abuse Web site. http://www.casacolumbia.org/absolutenm/templates/Home.aspx?articleid=287&zoneid=32.

Premack, D. "David Premack." http://www.psych.upenn.edu/-premack/About.html.

Rawls, J. 1971. *A Theory of Justice.* Harvard University Press.

Rhodes, J. E. 2002. *Stand by me: Risks and rewards in youth mentoring.* Cambridge, MA: Harvard University Press.

Steinberg, L. 2004. *The ten basic principles of good parenting.* New York: Simon & Schuster.

———. 2005. *Adolescence.* 7th ed. New York: McGraw-Hill.

Steinberg, L., N. S. Mounts, S. D. Lamborn, and S. M. Dornsbusch. 1991. Authoritative parenting and adolescent adjustment across varied ecological niches. *Journal of Research on Adolescence* 1 (1): 19–36.

Theokas, C., and R. M. Lerner. 2006. Observed ecological assets in families, schools, and neighborhoods: Conceptualization, measurement and relations with positive and negative developmental outcomes. *Applied Developmental Science* 10 (2): 61–74.

Thomas, A., and S. Chess. 1977. *Temperament and development.* New York: Brunner/Mazel.

Thomas, A., S. Chess, and H. G. Brich. 1970. The origin of personality. *Scientific American* 223: 102–9.

Thomas, A., S. Chess, H. G. Brich, M. E. Hertzip, and S. Korn. 1963. *Behavioral individuality in early childhood.* New York: New York University Press.

Tobach, E., and T. C. Schneira. 1968. The biopsychology of social behavior of animals. In *Biologic basis of pediatric practice,* ed. R. E. Cooke and S. Levin, 68–82. New York: McGraw-Hill.

Weinstock, A., and R. M. Lerner. 1972. Attitudes of late adolescents and their parents toward contemporary issues. *Psychological Reports* 30: 239–44.

7. CARING

Block, J. H. 1973. Conceptions of sex role: Some cross-cultural and longitudinal perspectives. *American Psychologist* 28: 518–29.

Broverman, I. K., S. R. Vogel, D. M. Broverman, F. E. Clarkson, and P. S. Rosenkrantz. 1972. Sex-role stereotypes: A current appraisal. *Journal of Social Issues* 28: 59–78.

Damon, W. 1990. *The moral child: Nurturing children's natural moral growth.* New York: Free Press.

Eisenberg, N. 2006. Introduction. In *Social, emotional, and personality development,* ed. N. Eisenberg, 1–23. Vol. 3 of *Handbook of child psychology,* 6th ed., ed. W. Damon and R. M. Lerner. Hoboken, NJ: Wiley.

Galambos, N. 2004. Gender and gender role development in adolescence. In *Handbook of Adolescent Psychology,* ed. R. M. Lerner and L. Steinberg, 233–62. New York: Wiley.

Kutcher, S. 2006, March 19. Adoptions, the church and children [Letter to the editor]. *The Boston Globe,* p. C10.

Lee, H. 1960. *To kill a mockingbird.* New York: HarperCollins.

Saarni, C., J. J. Campos, L. A. Camras, and D. Witherington. 2006. Emotional development: Action, communication, and understanding. In *Social, emotional, and personality development,* ed. N. Eisenberg, 226–99. Vol. 3 of *Handbook of child psychology,* 6th ed., ed. W. Damon and R. M. Lerner. Hoboken, NJ: Wiley.

Theokas, C., and R. M. Lerner. 2006. Observed ecological assets in families, schools, and neighborhoods: Conceptualization, measurement and relations with positive and negative developmental outcomes. *Applied Developmental Science* 10 (2): 61–74.

8. CONTRIBUTION

Applebome, P. 2006. "When saving lives is more than child's play." *New York Times,* June 25.

Common Cents Web site, https://www.commoncents.org.

Gestsdottir, S., and R. M. Lerner. In press. Intentional self-regulation and positive youth development in early adolescence: Findings from the 4-H Study of Positive Youth Development. *Developmental Psychology.*

Global Youth Action Network Web site, http://www.youthlink.org/gyanv5/programsother.htm.

Global Youth Service Day Web site, http://www.ysa.org/nysd.

Jelicic, H., D. Bobek, E. Phelps, J. V. Lerner, and R. M. Lerner. 2007. Using positive youth development to predict contribution and risk behaviors in early adolescence: Findings from the first two waves of the 4-H Study of Positive Youth Development. *International Journal of Behavioral Development* 31 (3): 263–273.

King, P. E., E. M. Dowling, R. A. Mueller, K. White, W. Schultz, P. Osborn, E. Dickerson, D. L. Bobek, R. M. Lerner, P. L. Benson, and P. C. Scales. 2005. Thriving in adolescence: The voices of youth-serving practitioners, parents, and early and late adolescents. *Journal of Early Adolescence* 25 (1): 94-112.

Kingdom of Heaven. 2005. DVD. Directed by Ridley Scott. Los Angeles: 20th Century Fox.

Lerner, R. M. 2004. *Liberty: Thriving and civic engagement among America's youth.* Thousand Oaks, CA: Sage Publications.

Lerner, R. M., J. V. Lerner, J. Almerigi, C. Theokas, E. Phelps, S. Gestsdottir, S. Naudeau, H. Jelicic, A. E. Alberts, L. Ma, L. M. Smith, D. L. Bobek, D. Richman-Raphael, I. Simpson, E. D. Christiansen, and A. von Eye. 2005. Positive youth development, participation in community youth development programs, and community contributions of fifth grade adolescents: Findings from the first wave of the 4-H Study of Positive Youth Development. *Journal of Early Adolescence* 25 (1): 17–71.

Phelps, E., A. Balsano, K. Fay, J. Peltz, S. Zimmerman, R. M. Lerner, and J. V. Lerner. In press. Nuances in early adolescent development trajectories of positive and of problematic/risk behaviors: Findings from the 4-H Study of Positive Youth Development. *Child and Adolescent Clinics of North America.*

Theokas, C., and R. M. Lerner. 2006. Observed ecological assets in families, schools, and neighborhoods: Conceptualization, measurement and relations with positive and negative developmental outcomes. *Applied Developmental Science* 10 (2): 61–74.

9. WHEN REAL TROUBLE BREWS

American Psychiatric Association. 2000. *Diagnostic and Statistical Manual of Mental Disorders,* 4th ed., Text Revision. Arlington, VA: American Psychiatric Publishing, Inc.

Child and Family WebGuide, www.cfw.tufts.edu.

Children's Defense Fund Web site, http://www.childrensdefense.org.

Dryfoos, J. 1990. *Adolescents at risk: Prevalence and prevention.* New York: Oxford University Press.

Gore, A., and T. Gore. 2002. *Joined at the heart: The transformation of the American family.* New York: Henry Holt.

Lerner, R. M. 1984. *On the nature of human plasticity.* New York: Cambridge University Press.

———. 1998. Theories of human development: Contemporary perspectives. In *Theoretical models of human development,* ed. R. M. Lerner, 1–24. Vol. 1 of *Handbook of child psychology,* 5th ed., ed. W. Damon. New York: Wiley.

———. 2002. *Adolescence: Development, diversity, context, and application.* Upper Saddle River, NJ: Prentice-Hall.

———. 2004. *Liberty: Thriving and civic engagement among America's youth.* Thousand Oaks, CA: Sage Publications.

Lerner, R. M., and N. Galambos. 1998. Adolescent development: Challenges and opportunities for research, programs, and policies. In *Annual Review of Psychology,* vol. 49, ed. J. T. Spence, 413–46. Palo Alto, CA: Annual Reviews.

Perkins, D. F., and L. M. Borden. 2003. Risk factors, risk behaviors, and resiliency in adolescence. In *Developmental psychology,* eds. R. M. Lerner, M. A. Easterbrooks, and J. Mistry, 273–419, Vol. 6 of *Handbook of Psychology,* ed. I. B. Weiner. New York: Wiley.

10. BEYOND OUR OWN FAMILIES: A CALL TO ACTION

Cummings, E. E. 2003. Foreword. In *Handbook of applied developmental science,* vol. 2: Enhancing the life chances of youth and families: Contributions of programs, policies, and service systems, ed. R. M. Lerner, F. Jacobs, and D. Wertlieb, ix–xi. Thousand Oaks, CA: Sage Publications.

Gore, A. 2003. Foreword. In *Developmental assets and asset-building communities: Implications for research, policy, and practice,* eds. R. M. Lerner and P. L. Benson, xi–xii. Norwell, MA: Kluwer.

———. In preparation. Vision for family centered community building. In *Family-Centered Community Building,* ed. A. Gore, R. M. Lerner, S. Shields, B. Holland, and I. Katz.

Gore, A., and T. Gore. 2002. *Joined at the heart: The transformation of the American family.* New York: Henry Holt.

Hamburg, D. A. 1992. *Today's children: Creating a future for a generation in crisis.* New York: Time Books.

Jonathan M. Tisch College of Citizenship and Public Service Web site, http://activecitizen.tufts.edu.

Lerner, R. M. 2004. *Liberty: Thriving and civic engagement among America's youth.* Thousand Oaks, CA: Sage Publications.

Mentor Web site, http://www.mentoring.org.

O'Connell, B. 1999. *Civil society: The underpinnings of American democracy.* Hanover, NH: University Press of New England.

Taylor, C. 2003. Youth gangs and community violence. In *Handbook of applied developmental science,* Vol. 2: *Enhancing the life chances of youth and families: Contributions of programs, policies, and service systems,* eds. R. M. Lerner, F. Jacobs, and D. Wertlieb, 65–80. Thousand Oaks, CA: Sage Publications.

Taylor, C. S., R. M. Lerner, A. von Eye, A. B. Balsano, E. M. Dowling, P. M. Anderson, D. L. Bobek, and D. Bjelobrk. 2002. Stability of attributes of positive functioning and of developmental assets among African American adolescent male gang and community-based organization members. In *Pathways to positive development among diverse youth,* ed. R. M. Lerner, C. S. Taylor, and A. von Eye, 35–56. Vol. 95 of *New directions for youth development: Theory, practice and research,* ed. G. Noam. San Francisco: Jossey-Bass.

UNICEF, Convention on the Rights of the Child, http://www.unicef.org/crc.

Acknowledgments

Across my career I have learned that a book is a product of the vision, creativity, and passion of many people other than its author. *The Good Teen* is certainly an example of this group effort. The idea for the book, and the person chiefly responsible for convincing me to write it, was Judy Linden, vice president and executive editor at Stonesong Press. I appreciate greatly her confidence in me and all her good advice and editorial skills. She and her colleagues at Stonesong Press, Alison Fargis and Ellen Scordato, were invaluable assets and wonderful colleagues throughout the development of the book.

I am also deeply grateful to Roberta Israeloff for her talent and collaborative spirit. The excellence of her writing and her unflagging commitment to the message of positive and healthy teens were vital to the quality of this work.

My colleague Jennifer Davison, managing editor at the Institute for Applied Research in Youth Development, was my muse throughout the entire project. It was her enthusiasm for this book and her unfailing good spirit, professionalism, and understanding of my goals and my commitment to both good science and good service for adolescents that got me going, that kept me going, and that enabled the project to be completed on time and with high quality.

Both Jennifer's assistant, Lauren Sweeney, and my assistant, Nancy Pare, played vital roles in organizing my work, in following up on the details of hundreds of tasks, and in keeping me on target and on time. I am grateful to both of them.

My faculty colleagues and students at the Institute deserve recognition and my deep gratitude as well. Erin Phelps, Lawrence Gianinno, Heidi Johnson, Robert Roeser, Jacqueline V. Lerner, Deborah Bobek, Amy Alberts, Pamela Anderson, Neda Bebiroglu, Jeannette Belcher-Schepis, Aerika Brittian, Jennifer Carrano, Elise DiDenti Christiansen, Alicia Doyle, Dan Du, Kristen Fay, Sonia Isaac, Katie Leonard, Yibing Li, Lang Ma, Jack Peltz, Mona Abo-Zena, Stacy Zimmerman, Yulika Forman, Nicole Zarrett, Maria Mallon, Marie Pelletier, Aida Balsano, Elizabeth Dowling, Helena Jelicic, Christina Theokas, Sophie Naudeau, and Steinunn Gestsdottir read, discussed, and critiqued drafts of parts of the book, assisted me in locating elusive citations, and helped me find engaging anecdotes and epigraphs for the book. These superb colleagues are my scientific collaborators on many of the studies I discuss in this book. To them, and to literally hundreds of other colleagues and former students, I express my sincerest appreciation for over thirty years of productive partnerships.

The research on adolescent development that I have conducted for more than three decades has been generously supported by grants from numerous federal agencies and private foundations, including the National Institute of Health and Human Development, the National Institute of Mental Health, the William T. Grant Foundation, the John Templeton Foundation, and the National 4-H Council. The National 4-H Council has been incredibly generous in its support of the 4-H Study of Positive Youth Development, data from which provide an essential part of the story of what it means to be a healthy, positive teen in contemporary America. I am grateful to Don Floyd, president and CEO of the National 4-H Council, and his colleagues at the Council—Michael Carr, Jennifer Sirangelo, and Adele Whitford—and to Cathann Kress, director of Youth Development at the U.S. Department of Agriculture, for the faith they placed in my work. I am also grateful to our colleagues at the Philip Morris Youth Smoking Prevention Department, Jennifer

Hunter, Melissa Hough, and Darlene Moehling, and to Howard Willard, executive vice president, corporate responsibility, for having the integrity, vision, and generosity in joining the National 4-H Council in supporting work that would tell the story of how to promote health and positive development among today's teens.

Colleagues at Tufts University have also provided superb support of my work. I am grateful to Kim Thurler, associate director of public relations, Ellen Pinderhughes and Fred Rothbaum, the present and past chairs of my academic department, the Eliot-Pearson Department of Child Development, and to Susan Ernst and Robert Sternberg, the past and present deans of the College of Arts and Sciences, for their enthusiasm for and championing of my scholarship.

Two families merit very special thanks. I am deeply grateful to Drs. Joan and Gary Bergstrom for their warm friendship and for their boundless generosity in supporting my scholarship at Tufts. Their warmth and kindness are extraordinary. My wife, Jackie Lerner, and our children, Justin, Blair, and Jarrett, are—as always—the true energy behind this book. Their love and their unfailing devotion are the core strengths of my life.

I want to express my gratitude to my mother, Sara Lerner, for her love and devotion as well. She has always given me lessons about parenting that, as my years progress, I find are rich and instructive. My mother-in-law, Pauline Verdirame, has also been a source of great warmth and support. I deeply appreciate her affection and love.

Finally, I am very grateful to Heather Jackson, my editor at the Crown Publishing Group. Her excitement about this project and her great insights about the message I have presented enhanced in deep and important ways the value of this work.

Index

Printed in the United States
by Baker & Taylor Publisher Services